TEN PAST NOON

Focus and Fate at Forty

Tucker Lieberman

Copyright © 2020 Glyph Torrent (Bogotá, Colombia)

Cover design: Arturo Serrano and Tucker Lieberman.
Fonts: Montecatini (headings) and Sabon LT (body).

All rights reserved. This book or any portion thereof
may not be reproduced or used in any manner
whatsoever without the express written permission of
the publisher except for the use of brief quotations in a
book review or scholarly journal.

First printing (paperback): February 2020
ISBN-13: 978-1-7329060-4-4

ARCHITECTURE

NOW DEPARTING FROM TRACK 1   PAGE 1

TRACKS 1-28: ORIGIN STORY   PAGE 31
Was the Superintendent Deceived? ### The Turn of the Century ### The Trains of Ned's Childhood ### Industry, Thoroughness, Purpose ### Entering the Great Depression

TRACKS 29-36: THE CART   PAGE 161
By Subject Not Alphabetical ### Damn the Surgeons! ### Thought Processes ### Hypothetics and Hoarding ### Correspondence ### Where to Begin? Will It Ever End? ### What We Can Stop Today ### Nothing? Or Almost Anything? ### 'Little Infinite Poem' ### Tell Me, How's It Going? ### Every Effect Is Itself a Cause ### Testosterone

TRACKS 37-39: NO BOOK   PAGE 303
Unanswered Questions ### Impulse, Obsession, Doubt ### Monster Manuscripts ### Molossus ### End of a Decade ### Suicide Note

NOW ARRIVING ON TRACK 40   PAGE 423

CABOOSE   PAGE 463
Acknowledgments ### About the Author ### Primary Texts ### Selected Books

IMAGES

Figure 1 – The *Eunuchry* manuscript.
Figure 2 – Illustration from G. Frederick Wright's 1890 monograph, *The Nampa Image*.
Figure 3 – Photograph of George Cumming (Harvard AB 1876).
Figure 4 – Ned Cumming's birth certificate, 1901.
Figure 5 – George Cumming's passport photo, 1919.
Figure 6 – Benjamin [Felix] Kittredge and Ned Cumming in a school play, 1916.
Figures 7, 8, 9, 10 – Four photographs of Ned Cumming: 1915, 1916, 1919, 1920.
Figure 11 – L. L. Nunn, undated.
Figures 12 and 13 – Charley Walcott, 1908.
Figure 14 – Seven boys on the dynamo.
Figure 15 – Charles Loomis Dana.
Figure 16 – The manuscript (most of it, anyway) on the cart at the New York Academy of Medicine.
Figure 17 – The third draft of the manuscript.
Figure 18 – Lange's monograph included the shirtless portrait of a man reportedly castrated at age four.

Figure 19 – Source number 1,043 by an author named Lewis about squirrel fights.

Figure 20 – A rare piece of typed material in Ned's manuscript. He classifies the information he's collected: "preliminary," "miscellaneous," "loose," "sketchy," "doubtful."

Figure 21 – The chemical structure of testosterone.

Figure 22 – An index card listing several 1937 publications.

Figure 23 – Handwritten goals.

Figure 24 – Ned Cumming's death certificate.

Figure 25 – A newspaper report of the death. *New York Herald-Tribune,* October 27, 1940.

Figure 26 – My husband's wedding ring.

Figure 27 – "Ring of Fire," December 26, 2019. U.S. National Weather Service.

NOW DEPARTING FROM TRACK 1

NOW DEPARTING
FROM TRACK I

For nearly eighty years, *Eunuchry* has endured in five dozen binders and boxes, housed in a building faced with limestone and sandstone. To better direct you, I can reveal that *Eunuchry* is in the Rare Book and Manuscript Collection at the Library of the New York Academy of Medicine on Fifth Avenue in Manhattan, on the north end of Museum Mile. You make an appointment and, when you arrive, the guard makes a call to announce you. You take an elevator, then a staircase up. The Rare Book Reading Room has a high ceiling. Its shelves are made of dark wood, the contents protected by a grill and accessed by a ladder. The librarian has already retrieved your requested items and rolled them out on a cart. The cart is like a little train car with no motor.

The author of *Eunuchry*, Edward Dilworth Cumming, writing during the Great Depression, hoped to illuminate "a right understanding of the eunuch character."

TEN PAST NOON

Figure 1 – The Eunuchry *manuscript.*

The first draft of *Eunuchry* is divided among nineteen loose-leaf binders, each identified as its own "volume." Additional binders hold a second draft. A third draft manifests as a stack of one or two thousand sheets of paper—they aren't numbered, and I chose not to count them—bound with brads. Numbered index cards were used to record quotations and bibliographical sources so the main text could be footnoted to the number of the card. The information on the cards was then compiled and presented in a different format: the 87-page "List of Reference Works" with 1,239 numbered sources. All of this is handwritten.

Some correspondence also survives. These letters are copies of the author's inquiries with fellow scholars and librarians regarding some of the harder-to-find texts. None of these letters have personal content.

No one knows what motivated Edward Cumming to write so much about eunuchs. I know, however, how his life began and ended, and that's how I've planned the journey of this book. The mountain has a gap in it, and the gap is a tunnel through which we can ride.

This book is about the mystery of one man's suicide, the wars he experienced only as a backdrop to his life in early 20th-century New York, his portrayals of castration, the workings of whiteness, and the history of trains. Throughout the story, images repeat. The repetition is the story.

~~~~~~~~~~

I have always been drawn to literature about eunuchs. As I explained in the introduction to my 2018 book *Painting Dragons:*

> I transitioned to a new gender as a teenager in the late '90s when there were fewer books about transgender identity and they were difficult to find. While I knew of a few nonfiction titles (clinical, political, memoir), I yearned for the kind of truths that are more commonly and more powerfully conveyed through narrative. I hadn't yet been exposed to many strong, mythic interpretations of gender-crossing people, certainly not as many as I personally wanted and needed, and I hadn't yet lived long enough to give them the complex interpretations that

> would make them relevant to me. I didn't have stories or language with which to interpret myself and the specific way in which I felt different.
>
> I didn't expect to find any stories about transgender men in fiction, and, since I did not look for them, I did not find them. What I found, instead, were eunuchs, and they immediately captured my attention.[1]

To be more specific, much of the literature I found was written by white men—Orientalist scholars tunneling through mountains, constructing mazes for their own fascination—and their perspectives rubbed off on me. I can't say I was influenced by any of their specific opinions. Rather, my perspective was shaped by their more general assumptions about how a white person in the West (like myself) might go about learning, especially learning about the East. One of their biggest assumptions: the more facts we can retrieve and catalog, the more complete and transformative our knowledge will be.

I developed a habit of cataloging facts on a variety of subjects, especially eunuchs. In Norman Mosley Penzer's 1936 book *The Harem,* he acknowledges help from an E. D. Cumming who, he claimed, also had a book in progress. I knew since the early 2000s that the unpublished Cumming manuscript was in the New York library, but I do not recall exactly how I learned it was there. One of my colleagues visited it, so perhaps he was the one who told me its location; he reported to me that it was long, disorganized, and in multiple languages. This made me want to read it more. It is my habit to "save the best for last," and it was years until I made my own trip to see it.

Since Edward Dilworth Cumming's fustian scribblings had more than one thousand sources, I assumed he must have gleaned a treasure vault of knowledge. I was curious about his findings and more curious about their unpublished status. His papers are in a literal vault: an archives library. They don't circulate, which amplified their mystique. I became increasingly fixated on the idea that his manuscript held captive some jewel of wisdom that I had to liberate.

The jewel was not readily available to me. I had to make separate short trips to Manhattan during which I could read only portions of the manuscript. Years passed before I felt I was finally grasping what I was reading. This was partly due to the attitude and assumptions with which I approached what I was reading; it turned out that I had been somewhat of a barrier to my own learning. I had a lot to learn about why the author couldn't complete his book. A long time passed, too, before I began to see the book more clearly and to have better ideas about what to do with it.

First I had wanted to mine the author's data. Then, I had wanted to finish and publish his book for him. My revised goal became to write a study of his life, his personal reasons for failing to finish his book, and my personal reasons for choosing not to finish it for him. Light at the end of the tunnel.

############

I decided that we—Edward Dilworth Cumming and I—could be on a first-name basis. I call him Ned, as his father and school headmaster did. I know of no other name he went by.

############

Ned's text on eunuchs doesn't explain his motivations for writing it, nor are there other surviving writings that make those motivations visible, and this makes it hard for me to interpret his text. Using what I've learned about him from other sources, I've brought my version of his life story into my discussion of his text.

I've also put some of myself in here.

I allowed myself a creative approach. I tried to stay open to new sources of information. I had to be responsible for my book's architecture from start to finish, but I stayed responsive to new information that arrived as I was designing. My work's characteristic stamp is less a methodology and more the deliberate lack thereof. An explanation I like comes from Eileen Pollack:

TUCKER LIEBERMAN

> What's creative about creative nonfiction is the writer's determination to speak in a natural voice rather than hide behind the manufactured doublespeak of the military-industrial-governmental-academic complex. What's creative is the choice to structure one's meditations according to a natural, organic form—a narrative, a journey, an experiment, a day spent with an expert violin-maker or embalmer—rather than jam that same experience into a prefabricated container—the five-paragraph essay, the lab report, the news article forced to stand on its head in some bizarre "inverted pyramid." What's creative is the decision to bring an authentic question to one's experience rather than force it to conform to a pre-approved political principle or religious moral or hackneyed proverb.[2]

The early 20th-century history surrounding Ned's manuscript is important, but it is challenging, to say the least, to put it in any kind of order. I can only give my view of the history, and that by evoking some of the collective feelings: the amazement at technology, the grimness of ethical failure. There are still gaps here. They are supposed to be here. The world has always been made of gaps. Traversing the tunnels, I present what I find in my own impressionistic, poetic way.

Giving myself permission to speak from my

own viewpoint is helpful, and yet first-person writing is still difficult for its own reasons. To draft an "I statement," one has to hold two competing ideas: the fact of one's limited perspective and the conviction that one's uniqueness is terribly important.

≠≠≠≠≠≠≠≠≠

For research, I traveled.

To read Ned's writing, as I already described, I visited the New York Academy of Medicine in 2012, 2013, and 2019.

To learn more about his family and early life, I visited the South Carolina Historical Society in Charleston in 2013; the Massachusetts Historical Society in Boston in 2014; and the Division of Rare and Manuscript Collections at Cornell University in Ithaca, New York in 2014. I reconstructed his family tree using online sources that eventually yielded profiles of nearly five hundred people, though hardly any of their names made it into this book. (Not everyone is invited to the church for the wedding and still fewer are invited for cake afterward, to use an image from the Vanderbilt wedding that will appear later.)

For background on people with whom he corresponded, I consulted the N. M. Penzer papers in 2013 and the Errol T. Engle papers in 2014, both at Columbia University in Manhattan. I also tried the John Rodker papers at the Harry Ransom Center at the University of Texas—Austin in 2018; although this did not bear fruit for this book, it was nevertheless part of my journey.

To get a new perspective on the trains, I visited the New York Transit Museum in 2015.

I drove to Ithaca. I flew to Austin. I made the other journeys by train.

#########

"Information architecture" is a modern term used to observe how we organize complex information to make it more accessible.

This book has three parts.

The first part, "Tracks 1–28: Origin Story," begins with Ned's birth in 1901 into a wealthy family and covers his childhood through his teenage years. None of his first-person writings on personal topics seem to have survived, nor did I find writings of others who knew him during his lifetime that might have given insight into his personality. I know, however, that Ned's father was an executive with railway companies; this is important to understand Ned's trajectory.

The second part, "Tracks 29–36: The Cart," examines Ned's project in the 1930s to create a sort of encyclopedia of eunuchs. My investigation is based on the unpublished text he left behind: a project he worked on in his thirties, after his family's living quarters downsized

TEN PAST NOON

during the Great Depression.

The source material speaks bluntly about castration in the eras before anesthesia, with and without the person's consent, as well as about reported physical consequences. This may be difficult for some people to read. A lot of Ned's sources described violence, and many were racist. His notes did not challenge these attitudes. This problem—his own attitude of not challenging the attitudes of his sources—would not have been easily scrubbed off if he'd simply hired a copyeditor. It was foundational to his entire approach.

There's no one else's handwriting on the drafts, nor any mention that Ned ever showed the drafts to anyone for their feedback. Did he try to keep his project private? Perhaps. But people demand privacy in degrees. He didn't destroy his text. I suppose he wanted it eventually to be found as is. Sometimes we keep secrets while we are alive. We might have a different opinion about what should happen to the information after our deaths.

Ned took a special interest in eunuchs' characters and personalities, although this material was hard for him to find. In the later part of the decade, his interest shifted toward writing about mental illness. He rolled these notes into the same project and called them "supplementary" to *Eunuchry* as they remained on the same general theme of human character and personality. He was searching for the answer to something. Perhaps he was trying to diagnose his own problems. He was on a Grail quest, though his research question was always unclear. He didn't have an image of the Grail he was looking for.

An unfinished text is made of loose ends, and I've had to decide what to make of them. It is possible that under some circumstances—had Ned lived to do more work, and had he found mentors, editors, and publishers to encourage, challenge, and reward him and hold him accountable—he might have developed a better text. He might have evinced more sensitive awareness, original opinions, thoughtful phrasing, and valid arguments. But there is no evidence that he was maturing in this way—not even so much as "note to self" marginalia. So, rather than indulging in an imagined text that might have been, I contend with the text he left behind.

The third part, "Tracks 37–39: No Book," examines the uncertainties surrounding Ned's death by suicide at age 39. I don't know exactly why he died this way. For roughly a couple years, he'd been making lists of mental illnesses, but these lists were wide-ranging and there is no hint of what type of instability or pain might have afflicted him. Instead, I focus on a different sort of pain he could have suffered: I argue that his unexamined racism may have contributed to his unhappiness and his inability to help himself, as well as his sense of otherness because of something related to his gender or sexuality that he couldn't express.

※※※※※※※※※

As suggested above, I've ordered the story chronologically. Sometimes it takes a while to see how an event's meaning plays out. Some information may seem irrelevant when it is first presented, and readers may make their own connections later. This format may resemble the diverse information streams of real life. This literary style—or at least my deliberate use of it—may be owed to my place in the early 21st century. The text may appear, at times, like the accumulation of headlines as one scrolls through a social media feed: a mix of family updates and local and global news. Many of us are now accustomed to offering and receiving important facts and opinions this way. We accrue items without expectation that they will ever be sorted. This modern format may be an anachronistic way to engage the story of a man living more than a century ago, but then again, history lives through us.

While the story is chronologically linear, it may not feel like what we usually mean by a "linear narrative." Two people alive at the same time may not know each other. A small event nearby, or a large event in a far-off place, may go unnoticed. The people may meet someday, or not. The event may change their lives, or not.

When the story is told purely chronologically, we aren't given the connections and the outcomes until they happen. A line is drawn through history, but it takes a long time to follow that thread. As long as we can't see the end of the thread from where we stand, it doesn't look linear.

One benefit of writing that doesn't adhere to a linear narrative is that it allows and encourages the repetition of images so that their meaning slowly changes. This literary technique goes back to Greek tragedy, in which recurring words pointed to the audience's existing metaphysical concepts. That was how the poetry worked. The word "fate" in Greek, for example, was "a topographical or territorial metaphor" for the limits of human life and was often tied to images of "enclosure, encirclement, binding, restriction, circumscription, and the like," the classicist Jules Brody said.[3] The repetition of common words can expose other ideas that the words already contain for us.

In this book, I use: *Train. Light. Hands.* And, of course, to different effect: *Eunuch.*

###########

The title of this book, *Ten Past Noon,* relates to time. It suggests that we are halfway through a process. More than that does not need to be said right now.

The subtitle, *Focus and Fate at Forty,* introduces two key concepts that are worth discussing here.

Focus is about an author's persistence. More generally, it is about a person's ability to identify their mission and pursue their project to completion. A problem with focus—its under- or overdevelopment, the oddness of its manifestations, or the corruption of its purpose—affects the meaning of a life.

Except in two quotations of others' words, I have deliberately avoided the word "obsession." It is possible that Ned may have suffered from what we understand today as "obsessive-compulsive disorder." However, I cannot prove that. He may have been finicky about making footnotes, but that is not necessarily pathological. He may have enjoyed making footnotes, and he may have appreciated the overall result. I would like to avoid being overly specific about Ned in this regard and also to avoid watering down the meaning of this disorder for those who use the term to refer to something specific in their lives.

Nonetheless, it is important to note that Ned's passion project could only have been made possible by an unusual attention capacity. Most people do not wish to make lists of eunuchs. Most people do not have folders stuffed with handwritten papers about anything whatsoever, let alone on a single theme, with citations. A particular type of attention enables the collection of an enormous amount of raw material for such a project. Other types of attention would have been needed for changing the thesis and methodology in response to new information and feelings and for seeing the project to completion.

Fate is about the constraints placed on a life. For Americans, the notion that there are constraints at all is unpopular. Liberal democracy has, for hundreds of years, been premised on the importance of individual freedoms. It may be hard to imagine that we are not free—that fate has got us in its clutches.

This is part of the reason I employ an unusual narrative style in this book. Had I written in a style more common to nonfiction, readers might rely on their own existing metaphysical assumptions that my historical subjects could have chosen differently because all options were always open to them. Instead, by using some techniques that are more common to fiction, I hope to prompt different questions.

We often assume that fictional characters—who exist only on the page—have fates that are constrained by what we already know about them, because we wouldn't have been given that information if it were not going to be relevant later. (It's the law of "Chekhov's Gun," but from the reader's perspective rather than the writer's.) The characters are given guns, and then they do what they are bound to do.

The individuals described in this book were all real. The question, then, is whether *real* human lives are circumscribed by fate. Do we have orbits or trajectories because of where we are born? Does one choice lock us in forever? Do some actions appear free while actually being the way we act out our predetermined drama?

Having discussed *focus* and *fate*, it is worth mentioning their relation. We adjust our focus because we wish to control our experiences. We believe that we exercise free will, first by choosing what to pay attention to, then by deliberating and making free choices about that subject matter. But sometimes our focus becomes so intense that it feels unfree. We might feel that we can choose neither the object nor the intensity of our attention. Our focus might, in that case, be a major constraint that determines our fate.

#########

"Interdependence" is a notion that influenced me as I wrote this book. I attended a talk by Gish Jen (who, I later learned, spent some of her childhood in Scarsdale, New York, where Ned also lived for a time)[4] at a public library in Cambridge, Massachusetts in 2013. In her book *Tiger Writing*, she describes her father's attitude in penning his autobiography.

> In 2005, when he was eighty-five, my father sat down to write his life story. This begins simply: 'It is few days before my 86th birthday. I am writing my personal history for my family.' As for

what follows, it is notably un-self-centered. Written over the period of a month and totaling thirty-two pages, it does not begin à la David Copperfield with 'I was born'; in what we will come to recognize as true interdependent style, my father does not, in fact, mention his birth at all. We do not hear how much he weighed or whether he peed on the nurse, much less anything remotely like 'the clock began to strike, and I began to cry, simultaneously.' In fact, he does not even give his birth date until page eight, when he includes 'Norman Chao-Pe Jen, June 26, 1919' in conjunction with another event, and in parentheses.'[5]

Jen drew my attention to the distinction between biographical elements that are driven by personality and character and those that are driven by the more wide-angle lens of a sociological or historical perspective. It was helpful for me to understand that a story can be written in the latter way, especially given that I was frustrated at finding relatively little information directly about my biographical subject himself. Ned's birth occurs about seventy pages into this four-hundred-page book, and though in some senses I've pinned the beginning of the story there, in many respects the story hovers *around* my subject. The result is something simultaneously less and more than biography. It awakens us to our interdependence.

TEN PAST NOON

#########

"**B**iomythography," a word coined by Audre Lorde for her own work in *Zami*, might fit. On a couple criteria, though, it could be argued both ways.

First is the element of speaking from the margins. Lorde's memoir speaks from her social marginalization as a black lesbian from an immigrant family, and so the genre of biomythography patterned after her work is usually understood to take aim at "colonial modes of cataloging difference" (as C. Riley Snorton put it, citing Sylvia Wynter).[6] This is on point here because the problem of racist otherization is central to my *Ten Past Noon*. To be more precise, though, my biographical subject was the one doing the cataloging of others' differences, and I am not sure if it is proper for me to take this word "biomythography" and apply it to someone who was generally privileged. I know the exact ways in which Ned was privileged: he was a white American man raised in inherited wealth, with access to elite education, business connections, and travel opportunities. I have been unable to determine the exact ways in which he may have been marginalized. He likely experienced mental illness and financial strain later in life, and he was perhaps disabled or queer, but I don't know any of that for certain.

Second is the element of fiction. Lorde's

autobiographic "myth" doesn't reveal which strands of her story may have been rewoven, embellished, or outright invented, and we are left to trust the way she has chosen to tell it, understanding and accepting that some of it might be fiction. By contrast, none of the strands I provide in *Ten Past Noon* are fictional. I quote from fiction for literary effect, but I indicate when I am doing so. I don't intend to sow a fictionalized version of Ned's story in the readers' imaginations, although readers may make their own leaps of fantasy across the gaps in the history.

What I have written is some kind of saga: biographical but also genealogical, tied into the identity of a people, and at times trying to evolve into a poem. It follows one man from birth to death, his enormous manuscript being a Herculean, if not quite heroic, feat. I wish to neither hagiographize nor vilify Ned. Rather, I use his life and text as an opportunity to reflect upon and interpret other matters.

Ted Warburton explained biomythography as "the weaving together of myth, history and biography in epic narrative form, a style of composition that represents all the ways in which we perceive the world around us."[7] In this book, I open conversations about how the era in which we live might affect us, how we know what we know, and about what we might choose to do better with the time we have. The genre of biomythography is, in David Marriott's estimation, a form "whose introduction necessarily never arrives and does not stop arriving, and whose destination cannot be foreseen, or anticipated, but only repeatedly traveled."[8] I can't foresee all the places the reader might travel with my work.

In sum, this may be a biomyth or something else, and the reader may judge.

≠≠≠≠≠≠≠≠≠

"Chronotope" is an idea used by the philosopher and classicist Mikhail Bakhtin. He coined the term from the Greek words for time and space. Each chronotope is a mini-genre. The system classifies how time and space operate in fiction—that is, how a novel's narrative motion is related to its setting.

I feel that the idea is useful for nonfiction, too, since in writing this history I felt (conceptually, not physically) a slight disorientation of myself and my biographical subjects in time and space. I don't meticulously analyze or name my own literary chronotope here, but it does seem useful to note that there always is a chronotope, and that how we use language to describe time and space can have an important effect on our stories.

Born in 1895 in Russia, Bakhtin's young adulthood was shaped by war, famine, and exile to Kazakhstan. His publishers were shut down, and one was torched by the Nazis. Nevertheless, he kept at his scholarship. One of his most famous long essays, written in the late 1930s, focuses on the chronotope in different genres of fiction. In ancient Greek romances, for example, he points out that the lovers "experience a most improbable number of adventures" that don't sum coherently or plausibly. "All the days, hours, minutes that are ticked off within the separate adventures...do not become the days and hours of a human life. These hours and days leave no trace, and therefore, [within the story,] one may have as many of them as one likes."[9] Reading such adventures, we might imagine that a great deal of time is passing for the characters, or that, as if they were in a dream, no time is passing at all.

The narrator of Thomas Mann's novel *The Magic Mountain [Der Zauberberg]* explains that, unlike musical compositions, which fill a fixed amount of time, narrative descriptions do not fill the exact time they describe.[10] I imagine this must be evident to psychoanalysts. The story of a train crash may be drawn out for hours on the therapeutic couch, while the story of a chronic illness may be dismissed with a "So that happened, and anyway..."

As an author of nonfiction, I choose to skip over some parts and draw out others, but I know the direction in which we are going: the 20th century will end and the 21st century will begin. Ned is born at the beginning of this story, and then he will die, and then I will be born. The real-world constraints of time and space make their demands. Past events cannot be changed. It is my task to put the past in some kind of order. I can play with the chronotope somewhat by delaying or accelerating the action or by shifting to a new location, but still the outcome is constrained by fate. Readers may develop their understanding of this book's experimental genre by thinking about its chronotope.

++++++++++

"Hypnagogy" is the effort to put someone else into a trance. I hope this book works not only through its content and structure but also through the feeling it produces in the reader.

"It doesn't really matter what any given experimental film is 'about,'" Gemma Files wrote in her novel, "because the genre as [a] whole rejects narrative, conventional or otherwise, in favour of hypnagogy; it wants to bore you, to annoy you, to put you in a trance and force you to meet it halfway."[11] Repetition may tend to irritate or confuse, but it is through those sensations that one passes into a trance state.

You can sleep on the train and still your journey continues. It is a hypno-saga.

++++++++++

Parallels between Ned's life and my own influenced the way I developed this story.

Both of us were born into affluent white families in the northeastern United States.

We spent time at Ivy League colleges. We avidly collected facts and anecdotes about the history of eunuchs and aspired to write enormous, comprehensive books, but we did not have good thesis statements. When we were in our mid-thirties, we had concerns about mental illness, refocusing our writing on that area.

When I began reading Ned's papers, I was in my early thirties, the same age at which he had begun writing them eighty years earlier. Therefore, I thought of him as more advanced than I, as he had eventually reached a later age, his late thirties, by which point he'd written something that I hadn't yet fully read. I was nonetheless aware that I was slowly catching up to him in age and making progress reading his papers. I took long breaks from my research. It was as if I sensed that I would eventually catch up to him one way or another, whether I liked it or not, whether I tried to focus on it or not. I knew what ultimately happened to him because his fate was written, but I didn't know what would happen to me. Someday I might be older than he, and then I might finally have the wisdom to crack his puzzle.

Ned remained single, though his cousin married at 36. I, too, married at 36. Ned committed suicide at 39; I did not.

"Just as it is natural in the modern languages to speak of old age as 'creeping up' on us, and eventually 'overtaking' us," said Brody, the ancient Greeks understood age as "a τέλος [*telos*], a 'fate' or circumscription that separates and closes people off from youth, an outer limit that completes or rounds off a portion of time and a vital space."[12]

In describing Ned's formation in early 20th-century New York, I am illustrating the circumscription of his particular life and thus hinting at what his destiny may be as well as what it cannot be. In following the history through to my own lifetime, I describe my own circumscription, too. Examining how we are part of history is a way of acknowledging our limits.

Ned tried to write a book and ended his life. Now I've written a book about what he did.

✝✝✝✝✝✝✝✝✝✝

Had Ned left descendants, I probably would have approached this project differently. However, neither he nor his sister had children. I located only one cousin; she had been a baby when Ned died and did not recall ever being told of his existence. (She is quoted briefly at the end of this book.) A ghost and a living person may glom on to each other, and in that sense Ned is "mine." We have claimed each other: he has attracted my attention, and I have asserted the prerogative to discuss him and his work. I am not aware that anyone else today takes such an interest in him.

His lack of present-day family, people who might have been stakeholders of sentiment about him, releases a social obligation that would otherwise constrain me as an author. I've gotten creative in leveraging his story for my own ends because there is no one to object.

I am not sure if he himself would be pleased by what I've done here with his story. He is not here to ask. I don't know who could possibly want an apology, and I am not sure if the idea of apology makes sense in this context. Hauntings are unfree scenarios. A ghost is dispatched so that both the haunter and the haunted can regain their freedom.

#########

The modern form of the "trolley problem"—as originally posed by the philosopher Philippa Foot and as modified by countless others in philosophy classrooms—asks us to imagine that someone is going to die on the train tracks and that we can influence the outcome by sacrificing someone else. It asks whether the details make a difference:

How many people are involved.
If we know them.
If we like them.
If we must select the substitute victim.
If the outcome is probability or certainty.
If it is better to sit passively and watch the scene spool out.
If it will feel worse to push someone with our

TEN PAST NOON

bare hands because we will feel our crime within our flesh.

If we can instead antiseptically pull a lever to direct the murder-vehicle.

If we may be forgiven.

The moment for decision is up.

++++++++++

"If there's a book you want to read, but it hasn't been written yet," Toni Morrison advised us, "then you must write it."[13]

++++++++++

The lever is pulled. The time is ten past noon, and the train is on the move.

NOTES TO
"NOW DEPARTING FROM TRACK I"

[1] Tucker Lieberman. *Painting Dragons: What Storytellers Need to Know About Writing Eunuch Villains.* Bogotá: Glyph Torrent, 2018. p. 4.

[2] "How to Tell the Truth." Eileen Pollack. *Human Parts.* October 16, 2019. https://humanparts.medium.com/how-to-tell-the-truth-7139aaf6aa9 Accessed October 21, 2019.

[3] Jules Brody. *'Fate' in* Oedipus Tyrannus: *A Textual Approach.* (Arethusa Monographs, XI.) Buffalo, N.Y.: SUNY Buffalo, 1985. pp. 9, 10. Brody was paraphrasing (and agreeing with) the thesis of Richard Broxton Onians,

TUCKER LIEBERMAN

The Origins of European Thought about the Body, the Mind, the Soul, the World, Time, and Fate. New Interpretations of Greek, Roman and Kindred Evidence, also of Some Basic Jewish and Christian Beliefs (1951). Cambridge University Press, 2nd edition 1954.

[4] "About Gish Jen: A Profile." Don Lee. *Ploughshares.* Issue 82, Fall 2000. https://www.pshares.org/issues/fall-2000/about-gish-jen-profile Accessed October 16, 2019.

[5] Gish Jen. *Tiger Writing: Art, Culture, and the Interdependent Self.* Cambridge, Mass.: Harvard University Press, 2013. p. 11.

[6] C. Riley Snorton. *Black on Both Sides: A Racial History of Trans Identity.* Minneapolis: University of Minnesota Press, 2017. He cites the idea to Sylvia Wynter, "Unsettling the Coloniality of Being/Power/Truth/Freedom: Towards the Human, after Man, Its Overrepresentation—an Argument," *CR: The New Centennial Review* 3, no. 3 (2003): 257-337.

[7] Prof. Edward (Ted) Warburton, University of California, Santa Cruz. Course description for "Movement Research in the New Arts Praxis." Spring 2005.
http://www.nyu.edu/classes/gilbert/collaboration/pdf/newartspraxis.pdf Accessed October 16, 2019.

[8] David Marriott, "Inventions of Existence: Sylvia Wynter, Frantz Fanon, Sociogeny, and 'the Damned.'" *CR: The New Centennial Review* 11, no. 3 (2011): 53-54. Quoted in C. Riley Snorton, *op. cit.*

[9] M. M. Bakhtin, "Forms of Time and of the Chronotope in the Novel: Notes toward a Historical Poetics." Essay 3 of 4 in *The Dialogic Imagination.* Translated from the Russian by Caryl Emerson and Michael Holquist. (1981) Austin, Texas: University of Texas Press, 2008.

[10] Thomas Mann. *The Magic Mountain* (originally S. Fischer Verlagberlin, 1924). Translated from the German by H. T. Lowe-Porter. England: A. Wehaten and Co., Exeter, 1971. pp. 541-542.

[11] Gemma Files. *Experimental Film.* Toronto, Canada: ChiZine, 2015. p. 38.

TEN PAST NOON

---

[12] Brody, *op. cit.* p. 19. He cites this idea to Onians, *op. cit.,* pp. 429-430.

[13] Toni Morrison, @ToniMorrison, Twitter, Oct. 30, 2013. https://twitter.com/tonimorrrison/status/395708227888771072 Accessed Sept. 1, 2019.

TRACKS 1-28
ORIGIN STORY

WAS THE SUPERINTENDENT DECEIVED?

It bubbled up from the unconscious: genderless, ageless, made of the stories we project upon it.

The clay figurine was sucked out by a sand pump, we are told, dredging the Pliocene-Pleistocene era layer of clay[1] three hundred feet underground in Nampa, Idaho to create an artesian well as a water source. The drilling company owner noticed the artifact and called over the superintendent of the Oregon Short Line Railroad who happened to be in town. As the men had no way to take a photograph that day in 1889, the figurine was sent to George Frederick Wright, a geologist and author on the East Coast.[2] "It represents a human body; and from the slight depression between the breasts it is evident that a female figure is intended," Wright opined in a dedicated monograph.[3] If this had been a genuine find, it might be the oldest artifact known to humanity, dating back to the first use of fire and stone tools.

Figure 2 – Illustration from G. Frederick Wright's 1890 monograph, The Nampa Image.[4]

Should we suspect a hoax? To avoid this, Wright included third-party testimony for the character of the railroad superintendent. The superintendent's word should receive "as much consideration as the evidence of any scientific man," readers were assured, as "he was on the spot the day the 'find' was made, and his estimate of it would in my mind carry very great weight. He is, as you are aware, not only a graduate of the college [Harvard], but he was educated as a lawyer, passed several years of study in Europe, and is a man of the highest personal character, accustomed to weigh evidence, and not likely to be deceived."

That character testimony notwithstanding, the Nampa figurine *was* a hoax, according to an expert on anthropomorphic figurines of the

Neolithic.[5]

Imagine how bright the stars were, though, that night over the empty desert, winking like gaslights. *The train runs on its appointed time.* Everything will become clear in the end.

✝✝✝✝✝✝✝✝✝

From New York City, if you travel 130 miles west, you arrive at Pottsville, within Pennsylvania's anthracite coal region where German immigrants settled. There, in 1854, a wealthy family of Scottish descent welcomed an infant they named George Miller Cumming. The father was an attorney; an uncle was a bank president and a member of the Potts family who had lived in the area for two centuries and given their name to the town.

From Pottsville, if you travel another 230 miles northwest, you arrive at Titusville, where in 1859 the first oil well was drilled. "That discovery, like the big bang itself, is but a subatomic pinhole in space," the political commentator Rachel Maddow recently wrote of this oil well, "compared with all that has followed."[6]

And from the pinhole, how did the universe expand? By train. "With the advent of the speed and power of mechanical travel using the powerful steam engine, the sense of time, the ordering of life, and the possibilities of human reach," the historian Gordon H. Chang said, "quickened and expanded in previously

TEN PAST NOON

unimaginable ways."[7]

While George was still a boy, Chinese men began leaving Guangdong Province's Pearl River delta for railroad work in the United States. This was their preferred destination, although they would be paid less than white American laborers and "every Chinese community in America in the mid- to late nineteenth century suffered arson, looting, and other forms of obliteration."[8] (Another common destination for Chinese migrants was Cuba, but those recruiters were yet more exploitative, sending the men to work in the sugar fields.)[9] Meanwhile, the Civil War ended and the Emancipation Proclamation was signed. Everyone wanted to go somewhere. Congress had required the track to be laid for a transcontinental railroad that would run between the East and West Coasts. The Chinese laborers got it done in five years. Their work often involved dangerous tasks: lowering a man in a basket so he could light a dynamite fuse, then quickly pulling the ropes to raise him again, for example. Even though the government's land grants to the railroads displaced indigenous people, the Chinese immigrants themselves generally had friendly interactions with the Native Americans, with whom they sometimes lived and worked.[10]

On May 10, 1869, Leland Stanford, governor of California and president of the Central Pacific railroad, prepared to hammer the final spike in the transcontinental track "as the trains drew close to each other at a few minutes after noon..." Now, "two locomotives finally meet, pilot to pilot," Richard Francaviglia wrote, "after years of anticipation."[11] The system was not even built yet, and we already needed the train to run on time.

--*-*-*-*-*-*-*-*

Across the pond, London had already put trains underground. It called its system "The Metropolitan."

"Wide, spacious, clean and luminous," the *Illustrated London News* promised in 1862. Reader, it was not. The trains ran on coal, and there was no electricity to help ventilate the tunnels, which were filled with pollution called "choke damp" that contributed to several deaths. The company tried arguing that the fumes were actually beneficial for asthmatics and that the subway was therefore "a sort of health resort."[12] To sell the concept to the public, artists' engravings showed men in fancy clothes riding experimental "smokeless" engines on outdoor tracks, though these were not the trains that were actually used underground. And while tobacco was initially banned on the trains, "smoking carriages" were soon required by law, at least, by custom, for gentlemen passengers (as the railways generally excluded ladies from the smoking cars).[13] The Metropolitan commissioned a hundred and twenty engines with "enormous external cylinders" that condensed steam to lessen pollution.[14]

England's railway projects were entirely privately funded, with no government support, though "the banking system was still in its early stages of development," Christian Wolmar said. "It is no exaggeration to say that railways were the principal catalyst for the creation of capitalism."[15]

England, always seeking to enable international commerce, had also laid railways throughout India, with the first steam locomotive running near Madras in 1838.[16] Indian taxpayers guaranteed profit to British shareholders, so during their construction phases the railroad companies spent profligately.[17] These expenses did not necessarily go toward labor; magistrates were empowered in 1860 to resolve workers' complaints about wages.[18] Mostly the Indian railroads hired Europeans, anyway, and only 8 percent of engineers in 1886 were Indians.[19]

In the 1870s, a time of famine, railways were leveraged to export food more so than to distribute it within India.[20] Trains were also used in the service of the Second Anglo-Afghan War.[21]

Local trains connected many Indian cities by the 1880s.[22] They were built with the Indian broad gauge, as Lord Dalhousie had decreed that India's tracks should be nine-and-a-half inches wider than England's on his assumption that bigger trains would be better.[23] By 1900, thirty-three railway companies were operating in

India.[24]

These machines, according to some early rumors, were powered by human sacrifices. Other rumors had it that a train passenger would age faster than a pedestrian since the train passenger ought not to be able to cheat destiny of the journey's allotted duration.[25]

In some ways, the train in India might have been a social equalizer: A wealthy person who previously would have insisted on "a palkhee and bearers [i.e. a litter or palanquin carried by four servants], now cheerfully marches to the station with a carpet bag," according to an 1868 report.[26] On the other hand, passengers were racially segregated in the stations and vehicles, and workers were treated according to a racial hierarchy as well,[27] so ultimately the trains merely changed how the social stratification manifested.

British efforts were not so successful everywhere. A British company brought a locomotive to Shanghai in 1876, and this surprise was not appreciated. The company had claimed to be building an ordinary road. When the "fire cart" appeared and promptly killed a Chinese soldier, Chinese officials (sitting on palanquins to underscore their anti-technological position) personally oversaw the destruction of the tracks.[28] China eventually built railways on its own terms. In 1889, the Empress Dowager Cixi had a train built by a French company, but, deciding that the noise and smoke were threats to *feng shui,* she preferred to have the train carriage pulled on silken ropes by her eunuch servants.[29]

#########

George, the boy from Pottsville, went to Phillips Exeter Academy and rowed crew in the summer after his first year at Harvard. In his final year, he received a distinguished mark in history from Prof. Henry Adams.[30] He attended Harvard Law for a few months,[31] finished his law studies in Germany, and was admitted to the New York Bar in 1881, after which he lived in Wisconsin, Minnesota, and Manitoba for a couple years, earning a two-thousand-dollar salary as a land agent for the Northern Pacific Railroad. He practiced law in New York with Mr. Critchlow, the future assistant U.S. Attorney for Utah.

New York City at this time was illuminating. Thomas Edison launched his central power station on Pearl Street in 1882, replacing gas lamps with electric bulbs and, one evening, making a big demonstration of direct current that lit up a large portion of the district that included the Drexel, Morgan building on Wall Street and the desks of the *New York Times*. The newspaper described Edison's light bulb as "a glass globe about four inches long, and the shape of a dropping tear, broad at the bottom, narrow in the neck, in which is inclosed the carbon horseshoe that gives the light," producing light admired as "more brilliant than gas and a hundred times steadier...with no nauseous smell, no flicker and no glare...soft, mellow, and grateful to the eye," so that it was "almost like

Figure 3 – Photograph of George Miller Cumming (Harvard AB 1876), courtesy of Harvard University Archives.

TEN PAST NOON

writing by daylight to have a light without a particle of flicker and with scarcely any heat to make the head ache." The journalists on that first evening were "unanimously in favor of the Edison electric lamp as against gas."[32] By the end of the decade, enterprising companies had strung so many electrical wires throughout the city that it was common for utility poles to collapse under their weight.[33]

The sun rises on the East Coast, first over Boston and then, some minutes later, farther west in New York City. "Why, people are getting up in Boston while they sleep in New York," a mid-century comic dialogue wagged. When New Yorkers look at the sun overhead and set their watches for noon, it is already ten past noon in Boston. So, if everything happens "earlier" in Boston, why is the Boston clock's hour "later"?[34]

There's a reason this is intended as comic dialogue. It's not a paradox. The problem is in the way the question is asked.

In 1883, the American railroads agreed to four time zones: Eastern, Central, Mountain, Pacific. The machines were moving quickly enough that it no longer served to look at the sun's position overhead. Train engineers needed to know the exact local time at which they would arrive in a faraway place.[35] The public adopted these time zones pretty much "within the week";[36] after all, if you promise a telephone call from Boston to New York, you aren't incurring that expense to waste ten minutes arguing about a ten-minute difference, and New Yorkers shouldn't be sleeping anyway when you are ready to call them. Besides, railways in England had long since agreed to operate on Greenwich Mean Time, and railways in India on Madras Time.

Out West, where Cumming also spent time seeking his fortune, industry had focused on laying railroad tracks and stripping metal from the earth. When many American mines closed in the late 1880s, it caused anxiety among investors in the big cities.

Thousands of immigrant Chinese workers had, by that point, spent years constructing the Western railroads, the first among them having begun work three decades earlier.[37] They were not well rewarded. The Chinese Exclusion Act of 1882 prohibited further immigration from China and denied U.S. citizenship to all Chinese immigrants already in the country.

#########

Around the end of the decade, George Miller Cumming was a director for the Nevada Pacific railroad. He managed the Utah Central Railway, a 280-mile corridor that, unlike those that covered longer distances, did not need to provide lodging for its employees. It merged with the Oregon Short Line and the Utah & Northern, both of which he also managed.[38] The railroads were doing this—connecting isolated pieces, then connecting the

TEN PAST NOON

connections, becoming a great network that made itself increasingly useful. From the official completion of the first transcontinental railroad track in 1869, the nation's miles of track more than tripled over the subsequent twenty years.[39]

That's when the Nampa figurine showed up one day in 1889 in Idaho under Cumming's superintendency and was sent away for inspection, discussion, and curation. The figurine was a mystery unsolved, one handful of hard clay, ancient and fragile, against the width of North America, traversed by modern train.

He is grasping and staring at the clay. He is not looking at what surrounds the clay.

╫╫╫╫╫╫╫╫╫

Trains changed people's perceptions of time. For safety, the machines' schedules were coordinated not just by the minute, but by the second; therefore, passengers, people expecting visitors, and merchants waiting for deliveries had to conform to the new regime.[40]

Trains also changed the way human eyes apprehended things. "No object out the window," as Tom Zoellner described viewing a landscape from a train, "could be watched for very long."

> Trees, flowers, houses, horses, waving children—all of them receding as quickly as they were seen, gone down the backward-spooling time funnel. Travelers complained of headaches and

nervousness...The flickering quality of the landscape made the foreground virtually disappear and brought a new method of 'seeing' into the vocabulary of the brain. In many ways the advent of the railroad in the mid-nineteenth century helped prepare humanity for the coming of the motion picture at the end of the century.[41]

"Nothing but picture after picture," Rabindranath Tagore would write near the end of his life about people-watching on a platform in a train station. "Whatever catches the eye for a moment / Is erased the next moment after."[42]

Chronotope, again, is the word with which Mikhail Bakhtin referred to the relative movements of time and space. He was analyzing fictional narratives. But reality changes its chronotope, too.

‡‡‡‡‡‡‡‡‡

George Cumming married. He had come to know the four Kittredge siblings, all of whom had been born in Ohio but who had generally returned to their parents' roots in the Northeast. The youngest Kittredge became George's bride.[43]

The eldest, Sarah, had married one of George's Exeter and Harvard classmates,[44] a lawyer by the name of Canfield who now taught at Columbia Law School in Manhattan.

The second was Samuel, affectionately called

by his middle name "Dana," who, as an undergraduate at Harvard in George's class, had set a student record of eleven-and-a-half seconds for the 100-yard dash.[45] He went on to organize residents of suburban New York against horse theft.[46]

Third was Benjamin, who moved to California with his wife Bessie. In late 1900, Benjamin wrote to inform his brother Dana of the birth of his only child. Bessie had, naturally, been asking her attending physicians "about every two minutes whether they could tell yet whether it was a boy or girl." It was a boy, "about 8 pounds" and with "nice ears." The boy received his father's name, Benjamin Rufus Kittredge. This "Junior" was immediately nicknamed "Felix."[47]

And the youngest of the four Kittredge siblings was Lucy. In the spring of 1891, George was hired to teach at Columbia Law, having been recommended by his former classmate who was married to the eldest Kittredge sibling. George married Lucy a couple months after he got the job as a professor. They had a daughter, Emily, in 1894. He continued teaching business law for several more years at Columbia[48] alongside his former classmate who was now his brother-in-law.

The population of New York City was growing rapidly. The city's streets were increasingly clogged with horse-drawn traffic (and its odorous, infectious remainders), including large, unheated carriages for public transportation operated by dozens of unregulated companies.[49] New York planned to build a subway, as did Boston. During an 1887 test run in Boston that looped around Beacon Street and Harvard Square, Doug Most wrote, "as the electric streetcar rolled by, horses could be seen flinching and fidgeting, pricking up their ears and tossing their heads high in the air, as if they sensed their pending demise."[50]

Russia began construction on the Trans-Siberian Railway in 1891. Czar Alexander III put thousands of prisoners to work, Count Sergei Witte printed extra rubles to pay the engineers, and it got done. Millions of people subsequently took the train to settle in Siberia.[51]

London also continued to innovate. As long as coal burned inside the trains to heat water for steam engines, the air in the tunnels would be dirty, so the next step was to burn coal at a central power station from which electrical wires could run. If they could electrify the underground train, the air in the tunnels would be cleaner. This would also enable the installation of electric lights inside the carriages so a few lucky passengers could read the newspaper. The passengers would just have to learn that the extra rail under the electric train delivered 160 amperes and would therefore, as one engineer explained briefly, electrocute anyone who touched it so that they would be "killed very dead."[52] *One should*

TEN PAST NOON

not play on the tracks. One should sit quietly in one's seat. The windows in the cars let in a little breathable air but were too small and positioned too high for passengers to see through.[53]

In 1890, the Prince of Wales lifted a golden key at the City & South London line, a deep tube line to Stockwell via Kennington.[54] The key wasn't merely ceremonial. By his hand, the electric current switched on.

The electric trains couldn't always make it uphill at King William Street "and had to be allowed to roll back down again for a second attempt."[55] The passengers who hadn't gotten a seat and who stood in the aisle had nothing to which to grab on.[56]

NOTES TO
"WAS THE SUPERINTENDENT DECEIVED?"

[1] "Forbidden Archaeology? The Nampa Image Hoax." Carl Feagans. *A Hot Cup of Joe.* July 30, 2018. https://ahotcupofjoe.net/2018/07/forbidden-archaeology-the-nampa-image-hoax-3/ Accessed February 22, 2020.

[2] "The Nampa Figurine." Keith Fitzpatrick-Matthews. *Bad Archaeology.* 3 January 2011.
http://www.badarchaeology.com/out-of-place-artefacts/very-ancient-artefacts/the-nampa-figurine/
Accessed February 22, 2020.
"Nampa Image." UnMyst3. September 21, 2015.
https://www.unmyst3.com/2011/07/nampa-image.html
Accessed February 22, 2020.

[3] The testimony for the character of George Miller Cumming was provided by Charles F. Adams.

G. Frederick Wright. *The Nampa Image.* Boston Society of Natural History. Jan. 2, 1890. p. 440. https://archive.org/details/nampimagecorresp00wrigrich/page/439 Accessed October 16, 2019.

[4] Wright, *ibid.,* p. 424.

[5] "Forbidden Archaeology? The Nampa Image Hoax." *op. cit.*

[6] Rachel Maddow. *Blowout: Corrupted Democracy, Rogue State Russia, and The Richest, Most Destructive Industry on Earth.* New York: Crown, 2019. p. 3.

[7] "Chinese Railroad Workers and the US Transcontinental Railroad in Global Perspective," by Gordon H. Chang. *The Chinese and the Iron Road: Building the Transcontinental Railroad.* ed. Gordon H. Chang and Shelley Fisher Fishkin, with Hilton Obenzinger and Roland Hsu. Stanford, Calif.: Stanford University Press, 2019. Chapter 1, p. 27.

[8] Introduction by Gordon H. Chang, Shelley Fisher Fishkin, and Hilton Obenzinger. Chang, Fishkin, Obenzinger, and Hsu, *ibid.,* p. 4.

[9] "Chinese Labor Migrants to the Americas in the Nineteenth Century: An Inquiry into Who They Were and the World They Left Behind," by Evelyn Hu-Dehart. Chang, Fishkin, Obenzinger, and Hsu, *ibid.,* Chapter 2, p. 51-52.

[10] "Tracking Memory Encounters between Chinese Railroad Workers and Native Americans," by Hsinya Huang. Chang, Fishkin, Obenzinger, and Hsu, *ibid.,* Chapter 11, p. 186.

[11] Richard V. Francaviglia. *Over the Range: A History of the Promontory Summit Route of the Pacific Railroad.* University Press of Colorado/Utah State University Press, 2008. Chapter 4, "A Moment of Glory: Promontory, 1869," pp. 101, 102. https://www.jstor.org/stable/j.ctt4cgp3p.8?seq=2#metadata_info_tab_contents Accessed October 19, 2019.

[12] Christian Wolmar. *The Subterranean Railway: How the London Underground Was Built and How It Changed the City Forever.* London: Atlantic, 2004. p. 45.

TEN PAST NOON

[13] The new legal clause was in the Railway Regulation Bill of 1868. Wolmar, *ibid.,* p. 137.
Danielle K. Dodson. "Minding the Gap: Uncovering the Undergroun's Role in the Formation of Modern London, 1855-1945." "Chapter Four: Underground: The Way For All?" University of Kentucky, 2016. p. 154.
http://dx.doi.org/10.13023/ETD.2016.339
Accessed January 16, 2020.
[14] Wolmar, *op. cit.* p. 47.
[15] Wolmar, *ibid.* p. 30. See also p. 144.
[16] Rajendra B. Aklekar. *A Short History of Indian Railways.* New Delhi: Rupa, 2019. p. 8.
[17] Shashi Tharoor. *An Era of Darkness: The British Empire in India.* New Delhi: Aleph, 2016. pp. 208-209.
[18] Aklekar, *op. cit.,* p. 44.
[19] Tharoor, *op. cit.,* p. 212.
[20] Tharoor, *ibid.,* p. 214.
[21] Aklekar, *ibid.,* p. 81.
[22] Aklekar, *ibid.,* p. 64.
[23] Aklekar, *ibid.,* p. 84.
[24] Aklekar, *ibid.,* p. 102.
[25] Aklekar, *ibid.,* pp. 46, 50, 51.
(Velocity time dilation works the opposite way, and in any case is not a practical concern.)
[26] Credited to "Edwardson's account, written in 1868 with the aid of the Records of India Office." Quoted by Aklekar, *ibid.* p. 50.
[27] Aklekar, *ibid.* pp. 77-79. Citing: Veena Talwar, "The City Must Be Safe—Communications," *The Making of Colonial Lucknow, 1856-1877.* Oldenburg: Princeton University Press New Jersey, 1984.
See also:
Mukhopadhyay, Aparajita (2013) *Wheels of change?: impact of railways on colonial north Indian society, 1855-1920.* PhD Thesis. SOAS, University of London. pp. 59-60. http://eprints.soas.ac.uk/17363 Accessed February 16, 2020.

"All the World is India; India is a World Apart." ed. Matthew D. Esposito. *A World History of Railway Cultures, 1830-1930, Volume 2.* New York: Routledge, 2020.
https://books.google.com.co/books?id=jNTHDwAAQBAJ
Accessed February 16, 2020.

[28] Tom Zoellner. *Train: Riding the Rails That Created the Modern World—From the Trans-Siberian to the Southwest Chief.* New York: Viking, 2014. p. 228.

[29] Jung Chang. *Empress Dowager Cixi: The Concubine Who Launched Modern China.* New York: Anchor Books, 2014.
https://books.google.com.co/books?id=bp4toTYNDLkC&pg=PP117&lpg=PP117 Accessed February 22, 2020.

[30] Prof. Henry Adams was the younger brother of Charles Francis Adams, the author of the exposé "A Chapter of Erie" (1869) about Jay Gould's financial corruption involving the Erie Railroad. That G. M. Cumming would go on to become first vice-president of the Erie Railroad is a coincidence noted in Stewart Mitchell's article. Stewart Mitchell, "Henry Adams and Some of His Students," *Proceedings of the Massachusetts Historical Society.* Third Series, Vol. 66 (Oct., 1936 - May, 1941), pp. 294-312. (Cumming is mentioned on page 304 and in the table on page 311.)
https://www.jstor.org/stable/25080330
Accessed January 24, 2020.

[31] George Cumming rowed crew at Harvard in the summer of 1873 and attended Harvard Law in the Fall of 1877.

[32] "Miscellaneous City News. Edison's Electric Light: 'The Times' Building Illuminated by Electricity." *New York Times.* Sept. 5, 1882. p. 8.
https://timesmachine.nytimes.com/timesmachine/1882/09/05/103421635.html?pageNumber=8
Accessed Sept. 26, 2019.

[33] Doug Most. *The Race Underground: Boston, New York, and the Incredible Rivalry That Built America's First Subway.* New York: St. Martin's Press, 2014. p. 147.

TEN PAST NOON

[34] "A Muddle of Words." George Wakeman. *The Galaxy Miscellany.* September 1869. pp. 417-420. https://books.google.com.co/books?id=7xhLAQAAMAAJ&pg=PA418&lpg=PA418 Accessed February 17, 2020.
[35] "When did the United States start using time zones?" Elizabeth Nix. History.com. April 8, 2015. https://www.history.com/news/when-did-the-united-states-start-using-time-zones Accessed January 28, 2020.
[36] Zoellner, *op. cit.,* p. 154.
[37] "Chinese Railroad Workers in North America Project." https://web.stanford.edu/group/chineserailroad/cgi-bin/website/timeline/ Accessed Sept. 24, 2019.
[38] From a report by the Interstate Commerce Commission, the entry for Utah Central having been made by Francis Cope, general freight and traffic agent (and possibly a cousin, Cope having been the name of Cumming's maternal grandmother).
"Utah Central Railway Company," by Francis Cope, General Freight and Traffic Agent.
Third Annual Report of the Interstate Commerce Commission. U.S. Interstate Commerce Commission. December 1, 1889. pp. 382-383.
http://books.google.com/books?id=fpRCAQAAMAAJ&pg=PA383&lpg=PA383
[39] "The Chinese as Railroad Builders after Promontory," by Shelley Fisher Fishkin. *The Chinese and the Iron Road: Building the Transcontinental Railroad.* ed. Gordon H. Chang and Shelley Fisher Fishkin, with Hilton Obenzinger and Roland Hsu. Stanford, Calif.: Stanford University Press, 2019. Chapter 17, p. 278.
[40] Zoellner. *op. cit.,* Introduction, p. 68.
[41] Zoellner, *ibid.,* Introduction, p. xiii.
[42] Rabindranath Tagore. "Railway Station." *Selected Poems.* Translated by William Radice. London: Penguin, 2005. p. 225.
[43] The parents of the four Kittredge siblings were Benjamin L. Kittredge, born in Rockingham, New Hampshire, and Lucy (Dana) Kittredge, born in Waltham, Massachusetts.

[44] George Folger Canfield married Sarah Kittredge in 1884.
[45] The record was set in 1874. "Early Track Records Slow Compared to Existing Ones." Harvard University. *The Crimson,* May 25, 1916.
https://www.thecrimson.com/article/1916/5/25/early-track-records-slow-compared-to/
[46] S. D. Kittredge was the treasurer of the "Cortlandt Stock Protective Association." It sought $1 dues from residents of Cortlandt to support "the pursuit, arrest and conviction of such persons as shall steal horses, wagons, harness or cattle from members of the Association." From an ad in the *Highland Democrat* (Peekskill, NY), January 30, 1886.
[47] Letter from Benjamin Kittredge, Sr. to S. D. ("Dana") Kittredge, November 24, 1900. Kittredge family papers, South Carolina Historical Society. Although the younger Kittredge used the name Ben later as a schoolboy and for the rest of his life, I have chosen to use the name Felix in this book, partly to distinguish him from his father but mostly because it is the name by which Ned might have known him in childhood. Benjamin Jr. was called Felix by his father and by his father's friend, Herman Duryea.
[48] G. M. Cumming. *Cases on Private Corporations: Arranged for Use as a Text-Book.* St. Paul: West Publishing Company, 1894. This was simply a collection of judges' rulings without any added commentary by Cumming.
[49] Throughout the United States in 1888: "As for the streetcars themselves, 21,736 were pulled by horses, 2,777 by cable, 258 by steam, and just 166 by electricity."
Most, *op. cit.,* p. 106.
"More than thirty different street railway companies ruled the streets [of New York City], each independently owned, and they reported their business to nobody."
Most, *ibid.,* p. 135.
"The gap between one car and the next [as recorded at the corner of Broadway and Chambers Street one day in 1852] was usually thirteen seconds. Fifteen years later, in 1867...[this had increased to] the absurd equivalent of 17 every minute."

Most, *ibid.,* p. 53.

"...horse manure was a common source of tetanus, and in the days before vaccination, any open wound was an invitation for illness or death."

"The elevated era." James Nevius. *Longform.* June 27, 2018. https://ny.curbed.com/2018/6/27/17507424/new-york-city-elevated-train-history-transportation

[50] Most, *ibid.,* p. 96.
[51] Zoellner, *op. cit.,* pp. 190-191.
[52] Wolmar, *op. cit.,* p. 139.
[53] Wolmar, *ibid.,* p. 137.
[54] Wolmar, *ibid.,* p. 135.
[55] Wolmar, *ibid.,* p. 139.
[56] Wolmar, *ibid.,* p. 137.

THE TURN OF THE CENTURY

The U.S. Supreme Court ruled that passenger trains could be racially segregated.[1]

Several months later, Henry Ford brought his ethanol-powered automobile prototype to Long Island for the 1896 convention of the Association of Edison Illuminating Companies.[2] He called it a "quadricycle." Commercial availability and mass production were a few years away.

If you wanted fast, modern travel, you were taking a train, and trains enabled the phenomenon of the traveling circus, the sixty-five railroad cars of Ringling Brothers and a hundred other shows of its type.[3] Many of these shows exploited people with unusual bodies for the entertainment of the crowds. One circus performer who would later gain fame was Harry Houdini; he showed audiences that he could escape from chains, but he wouldn't reveal the secret of how they could do it for themselves. He performed at Coney Island early in his career and

TEN PAST NOON

toured Europe in 1900.

The British officer Barog shot himself after the humiliation of failing to tunnel through a mountain in northern India in what is today the state of Himachal Pradesh. His crew had been digging from both sides of the mountain, but they did not meet in the middle according to plan.[4] Another overseer eventually completed the tunnel in 1903. Many workers died on the job, too, but it is Barog's ghost who is said to haunt the tunnel today.[5]

Sigmund Freud slept on Austria's Southern Railway. It was a July 18. The conductor announced that the train would reach the next stop in ten minutes; Freud heard this real voice in his dream. He dreamt that he sleepwalked to another carriage and fit himself into an uncomfortably small seat from where he saw books, Adam Smith's *The Wealth of Nations* and James Clerk Maxwell's *Matter and Motion,* and felt an oscillating uncertainty of whether the books belonged to him. He included this anecdote in his turn-of-the-century book *The Interpretation of Dreams* with a note explaining that his verbal description, though "not intelligible even to myself," is nevertheless part of the dream's meaning.[6]

A sixteen-year-old boy picked up a copy of science fiction about a Martian invasion. The novel was *The War of the Worlds* by H. G. Wells. The boy was Robert Goddard, an American inventor who, nearly three decades later, would build and launch the first liquid-fuel rocket.[7] Years later, Goddard wrote to Wells thanking him for his novel, crediting the fiction with swiftly inspiring him to find his personal mission based on his feeling that "'high altitude research' was the most fascinating problem in existence."[8]

L. Frank Baum published his children's novel *The Wonderful Wizard of Oz* in which a girl walks in silver shoes on a yellow brick road. Many years later, a historian suggested that this was a political allegory for the debate over whether money should be pegged to silver or gold, metals that were being mined in the American West and were measured in ounces, abbreviated "oz."[9]

Spain invented concentration camps in Cuba. The Spanish general Arsenio Martínez Campos, realizing he was losing the war, suggested transporting rural Cubans to other towns and holding them behind barbed wire, but he felt uncomfortable carrying out this policy. He sailed home and took the train to Madrid, where "crowds gathered at each stop to insult him."[10] Spain replaced him with General Valeriano Weyler y Nicolau who in 1896 sailed from Madrid to Havana to serve as Cuba's governor and carry out the world's first *reconcentración*. The victims starved. A concentration camp is "a modern phenomenon,"[11] the researcher Andrea Pitzer says, and "as counterproductive as it is inhumane."[12]

TEN PAST NOON

Britain opened concentration camps in South Africa during the Second Anglo-Boer War. Trains had been running there since 1860, and projects to link them into a national system were completed in 1898. Britain's Imperial Military Railways was established in 1900 and began to take control of other lines; the Boers attacked the British railways with landmines and dynamite. Britain used the trains to move Boer and African civilians, mostly women and children, to concentration camps, where they died of disease.[13]

The American president William McKinley was shot by an anarchist. His successor, President Teddy Roosevelt, invited African-American leader and educator Booker T. Washington to dine at the White House. Washington had worked in a coal mine until he was sixteen (the same year that George Cumming was finishing prep school at Exeter).[14] Leaving the mine, determined to study, Washington boarded a train and disembarked multiple times to find odd jobs to obtain his full train fare just to reach the Hampton Institute.[15] Despite adversity, he rose. *Per ardua ad astra.* The memory of his invitation to the White House in 1901 angered racists for decades.

In 1903, Roosevelt traveled west with a conservationist and slept under the sequoias, and before the end of his second term he gave control of Yosemite Valley to the federal government to maintain it as a nature preserve.[16]

The Wright Brothers tested the first gasoline-powered airplane at Kitty Hawk, North Carolina. The first three flights lasted a matter of seconds each. The fourth and longest trip began at noon and lasted nearly a minute until the plane crashed, lightly damaging its frame.

The golfer Harry Vardon came from England to the US and won the US Open. Having grown up poor in the Jersey Islands, he learned the game by caddying for rich men, invented his own way of gripping the golf club, and catalyzed the sport's popularity. Now golf was no longer just a private pastime but also a professional spectacle.

The Kansas Supreme Court ruled that it was libelous for a newspaper to namecall a man a "eunuch" because the word falsely implied that the man was physically, not just symbolically, castrated.[17]

In 1908, the Young Turks changed the Ottoman empire into a constitutional monarchy. There was still a sultan, and it would be some years before Turkey became a republic.

In 1909, L. Frank Baum, writing under a pseudonym, released the fourth volume of his *Boy Fortune Hunters* series, in which three white American teenage boys sail for China with two South Sea Islanders in a support role. They raid the treasure of a dead Chinese prince out from under the nose of the chief eunuch of the palace who has given them hospitality.[18]

TEN PAST NOON

By 1911, railway projects in China were a source of tension. The government controlled them too tightly, construction was slow, and investors were displeased with their returns. The Railway Rights Protection Movement overthrew the last dynasty of imperial China, though the palace eunuchs and the former emperor would remain together in the Forbidden City for another decade. The disempowered emperor sometimes played tennis there.[19]

A high-altitude retreat in Davos, Switzerland was opened for tuberculosis patients. Travelers, upon very nearly reaching that destination, had to switch to a narrow-gauge train that could ascend the Alps. In the spring of 1912, Thomas Mann spent three weeks there visiting his wife, Katia, who was undergoing a six-month treatment. Mann was given the same diagnosis, but he, just turning thirty-seven, refused to remain in such an isolating place that, in his view, threatened to "wholly wean a young person from actual and active life."[20]

He began to write a novel—completed over the course of twelve years—about a man who arrives at the Davos sanatorium intending to stay for three weeks and who remains seven years until World War I breaks out. What will happen, one character speculates, if the Ottoman sultan falls, if Turkey becomes "a national, constitutional state," and if England "set[s] herself up as protector"?[21]

Forty years after that lung examination, Mann fretted that, had he been successfully recruited by the Davos doctor to move into the sanatorium, "who knows, I might still be there!"[22]

NOTES TO "THE TURN OF THE CENTURY"

[1] Plessy v. Ferguson, 163 U.S. 537 (1896)
[2] Ford Richardson Bryan. *Friends, Families, & Forays: Scenes from the Life and Times of Henry Ford.* Dearborn, Michigan: Ford Books, 2002. p. 153.
[3] Michael N. McGregor. *Pure Act: The Uncommon Life of Robert Lax.* Fordham University Press, 2015.
[4] "Tunnel Number 33." P. Krishna Gopinath. *The Hindu.* September 23, 2017.
https://www.thehindu.com/society/history-and-culture/tunnel-number-33/article19734497.ece
Accessed February 16, 2020.
[5] "Man behind Barog tunnel lies forgotten." Jagmeet Singh. *The Tribune.* June 15, 2002.
https://www.tribuneindia.com/2002/20020615/windows/main4.htm Accessed February 16, 2020.
[6] Sigmund Freud. *The Interpretation of Dreams* (1900). Chapter 6, Part 3: "The Dream-Work." G-VI-8.
https://psychclassics.yorku.ca/Freud/Dreams/dreams6c.htm Accessed February 18, 2020.
[7] "The Stuff of Goddard's Dreams: Goddard's Legacy & NASA's Journey to Mars." Remarks by NASA Administrator Charles Bolden at the Goddard Memorial Symposium, Greenbelt, Maryland, February 9, 2016.
https://www.nasa.gov/sites/default/files/atoms/files/bolden_goddard_2016.pdf Accessed January 16, 2020.
[8] "Goddard Deserves Niche as Father of Rocketry—A Scientist's Dream Outlasted the Taunts." Harry

Guggenheim. *Evening Star* (Washington, D.C.). July 16, 1969.
https://books.google.com.co/books?id=7_JT9lp0YSkC&pg=PA20022&lpg=PA20022 Accessed January 16, 2020.
[9] Littlefield, Henry (1964). "The Wizard of Oz: Parable on Populism." *American Quarterly.* 16 (1): 47–58. doi:10.2307/2710826.
[10] Andrea Pitzer. *One Long Night: A Global History of Concentration Camps.* Introduction: Sailing to Guantánamo. New York: Hachette, 2017. p. 21.
[11] Pitzer, *ibid.* p. 14.
[12] Pitzer, *ibid.* p. 16.
[13] "A South African Railway History." Christo Kleingeld. 2003.
http://mysite.mweb.co.za/residents/grela/transnet.html Accessed February 18, 2020.
"All the World is India; India is a World Apart." ed. Matthew D. Esposito. *A World History of Railway Cultures, 1830-1930, Volume 2.* New York: Routledge, 2020.
https://books.google.com.co/books?id=jNTHDwAAQBAJ Accessed February 16, 2020.
[14] "Booker T. Washington's West Virginia Boyhood." Louis R. Harlan. Volume 32, Number 2 (January 1971), pp. 63-85. http://www.wvculture.org/history/journal_wvh/wvh32-1.html Accessed June 29, 2019.
[15] The year was 1872. See: "Booker T. Washington Made School Janitors Cool Way Before Good Will Hunting." Michael Tunney. Nov. 16, 2018.
https://medium.com/profiles-in-action/booker-t-washington-made-school-janitors-cool-way-before-good-will-hunting-94f847a2760d
[16] Christopher Gergen and Gregg Vanourek. *Life Entrepreneurs: Ordinary People Creating Extraordinary Lives.* Jossey-Bass, 2008.
[17] Eckert v. VanPelt (1904). Kansas Supreme Court.
"Application of Libel Law Principles by Kansas Editors." Matthew D. Bunker (submitted as part of a postgraduate

degree). Manhattan, Kansas: Kansas State University, 1989. pp. 16-17. https://archive.org/stream/applicationoflib00bunk/applicationoflib00bunk_djvu.txt Accessed June 7, 2014.

[18] Floyd Akers [L. Frank Baum.] *The Boy Fortune Hunters of China.* Reilly and Britton, 1909.

[19] "The Death of the Last Emperor's Last Eunuch." Seth Faison. *New York Times.* December 20, 1996. https://www.nytimes.com/1996/12/20/world/the-death-of-the-last-emperor-s-last-eunuch.html Accessed February 19, 2020.

[20] "The Making of *The Magic Mountain.*" Thomas Mann. *The Atlantic,* January 1953. Reprinted in Thomas Mann. *The Magic Mountain* (originally S. Fischer Verlagberlin, 1924). Translated from the German by H. T. Lowe-Porter. England: A. Wehaten and Co., Exeter, 1971. p. 721.

[21] Mann, *The Magic Mountain, ibid.*, p. 379.

[22] A "narrow-gauge" train: Mann, *The Magic Mountain, ibid.*, Chapter 1, p. 3.

Also, Mann, "The Making of *The Magic Mountain,*" *ibid.*, pp. 720-1.

THE TRAINS
OF NED'S CHILDHOOD

The eldest Kittredge sibling, Sarah, died young, leaving one child. Her husband, George Folger Canfield—the man who had gotten George Cumming the job at Columbia Law—remarried, undeterred, back into her family. There were subsequently a prolific number of Canfield children, nieces and nephews to George and Lucy Cumming.[1]

A son was born to the Cummings in 1899, a little brother for four-year-old Emily, but he didn't survive a week.[2] He was given a large stone at his mother's family plot at Hillside Cemetery in Cortlandt Manor, New York, fifty miles north of the city.

The Cummings moved frequently around Manhattan: East 49th Street, West 55th Street. *The doors of the local train will open at every station.* Then there was East 35th Street between Lexington and Park, an extravagant address in the Murray Hill neighborhood, three blocks from

TEN PAST NOON

the future site of the Empire State Building, with four servants. Little Emily had a 19-year-old Swiss nurse named Clara, and, hailing from Ireland, 34-year-old Rose cooked the food, 24-year-old Mary brought the food to the table, and another woman did the laundry.[3]

At this time, Christian Wolmar wrote, New Yorkers still endured "noisy, steam-hauled trains passing their second-floor windows at all times of the day."[4]

New York's subway system broke ground in early 1900. The engineers aspired to build electric trains, just as London had already accomplished. The tunnels themselves, too, were a major engineering feat. Twenty-five thousand New Yorkers congregated early on a cold Saturday morning at City Hall Park to celebrate the groundbreaking, and the festivities were as loud as possible: church bells, dynamite, and a band conducted by the man who had recently composed the military march "The Stars and Stripes Forever," John Philip Sousa himself.[5] It was preparation for the noise of the next several years of construction. Manhattan's bedrock is mica schist that formed a few hundred million years ago[6] and, at any given street corner, the workers couldn't predict at what depth they'd reach the end of the soil and sand and hit the impassable rock.[7] Soon, there were thousands of workers underground, digging and blasting, building with ten million dollars' worth of steel, hammering the rails, their materials pulled in by mules.[8]

As the subway construction began, the Cummings moved out to the suburb of Cedarhurst, Long Island, and that's where their second surviving child, Edward, was born on July 18, 1901, the anniversary of Freud's dream on the train. The birth may have been at home, and there may not have been an attending physician. Dr. Pershing, a physician who hailed from George Cumming's hometown of Pottsville, Pennsylvania, dated the birth certificate two weeks after the baby's arrival.[9] Pershing began to handwrite the child's name as "Georg—," but this was the proud father's name. The error was crossed out, initialed, and corrected to "Edward," and informally the child would be called Ned; these happened to be Dr. Pershing's name and nickname.[10]

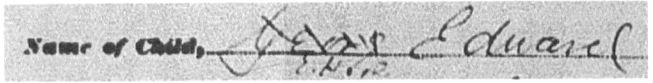

Figure 4 – Edward Cumming's birth certificate.

The following month, Lord Kelvin hit upon the answer to the question: *If there are an infinite number of stars, why isn't the night sky full of light?*[11] Perhaps unbeknownst to Lord Kelvin, Edgar Allan Poe had already answered the question in 1848 in his prose poem "Eureka." The reason is that it takes time for light to travel,

TEN PAST NOON

so, assuming there was a time before the stars existed, we simply have not reached the moment in time at which the infinite starlight has arrived to us. We must assume, Poe wrote, that "the distance of the invisible background [is] so immense that no ray from it has yet been able to reach us at all."[12] The current darkness of the sky is our proof of a time when the stars did not exist. Light, and therefore darkness, is a measure of time. Kelvin made the answer famous.

This is when Ned Cumming entered the world, under Lord Kelvin's star sign.

He was baptized on December 8 by the Rev. Edward Lincoln Atkinson at the Episcopal Church of the Epiphany in Manhattan. His uncle George Folger Canfield was inscribed as a witness, as were two of his Pottsville relatives: his father's mother and younger brother.[13] (This grandmother had, several years earlier, in her mid-seventies, applied for a passport to live in Cairo for "a year or two." Ned's maternal grandmother, by contrast, lived in the same house with his family in New York.)[14]

In those early years of the 20th century, George Cumming was vice president of the Susquehanna & Western Railroad, and of the Erie Railroad, and of the Black Rock Railroad, and of the Middletown, Unionville and Water Gap Railroad. He was chairman of the board of the Cincinnati, Hamilton & Dayton and of the Wisconsin Central.[15] For one month in 1905, he was president of the Detroit, Toledo, and Ironton Railway following the previous president's sudden death,[16] and he remained on the board for some years after that. He may well have aided coal and railroad interests to fix shipping rates; letters he signed in 1901 resurfaced a decade later when the Eastern railroads again proposed raising freight rates.[17] Add a monocle, and he was, down to his white handlebar mustache, the embodiment of the mascot of the Monopoly board game.

Figure 5 – G. M. Cumming passport photo, 1919.

I don't know what this old-school railroad man thought about the concept or logistics of the underground subway. Though the final product was of course essential for New Yorkers, the construction period made the city for several years a less pleasant place in which to live and work.

The New York City subway engineers quickly

TEN PAST NOON

realized that digging through rock would not form reliably smooth paths for the trains and that they would have to use dynamite to tunnel.[18] The Cummings' former neighborhood in Murray Hill was unstable in the geological sense, but the engineers nevertheless had to tunnel through it. "There was little to do to make the blasting more tolerable. It was loud, and the ground shook with terrifying vibrations each time there was a detonation," wrote Doug Most in his history of the subway.[19] Perhaps that was why the Cummings left for Long Island: so that Lucy could give birth and nurse in a quiet suburb.

It was a lucky choice. Only five or six short blocks from where the Cummings used to live, subway workers stored a quarter-ton of dynamite in a single shed, and, when the shed caught fire one day—January 27, 1902, at about ten past noon—the explosion shot smoke over the tops of the buildings, and window panes exploded. Dust, reaching the Cummings' former house on East 35th Street, was "so thick that it hurt to inhale."[20] The neighborhood was impacted twice again that spring: a lawyer's home was structurally damaged where the Park Avenue tunnel collapsed between East 37th and 38th Streets,[21] and another collapse at 39th Street killed the thirty-nine-year-old local project director.[22] In this manner, throughout the city, the subway incurred fifty-four fatalities before it ever opened for business.

Despite this recent safety record, a hundred

thousand rides were taken in the subway's first five hours of operation on October 27, 1904.[23] London had opened the dark tunnels of its primitive subway four decades earlier, but New York created a better customer experience by placing electric lights underground from the beginning. People could see where they were going.

※※※※※※※※※

So, Ned was born in a suburb, while his father continued to work in Manhattan. Of Ned's first years of life, nothing whatsoever is known directly. I can only give impressions.

He was eight months younger than his first cousin Felix Kittredge, the boy born to Benjamin and Bessie in California.

His family may have listened to G&T gramophone recordings from Europe, "with the recording angel on the label, red or black according to the prestige of the artist," as the novelist Roger Lewinter described them.[24]

Outside the city, he may have spotted one of the last wild Carolina parakeets: green, with a yellow head and red face. John James Audubon had once painted some of these parakeets, along with hundreds of other species, eventually published in his grand artistic catalog, *The Birds of America.*

If Ned's parents took him as a five-year-old to the Bronx Zoo, he might have seen Ota Benga, a twenty-two-year-old Mbuti man from the Congo, on display in the Monkey House.

Both of Ned's grandmothers died in 1907. His grandfathers had died before he was born.

When he was eight, he might have looked up and seen Halley's Comet swinging by as it does roughly once in every human lifetime, Earth touching the comet's tail.[25]

If his parents were invested in railroad stocks, those investments may have been shaky. When he was ten, his mother rented out her three-acre Irvington-on-Hudson estate. (This mansion with detailed brickwork was always identified as "her property.")[26]

They may have heard of a fossil excavation at La Brea in Los Angeles that began in 1913. As a natural underground source of crude oil bubbles to the surface, it becomes liquid asphalt, trapping any animal that touches it. The excavated tar pits yielded the skeletons of dire wolves, saber-toothed cats, and mastodons that were trapped between ten and twenty thousand years ago. Also, bears: the black, the grizzly, and the extinct giant.

If they attended a circus, they may have watched a magician who learned from the instruction book *The Expert at the Card Table*. It was published at the turn of the century by a pseudonymous S. W. Erdnase whose true identity remains unknown.[27]

There are hoaxes and illusions we can debunk,

and there are mysteries of which we must let go.

Ned's parents' activities, at least, are generally known. There was a house at Ardsley-on-Hudson. There were country club memberships at Ardsley, a society that offered golf and polo, recently founded by J. P. Morgan, John D. Rockefeller, and the late Cornelius Vanderbilt II;[28] Rockaway Hunt on Long Island with its fine horses;[29] and City Midday in Manhattan. George belonged to the Saint Andrews' Society, a mutual aid society for New Yorkers of Scottish descent.[30] As if the railroad business weren't enough, he was president of the US Mortgage and Trust Company, the United States Safe Deposit Company, and the Bronx Refrigerating Company; he was vice president of the American Telephone and Telegraph Company; and, along with two other men, he had a million-dollar business interest in the General Equipment and Construction Company. He had a law office on Wall Street and another address around the corner on Cedar Street. He dealt with occasional investigations and lawsuits.[31] He was perhaps not home very much.

###########

President Woodrow Wilson pressed a button at the canal in Panama. It was early afternoon on October 10, 1913. Explosives detonated at the Gamboa dike and made a pathway between the Pacific and Atlantic Oceans.[32]

TEN PAST NOON

#############

Ned's cousin Felix was already at a preparatory school—St. George's in Middletown, Rhode Island—by his early teens. There, Felix studied Latin, Greek, French, English, math, and religion.[33]

An hour's walk around the bay from St. George's stood the mansions in the city of Newport, with names like The Elms, Chateau-sur-Mer, and Rosecliff. They had gone up in the Gilded Age and were emblematic of late 19th century opulence. One mansion had been built by Cornelius Vanderbilt II. (He had been the grandfather of a boy Felix's age, also a Cornelius, who used the suffix "Jr.")[34] The house, called The Breakers, had seventy rooms, including living quarters for thirty-three staff. It was a summer home. The Vanderbilts had gained their astonishing wealth from railroads.

Felix's parents had been close with Nellie and Herman Duryea, a childless couple who had a New York house with five live-in servants, race horses in Europe, as well as a modern mansion (carbide lights, running water, indoor toilets) that they built on fifteen thousand acres in Hickory Valley, Tennessee in 1897 where they bred shorthorn cattle, dogs, and gamecocks and landscaped with imported Dutch tulips.[35] The men had corresponded at great length, especially about horse racing, livestock shows, and agricultural sales. Herman now sent a letter

TUCKER LIEBERMAN

about loneliness:

> It seems an age since I have either written or heard from you—It seems one of the hardest things of old age, coming on, that the oldest and best friends seem to see less and less of each other, and their interests that were at one time almost one, draw farther and farther apart. New ones spring up, but they are never the same...The old farm I haven't been near for over a year; the cocks might all be dead, for all I care for them; Santa B and all its life and fun and charms, died when we buried poor mother—now you are away and our old life seems only a dream—Well there's no use getting morbid, they will never come back again and I will try to write of the present. I have been down here for a month and have had a very good time—it's a very bad season for birds, owing to the drought, and lack of food, but there are lots of foxes, turkeys and rabbits-tracks...Nellie went to Boston to see her father...I wish that you and Bessie and Felix could be here for the next two weeks—It would be great fun, and we could talk each other to death but of course that's out of the question...I went in for dinner and received your letter...I take more interest in him [Felix], than I do in almost any human being—Having no son of my own, yours of course must be of interest. Years ago, and not so

many, anything that happened to anyone of my family was of the keenest interest to you...this damned age and separation seems to change things—It shouldn't and it mustn't.[36]

Meanwhile, Bessie wrote to her 13-year-old son Felix at his boarding school that his relatives, including his Uncle George, were proud of him for "trying to stick it out," "staying," and "going to try it again!"[37] She added, sharing information that she may have gained secondhand, that George and Lucy had just traveled to Europe and to "South America" (unlikely; Cuba is more probable), and that "Uncle Lucy [sic] said she was perfectly redicalous [sic] in her enthusiasm over standing on the highest peak of the world etc etc. She is very amusing..."[38] The young Felix responded frequently with an ebullient social diary in the form of letters addressed to his mother.

Ned followed his cousin Felix and entered St. George's in September 1914. The school headmaster, who had not yet met Ned nor his father, wrote to the father, "If he is not yet thirteen years old, he is very far advanced..." If Ned would also prove to be socially normal and reasonably athletic, "he must be a very interesting lad indeed." He added: "I also am very glad to know that the boy is a cousin of Benny [Felix] Kittredge, who is a boy that is doing very well with us, and is going to do still better."[39] (It was not the last subtle comment that people would make about the latter's grades having room for improvement.)

Ned's father and the headmaster decided he would skip the ordinary first year of study. His first year at St. George's was his Fourth Form (sophomore) year. He had begun a little Latin on his own (his father had suggested he should study at summer camp),[40] was signed up to study Greek, and won a geometry prize that year. A school photograph shows him, at age thirteen, a bit shorter than the boys next to whom he is standing.

In the drama club's performance of *Ici on Parle Français* in March 1915, Felix stole the show, the *Dragon* student newspaper calling him "the star, beyond all question" for his "most amusing and entertaining" interpretation of Mrs. Spriggins. Ned got an honorary mention for his "frenchified mannerisms" in the role of Victor Dubois.[41]

Students in 1915 requested military training. They fired guns, marched, drew maps, practiced first aid, learned radiotelegraphy, and cultivated an enormous "victory garden," as growing one's own food was then construed as indirect support for the troops.[42]

Lucy Cumming, with her daughter Emily turning twenty and her son Ned away at boarding school, once again leased her Irvington estate to Ardsley socialites on a seasonal basis.[43]

During Ned's second year at St. George's, he

TEN PAST NOON

compressed two years of study, accelerating through his Fifth Form and Sixth Form exams (junior and senior years).

While at home in Manhattan for Christmas in 1915, he played singles in a young men's tennis tournament.[44] One jumps to serve the tennis ball and tries to hit it while still in an upward trajectory, putting the whole body into the effort.[45]

In February 1916, the drama club put on *Foggerty's Fairy,* a farce in which Ned played a "mad doctor" while Felix once again donned a matronly dress to play "a matter-of-fact old lady."

Ned received his diploma that spring. He wasn't yet fifteen.

As his father had graduated from Harvard, and his great-great-grandfather Joseph Willard (on his mother's side) had served as the college's president in the late 1700s, it is perhaps unsurprising that his acceptance to Harvard was announced. He went first, however, to the Phillips Exeter prep school in New Hampshire for the Fall 1916 term, probably for a "postgraduate year" before beginning college, given his young age.

Figure 6 – Detail of some of the players in the February 26, 1916 performance of "Foggerty's Fairy," courtesy of St. George's School Archives. Benjamin [Felix] Kittredge is all the way on the left side of the image, and Ned Cumming is all the way on the right.

≠≠≠≠≠≠≠≠≠

When he was home in Irvington, he, his mother, and his sister sometimes attended St. Barnabas Episcopal Church.[46] The Book of Common Prayer, as it had done for centuries, translated the Gloria Patri's phrase *in sæcula sæculorum*, a lifetime of lifetimes, as "world without end," and specified that the funeral liturgy could not be recited for suicides.[47]

#########

Railway stocks had lost $3 billion in market value between 1906 and 1914. Effects on "commercial and industrial interests are just beginning to be felt," a Midwestern railroad president warned.[48] Shortly afterward, the Supreme Court ruled that the Interstate Commerce Commission should control the shipping rates charged by the railroads.[49] No longer was this an amount that George Cumming could change with a stroke of his pen.

#########

Kanan Makiya wrote in his 2016 novel *The Rope:*

> I don't know what Father would have done; I never knew him. I grew up with the fact of his disappearance...His body was never found. Not a trace of it anywhere; I know, I searched frenziedly...Still, I know it is out there somewhere. A fact that is also a non-fact never entirely goes away; it is like the dust that Mother battled with daily. Knowing that is not knowing continues to hang around in the air like dust, in the little nooks and crannies of our minds.[50]

#########

TUCKER LIEBERMAN

Felix was still at St. George's, playing two female characters in another school comedy[51] and, amidst rumors that the Germans would destroy Newport, Rhode Island, dreaming of joining the war as a surgeon: "I wish I were old enough to get a job on it!" He praised Hetty Hemenway's newly released novel *Four Days: The Story of a War Marriage* and bragged that he knew it to be a true story because his classmate's aunt knew the author. The school's battalion marched in a town parade on Decoration Day. That summer, he wrote home: "I howed [sic] potatoes yesterday all afternoon, and I feel every stroke you take with the hoe is one at the Kaiser's head!" He boasted of the continued purchases of Liberty Bonds by himself and his classmates.[52]

Ned, for his part, may have had his eye on the Canadian Royal Flying Corps, a program established by the British Royal Flying Corps in January 1917 to train Americans and Canadians.[53] His enlistment, with which he would have joined thousands of other young men in that program,[54] was announced in a St. George's Alumni Note, but he wasn't mentioned in the subsequent alumni veteran publication *St. George's School in the War*.[55] There's no other suggestion that he ever served. The military records for this year of this particular program—depending on whether you ask Britain, Canada, or the United States—were split, merged, destroyed in a fire, or perhaps never existed.

TEN PAST NOON

Ned might have been excited to try to sign up. "There wasn't a kid I knew that wouldn't lie, cheat, steal, anything to get into that war," one of his contemporaries recalled decades later of the U.S. Army/Navy recruitment. "If you went down the street with a band, you could pick up a thousand or fifteen thousand kids that wanted to get in. Opposite of what it is now."[56]

But adults knew differently. It was dangerous even to train during those early years of military aviation, especially in the snow. In Canada, during the two years before the armistice, fatal air crashes were, on average, a weekly event.[57] The Royal Flying Corps' motto was "*per ardua ad astra*": we go "to the stars," but only "through adversity."

And Europe knew differently.

> The Energy that belongs to the Universe says, 'I can't wait any longer. This is it.' The Universe writes a letter to you and leaves it with your tutor. The Woman with the Golden Hair and the thirty swan women sail away, and they will never come back. Something final has happened. The mood reminds one of that summer of 1914—some joy disappeared in England and never came again.
>
> —Robert Bly and Marion Woodman, *The Maiden King*[58]

Ota Benga, the man who had been held captive at the Bronx Zoo, longed to return to his homeland in the Ituri rainforest—which by then, after the colonization by King Leopold II, had become part of the Belgian Congo—and he was heartbroken when passenger ships to Africa were discontinued in 1914. Two years later, in Virginia, he shot himself in the heart.[59]

After Germany's intensive bombing of London in September 1917, residents of London developed the habit of sheltering in the subway system.[60]

Felix remained at St. George's in the Fall of 1917, enjoying a new Victrola phonograph, requesting recordings (likely by Enrico Caruso) of "Carmen" and "Santa Lucia." "I did not know anything could add to your fun as much as that has," he wrote. By spring, he seemed distressed by both academics and the war, writing home: "Things do look discouraging and I don't blame you for feeling downcast. If the war and all other horrors would be over! What is the use of struggling to pass college exams if as soon as the time comes for you to go college [sic], you have to go and fight."[61]

Ned joined the Harvard Class of 1921, beginning his first and only year at the university in the Fall of 1917, living in a freshman dorm, Persis Smith Hall, A21.[62] Standing five-foot-ten (six inches taller than his mother and also a full inch above his father), he played tennis. His grades were good.[63] Basing his character on his later writings—and extrapolating back to his teens—I imagine he was good at copying, making lists, keeping track of citations, and persisting in his interests; he was not afraid of long books nor of languages that were new to him; he maintained a detached tone that steered away from political statements; and he had legible handwriting. For all these reasons, academia would have rewarded him. But he did not want to stay with academia. Perhaps he accepted teachers' praise as evidence that he was already bright enough as he was and therefore felt he had license to quit.

Ned looked as though he could be Alan Turing's brother or, I also like to imagine, Federico García Lorca's cousin.

After that year at Harvard, Ned went home to New York City. The federal government had just given authority to the Interstate Commerce Commission to enshrine the American time zones that the railroads had already been using since before he was born.[64]

In August, he played singles in a national championship tournament at the West Side Tennis Club in Queens.[65]

Age 13   Age 14

Age 18   Age 18

Four photographs of Edward Dilworth Cumming.

Figure 7 (top left) – Student. Courtesy of St. George's School Archives. Detail of the 1915 "All School" group photo.

Figure 8 (top right) – Student. Courtesy of St. George's School Archives. Detail of his costume for the February 26, 1916 performance of "Foggerty's Fairy."

Figure 9 (bottom left) – Teacher. Courtesy of St. George's School Archives. Detail of a Fall 1919 faculty photo.

Figure 10 (bottom right) – Passport. February 1920.

TEN PAST NOON

Then he found an academic enterprise that interested him more than Harvard.

> But you were young, and you had
> Plenty of time:
> Going west,
>
> You slept on the train and did not smile.
> Under you the plains widened, and turned silver.
>
> —Larry Levis, "The Spirit Says, You Are Nothing"[66]

No, he had not started to write his book on eunuchs. Not yet. He was still forming. First, he would go westward into the desert to transmit the knowledge he had already acquired.

NOTES TO "THE TRAINS OF NED'S CHILDHOOD"

[1] Sarah Kittredge had one son, George Dana Canfield, born in 1887. Sarah died in 1897; the cause is unknown to me. Her widower, George Folger Canfield, then married Fannie Marshall. Fannie was the sister of Benjamin Kittredge's wife Bessie Marshall. From Felix's perspective, Canfield had been married first to his father's sister and then to his mother's sister, so Canfield was his uncle twice over.

[2] The infant was named Richard Cope Cumming. Cope was the maiden name of G. M. Cumming's maternal grandmother.

[3] In the 1900 census, Supervisor's District 1, Enumeration District 689, 156 A. The address was 113 East 35th Street. The servant in the laundry appears to be named Nunn

Duffy, but her first name is written unclearly and might have been Niamh or Nina. Her age was not recorded at all. https://www.ancestry.com/interactive/7602/4114674_008 25/53720510 Accessed February 21, 2020.
[4] Christian Wolmar. *The Subterranean Railway: How the London Underground Was Built and How It Changed the City Forever.* London: Atlantic, 2004. p. 127.
[5] Doug Most. *The Race Underground: Boston, New York, and the Incredible Rivalry That Built America's First Subway.* New York: St. Martin's Press, 2014. p. 306.
[6] "Manhattan Schist in New York City Parks—J. Hood Wright Park." NYC Parks. https://www.nycgovparks.org/parks/j-hood-wright-park/highlights/12369 Accessed Sept. 30, 2019.
[7] Most, *op. cit.,* pp. 156-158.
[8] Most, *ibid.,* pp. 324-325.
[9] Pershing, a Princeton graduate, was the cousin of the four-star General of the Armies known as "Black Jack."
[10] The middle initial on the birth certificate was "W."—perhaps intended to be Wilson or Washburn, family names on his father's side—but this was never seen again. The boy always used the middle name "Dilworth," another family name on his father's side, a name recorded at his baptism when he was four months old.
[11] Lord Kelvin published his answer in *The London, Edinburgh, and Dublin Philosophical Magazine and Journal of Science* in August 1901. Credit is usually given to Lord Kelvin for solving the paradox, but the cosmologist Edward Harrison (as Michio Kaku explains) found that Poe was "the first person in history to solve the paradox." Michio Kaku. *Parallel Worlds: A Journey Through Creation, Higher Dimensions, and the Future of the Cosmos.* (2004) Anchor eBooks, 2006.
Lord Kelvin published his "Lecture 16" as "On ether and gravitational matter through infinite space," *Philosophical Magazine,* August 1901.
https://books.google.com/books?id=Q1YwAAAAIAAJ&pg=PA161&lpg=PA161

TEN PAST NOON

This information is provided in Edward Harrison's book *Darkness at Night: A Riddle of the Universe,* Harvard University Press, 1989. p. 157.
https://books.google.com/books?id=IRKYueWVftYC
Accessed April 4, 2015.

[12] Edgar Allan Poe. "Eureka: A Prose Poem." Gutenberg, 2010. (Originally New York: Putnam, 1848).
http://www.gutenberg.org/files/32037/32037-h/32037-h.htm Accessed February 16, 2020.

[13] "New York, Episcopal Diocese of New York Church Records, 1767-1970." Manhattan: Church of the Epiphany: 1896-1927. pp. 22-23. Accessed on Ancestry.com, February 21, 2020.

[14] U.S. Passport Application for Emma Washburn Cumming. Feb. 14, 1898.
https://www.ancestry.com/interactive/1174/USM1834_15-0204/451378#?imageId=USM1834_15-0204
Accessed February 22, 2020.

[15] The Wisconsin Central had, in late 1905, suffered a stock drop. See: *The Commercial and Financial Chronicle,* Vol. 85. Oct. 12, 1907. p. 922.
See also: *Duluth Evening Herald.* Oct. 10, 1905.
http://www.mocavo.com/Duluth-Evening-Herald-Volume-October-6-1905/505063/62

[16] "G. M. Cummings [sic] to Head Reorganized Company—No Hitch in Ann Arbor Negotiations." *Brooklyn Daily Eagle.* June 3, 1905.

[17] "Charles E. Henderson, formerly Vice President of the Philadelphia & Reading Coal and Iron Company, was the chief witness [brought before the Commerce Board], and in the documentary evidence were letters written on July 9, 1901, and July 11, 1901, signed by G. M. Cumming, saying that at a meeting of the Temple Iron Company in New York it had been proposed to fix either a percentage or a flat rate to outside shippers...Mr. Henderson further testified that so far as he knew the proposed rates were not put into effect at that time."

"Gets Light on Coal Pool: Commerce Board Also Sifts Finances of the Reading Road." *New York Times,* 16 Jan 1914. https://www.nytimes.com/1914/01/16/archives/gets-light-on-coal-pool-commerce-board-also-sifts-finances-of-the.html?searchResultPosition=4 Accessed February 20, 2020.

"Shippers to Be Heard: Commerce Board courts specific objections to Rate Increase." *New York Times.* January 16, 1914. https://timesmachine.nytimes.com/timesmachine/1914/01/16/101913251.html?pageNumber=11 Accessed February 20, 2020.

[18] Most, *op. cit.,* p. 315.

[19] Most, *ibid.,* p. 316.

[20] The dust "blanketed a ten-block stretch between Thirty-fifth and Forty-fifth streets with air so thick that it hurt to inhale."

Most, *ibid.,* p. 319.

Regarding the timing of "about ten past noon":

"That day, just before noon, workers constructing the subway tunnel under Park Avenue set a small fire in the dynamite shed directly in front of the hotel to thaw out the explosives then walked away. A few minutes later master mechanic William Tubbs noticed that the fire had spread and rushed with a hose. It was too late."

"The Lost 1884 Murray Hill Hotel—Park Avenue and 40th St." Tom Miller. *Daytonian in Manhattan.* October 15, 2012.

http://daytoninmanhattan.blogspot.com/2012/10/the-lost-1884-murray-hill-hotel-park.html

Accessed Sept. 29, 2019.

"A few minutes after noon on January 27, 1902, the clamor from the digging along Forty-first Street near Park Avenue was suddenly drowned out by the frantic shouts of Moses Epps."

Most, *op. cit.,* p. 317.

[21] Most, *ibid.,* p. 320.

[22] Most, *ibid.,* p. 322.

[23] Most, *ibid.,* p. 346.

TEN PAST NOON

[24] Roger Lewinter. *The Attraction of Things.* (*L'attrait des choses: Fragments de vie oblique,* 1985) Translated from the French by Rachel Careau (2016). New York: New Directions, 2016. p. 1.

[25] "Observatory telescopes picked up the comet on April 9, 1910, and followed it as it reached perihelion on April 20." "May 19, 1910: Halley's Comet Brushes Earth With Its Tail." Tony Long. *Wired.* May 19, 2009. https://www.wired.com/2009/05/dayintech-0519/ Accessed November 12, 2019.
"...Earth actually passed through the comet's tail."
"Disappointed Comet-Gazers Bidding Halley's Farewell." Peter H. Lewis. *New York Times.* April 13, 1986. https://www.nytimes.com/1986/04/13/us/disappointed-comet-gazers-bidding-halley-s-farewell.html
Accessed November 12, 2019.

[26] "The Real Estate Field: Leases." *The New York Times.* September 7, 1911. https://timesmachine.nytimes.com/timesmachine/1911/09/07/106785298.html?pageNumber=16
Accessed February 20, 2020.

[27] "The magician who wants to break magic." Jonah Weiner. *New York Times.* March 15, 2017. https://www.nytimes.com/2017/03/15/magazine/derek-delgaudio-the-magician-who-wants-to-break-magic.html

[28] "New Club on the Hudson; The Ardsley Casino Will Soon Be Finished. Handsome and Complete Clubhouse Situated on a Bluff Overlooking the Hudson—Fine Golf Course and Polo Ground." *New York Times.* March 1, 1896. https://www.nytimes.com/1896/03/01/archives/new-club-on-the-hudson-the-ardsley-casino-will-soon-be-finished.html Accessed August 6, 2019.

[29] "Horses in the Five Towns." Hewlett-Woodmere Public Library. *Five Towns Local History.* April 26, 2011. http://ftlh.blogspot.com/2011/04/horses-in-five-towns.html

[30] "History of Saint Andrew's Society of the State of New York, 1756-1906." George Austin Morrison. New York,

1906. http://www.electricscotland.com/history/america/newyork/historyofsaintan00sainuoft.pdf

[31] "New York Produce Review and American Creamery." Vol. 34. New York, May 22, 1912, No. 5.
See also:
Cumming v. Middletown, U. & W. G. R. Co. et al. (Supreme Court Appellate Division, Second Department. June 11, 1912.) See also 135 N. Y. Supp. 1107.

[32] "Canal is Opened by Wilson's Finger." *New York Times.* October 11, 1913.
https://timesmachine.nytimes.com/timesmachine/1913/10/11/100651670.pdf Accessed January 20, 2020.

[33] Kittredge family papers, South Carolina Historical Society. Papers of Benjamin Kittredge, Jr., April 29, 1920.

[34] He was really the fourth Cornelius Vanderbilt, but he used the suffix "Jr." throughout his life due to a rupture between his father and grandfather. He married six more times, as mentioned in his *New York Times* obituary: https://www.nytimes.com/1974/07/08/archives/cornelius-vanderbilt-jr-newsman-author-dead-broke-family-tradition.html

[35] Whitney Hill. "Historic LaGrange & Hickory Valley." This was material I found online, accessed possibly in 2013, but I cannot identify the source again now in 2020.

[36] Herman Duryea, undated letter to Benjamin Kittredge, Sr. Kittredge family papers, South Carolina Historical Society. Duryea died in 1916.

[37] Letter from Bessie Kittredge to Benjamin Kittredge, Jr., October 14, 1913. Kittredge family papers, South Carolina Historical Society.

[38] The Chimborazo Volcano in Ecuador is sometimes said to be the world's highest peak because its location near the equator makes it the farthest point from the Earth's center. Reaching Chimborazo's summit, however, requires skill. The Cummings were 58 and 48 years old at the time of this trip, and even reaching Ecuador would have been a challenge, as Bessie Kittredge's report was written just ten days after President Wilson ceremonially opened the

TEN PAST NOON

Panama Canal. George traveled to Cuba for business in 1919, so it seems likely that this 1913 trip could also have been to Cuba. The highest mountain in Cuba is Pico Turquino.

Letter from Bessie Kittredge to Benjamin Kittredge, Jr., October 20, 1913. Bessie's information regarding the Cummings' visit to "South America" came from speaking to "Mrs. Otis"—possibly the wife of Walter Joseph Otis who had been in Cumming's freshman class at Harvard. Kittredge family papers, South Carolina Historical Society.

[39] Letter from John Diman to G. M. Cumming. May 23, 1914, courtesy of St. George's School Archives.

[40] Letter from John Diman to G. M. Cumming. June 3, 1914, courtesy of St. George's School Archives.

[41] *The Dragon*, April 1915, courtesy of St. George's School Archives.

[42] Christine Haverington, with the Middletown Historical Society and the Newport Historical Society. *Middletown.* Arcadia Publishing Library Editions, 2012. p. 100.

[43] Dr. and Mrs. P. F. Chambers leased it for the winter. "Ardsley Club Season Opens with Dance and Dinners." Dobbs Ferry Register, 1913.

http://fultonhistory.com/Newspaper%2017/Dobbs%20Ferry%20NY%20%20Register/Dobbs%20Ferry%20NY%20%20Register%201913/Dobbs%20Ferry%20NY%20%20Register%201913%20-%200186.pdf

Mrs. Charles E. Schafer leased it for the summer.

30 May 1914. Irvington, N.Y. Real estate record and builders' guide (v.93no.2390(Jan. 3 1914)-no.2415(June 27 1914)). New York, F. W. Dodge Corp.

http://www.columbia.edu/cu/lweb/digital/collections/cul/texts/ldpd_7031148_053/pages/ldpd_7031148_053_00001196.html

Today, in 2020, the building is divided into five residential units with a combined estimated market value of $3.6 million.

https://www.zillow.com/b/111-broadway-irvington-ny-BKccYb/ Accessed January 30, 2020.

[44] "Sixty Youngsters in Tennis Tourney: First National Junior Championship Attracts a Big Entry List." *New York Times.* December 25, 1915.

[45] "Jumping at the Right Time." Jeff Salzenstein. Tennis Evolution. https://tennisevolution.com/tennis-serve-how-to-jump-on-your-tennis-serve/ Accessed January 14, 2020.

[46] Ned, Emily, and Lucy Cumming were listed as "communicants" (people who regularly attended and received communion) on January 1, 1917. List provided to me courtesy of St. Barnabas.

[47] "Concerning Funerals." The Episcopal Diocese of New York. https://www.dioceseny.org/administration/for-clergy/liturgical-and-sacramental/funerals/ Accessed August 7, 2019.

[48] "$3,000,000,000 drop in railway stocks: Security values have declined that much since 1906, Newman Erb estimates." *New York Times.* April 7, 1914. https://www.nytimes.com/1914/04/07/archives/3000000000-drop-in-railway-stocks-security-values-have-declined.html?searchResultPosition=4&ip=0 Accessed February 20, 2020.

[49] Intermountain Rate Cases, 234 U.S. 476 (1914). https://supreme.justia.com/cases/federal/us/234/476/ Accessed February 20, 2020.
See: "Mountain Rate Case Goes Against Roads: Supreme Court Upholds Commerce Board's Power to Fix Long-and-Short Tariffs." *New York Times.* June 23, 1914. https://timesmachine.nytimes.com/timesmachine/1914/06/23/100322806.html?pageNumber=4 Accessed February 20, 2020.

[50] Kanan Makiya. *The Rope.* New York: Pantheon Books, 2016. p. 21.

[51] Program book for the performance on February 17, 1917 at St. George's of Charles Hawtrey's farce "The Private Secretary." Felix played the characters of Mrs. Stead and Miss Ashford. Courtesy of St. George's School Archives.

[52] Letters from Benjamin Kittredge, Jr.:
"I wish I were old enough…" February 5, 1917.

Hetty Hemenway's book: April 6, 1917.
Decoration Day: May 27, 1917.
"I howed potatoes..." June 14, 1917.
Purchases of Liberty Bonds: October 28, 1917.
Kittredge family papers, South Carolina Historical Society.

[53] The British Air Ministry created the Canadian Air Force in August 1918.

[54] "By the time the armistice was signed on 11 November 1918, the RAF establishment in Canada had a total strength 11,928 all ranks..."
"A History of the Air Services in Canada." Don Nicks. *CanMilAir.* c. 1990s.
http://www.canmilair.com/rcafhistory.htm

[55] Information provided by Valerie Simpson, St. George's School Archivist.

[56] Chet Dunn, Deep Springs alumnus, oral history transcript. Deep Springs College records, Cornell University. Box 23, Folder 22.

[57] "A History of the Air Services in Canada." Don Nicks. CanMilAir. c. 1990s.
http://www.canmilair.com/rcafhistory.htm

[58] Robert Bly and Marion Woodman. *The Maiden King: The Reunion of Masculine and Feminine.* New York: Henry Holt and Company, 1998. p. 31.

[59] "Taraji P. Henson's Groundbreaking Mental Health Summit Is Sure to Make an Impact on Black America's Quiet Crisis." Angela Helm. *The Root.* June 14, 2019.
https://www.theroot.com/taraji-henson-s-groundbreaking-mental-health-summit-is-1835513965

[60] Christian Wolmar. *The Subterranean Railway: How the London Underground Was Built and How It Changed the City Forever.* London: Atlantic, 2004. p. 212.

[61] Letter from Benjamin Kittredge, Jr. April 10, 1918. Kittredge family papers, South Carolina Historical Society.

[62] According to a Harvard College register of names, specifically for the 1917-1918 academic year beginning in Sept. 1917.
In the 1930s, the Smith Halls joined and became known as

Kirkland House. "Kirkland House celebrates 100th year, JCR Renamed." John P. Finnegan. *The Crimson.* Feb. 9, 2014. https://www.thecrimson.com/article/2014/2/9/kirkland-100-finnegan-celebration/

[63] "He was a member of the Freshman tennis team and was at the same time a high-ranking scholar," Harvard wrote in his obituary.

Harvard '21. A collective biography. Printed for the 20th anniversary. Cambridge, Mass. 1941, p. 143.

His height comes from his passport application in February 1920, as accessed through Ancestry.com.

Source Citation: National Archives and Records Administration (NARA); Washington D.C.; Passport Applications, January 2, 1906 - March 31, 1925; Collection Number: ARC Identifier 583830 / MLR Number A1 534; NARA Series: M1490; Roll #: 1071.

His parents' heights are on their respective passport applications: His mother's on October 28, 1882, and his father's on June 2, 1919.

[64] "President Wilson signs Standard Time Act, March 19, 1918." Andrew Glass. Politico.com. March 19, 2018. https://www.politico.com/story/2018/03/19/wilson-signs-standard-time-act-march-19-1918-467550
Accessed January 28, 2020.

[65] "Tennis Championship Starts This Afternoon." *The Daily Standard Union.* Brooklyn, August 26, 1918.

[66] "The Spirit Says, You Are Nothing." Larry Levis. *The Selected Levis.* ed. David St. John. University of Pittsburgh, 2003.
https://twitter.com/ChelsDingman/status/1166499581405753344 Accessed Nov. 10, 2019.

INDUSTRY, THOROUGHNESS, PURPOSE

That fall, sometime around the end of the war on Nov. 11, 1918, seventeen-year-old Ned rode the train to a remote area of California to teach at the Deep Springs school for boys.

> Uncertainty appears here [in Chapter 7 of Freud's 1900 book *The Interpretation of Dreams*] like a night-terror, something a child goes to sleep afraid of confronting in the dark: 'all our ways lead into the dark'. As soon as we take sleep as our focus, then fear of the dark, instead of a metaphor for the limits of knowledge, a salutary caution against psychoanalytic knowingness, turns real, becomes—precisely—fear.
>
> —Jacqueline Rose, *On Not Being Able to Sleep: Psychoanalysis and the Modern World*[1]

I have little information about Ned's personal

activity at the school, but I can tell the story of the school's founding, placing him in its context.

Deep Springs had been recently founded by Lucien Lucius Nunn, a Midwestern man who had grown up with ten siblings on a farm with a white picket fence. One of Nunn's formative experiences was a family hardship that struck when he was twenty. The family's bees, expected to produce thousands of dollars' worth of honey, died; his brother fell ill and could not work; and the family couldn't even sell off their hedge plants because local farmers were switching to wire fence. The young Nunn took it upon himself to pay off the family debt, spending two years "going without proper food and clothing, doing anything and everything to make or save a dollar which the stern principles of my father would permit, without once thinking of asking for assistance." His sister then offered to send him to study abroad at the Universities of Göttingen and Leipzig in the fall of 1876. "This year," he wrote,

> which cost less than $300, including passage both ways, was of the greatest benefit to me. I did not study. I made no effort. I just read, thought, and grew. The horizon cleared, the problem of my life took form, my health came back, and with the most complete contempt for any difficulty which could arise and with the feeling that success cannot be measured by locality or time, but alone belongs to

> eternity and the universe, I returned home to take up my work.[2]

This marked the development of Nunn's belief in the inherent value of hard physical labor combined with serious contemplation, a practice he aspired to teach and promote.

Nunn spent a brief time at Harvard Law (a couple years after Ned's father made his own appearance in the same program) and practiced law in Telluride, Colorado in the late 1880s. There, he took a controlling interest in the San Miguel Valley Bank which was promptly robbed of twenty thousand dollars by Butch Cassidy. Making his presence known at five-foot-one, Nunn had "something imperious" about him: not "a domineering temper," but something "of character, of the purpose of a man."[3]

He gambled on powering his Gold King mine with Tesla-Westinghouse alternating current, using a motor that Westinghouse built especially for him, rather than Edison's direct current. This greatly reduced his mine's power expenses. Moreover, it set a precedent for electric power in the United States, as it proved that alternating current could be used safely.[4]

TEN PAST NOON

Figure 11 – L. L. Nunn, undated.[5]

In 1897, he built a hydroelectric plant on Utah's Provo River just downstream of Bridal Veil Falls from where he stretched the longest and highest voltage electrical line in the country at that time. It powered another mine, the Golden Gate, for a client. "The power lines were so 'hot' that current sometimes arced to the cross arms on the power poles on foggy or rainy days, setting them aflame," wrote the historian L. Jackson Newell. To resolve this, new insulators and cooling mechanisms were developed. "This plant became Westinghouse Electric's showpiece."[6]

Nunn would eventually sell the hydroelectric plant to Utah Power and Light.[7] He built his own train station there, with service beginning in 1898. Travelers in hats lined up to board the train on a wooden platform near a "NUNNS" signpost. On the other side of the tracks was a sheer rock cliff. Only several hours' travel north was Promontory Summit, the junction of the

Central Pacific and Union Pacific railroads where the transcontinental track had been ceremonially completed three decades earlier.

The landscape was transforming. It meant different things to different people. Gordon H. Chang wrote:

> As late as the end of the nineteenth century, many Chinese believed railroads desecrated their natural world... Mountains, water, and trees had special meanings for the Chinese—we can wonder what they thought about what tunneling, blasting, massive tree cutting, and track laying meant for their cosmological universe, even if not being done in their native land.[8]

Environmental destruction may have implied social dissolution; as Zoellner pointed out, within China, it seemed to threaten the ancestral covenants that Confucius had called society's "glue."[9]

Nunn collected railroad passes in stacks as if they were baseball cards.[10] But he wanted something more from life, and he had very specific desires.

In 1916, he purchased a farm on the James River in Virginia, forty miles outside Richmond (and east of Lynchburg, where Ota Benga ended his own life that year), near a town with a population of six hundred, and he brought some boys there with the notion of forming a school.

TEN PAST NOON

Nunn found it to be insufficiently isolated; there was at least one incident where one of his boys got a girl pregnant. Making matters worse, the next year, most of them joined the war. He closed that school and planned a new one. To avoid the same outcome, he set his sights on more isolated areas, and, with the war still on, he determined to attract boys younger than sixteen.

He found a place out West. The Southern Pacific railroad's "Slim Princess" stopped on the narrow-gauge tracks at the express railroad station at the town of Big Pine, California, between Yosemite and Death Valley. There were still twenty-eight miles to go, no more towns, just wilderness. From Big Pine, one had to travel to Owens Valley, where the government had recently designated a reservation for the Paiute and Shoshone peoples,[11] and from there to climb up Westgard Pass to cross it heading east, then climb down again to reach Deep Springs Valley. The location was exactly what he wanted. In 1917, Nunn, then in his sixties and quite thin from his tuberculosis, purchased the cattle ranch at the Deep Springs Valley basin with water rights to an area as big as Boston.[12]

People had traveled this area for ten thousand years and lived there seasonally for three thousand years. On the west side of the valley, one still finds "petroglyphs (figures chipped or etched into the patina on rock surfaces) and pictographs (figures painted with dyes onto absorbent rock)," Newell wrote. The Paiute group that lived in the Deep Springs valley in Nunn's time called themselves and their land Patosabaya.[13]

California schools at the time were generally racially segregated, with separate schools for Native Americans, Asians, and Mexicans.[14] The students at Deep Springs were white. Dr. Charley Walcott, a former director for the U.S. Geological Survey, recruited the students, the first of whom began to arrive that summer with a planned focus on ranch work.

Nunn kept a photo of Walcott sitting outside a building, stretching a dead bear belly-up across his lap, bending over its cold nose and sneering lips, and slicing its hide open from neck to groin, extra six-inch knives at the ready.

The bear had been in the wrong place at the wrong time. Deep Springs is a couple hundred miles from the La Brea tar pits, but that didn't do any good for the bear; from the bear's perspective, if it isn't one thing, it's another.

To the west and northwest were the White Mountains; to the south, the Inyo Mountains; to the east, vast desert. Every place, no matter how big, has boundaries. That is what makes it a place.

News and mail service were limited. Nunn brought out a Buick touring car and two trucks, one emblazoned "FWD" for Four-Wheel Drive diagonally over its front grille, the other with "GMC" for General Motors Corporation.

TEN PAST NOON

Figures 12 and 13 – Charley Walcott, 1908.[15]

The student application form asked about immunity to measles, mumps, diphtheria, typhoid and smallpox, and included health questions such as "Have you a tendency to Colds... Tonsillitis... Rheumatism... Constipation?" "Are your teeth excellent?" and "Are you a mouth-breather, normally?" or "When exercising hard?" It also asked: "What profession or business have you in mind to follow?" "Which is your political party?" "Why?" "Why not be a Bolshevist?" and "Have you yet a 'Philosophy of Life'?" with a line and a half to "Explain briefly."

The revolutionary Bolsheviks had just gained power in Russia. They paved the way for what would become Stalin's Communist Party. In the United States, the new fear of "Bolshevism" related more narrowly to left-wing labor organizing that challenged the existing order, with immigrants from Eastern Europe as the stereotypical agitator culprits.

The Deep Springs academic program began early in 1918 with Ernest A. Thornhill and William L. Burgin as the only teachers for ten boys, one of whom left for the Navy[16] despite Nunn's general effort to avoid this sort of outcome. At first, Thornhill taught literature, and Burgin taught social science.[17] There was a Spanish class, and conversational German was required from all the boys in the first year. Nunn advised them not to attempt to study in their bedrooms as the rooms were not private. That first year, the Deep Springs library had a long rectangular table that a dozen boys could crowd around with their books piled in the middle of its peeling surface. The library's walls were concrete slabs decorated with school pennants.[18] The school was not accredited, although Cornell University conferred some course credit.

It was a bumpy start. This was the year of the Spanish flu. Hundreds of thousands of Americans died. Two boys at Deep Springs fell ill but recovered quickly; once immune, they tended to a sick adult, but they could not take him into town, and he died.[19] Another major disruption was the ongoing development of the Deep Springs campus buildings under supervision of power plant engineers.[20] (The man who died of flu on campus had been employed as a carpenter.) Thus academic work for the Fall 1918 term did not begin in earnest until December.[21]

Nevertheless, the population grew. By this time, there were three teachers and roughly a dozen staff for around twenty students.[22] An elderly Paiute couple, Mary and Captain Harry, helped maintain the ranch.[23]

The boys, who paid no tuition, were supposed to stay on-site, working eight-hour days: half academics, half ranch work, dressed in a collared shirt with a wide tie, billowy trousers tucked into tall workboots, and a belt.[24] Their names were written on their clothes to facilitate the garments' return from the staff-run laundry.[25] They were given pocket money, enabling them to travel back home to visit their relatives in summer.

They milked cows, separated the fat to make butter, and drank the skimmed remainder. They also had beef cattle.[26] They were permitted guns for the sole purpose of shooting gamebirds for food. A woman commanded a kitchen stocked with corn, peas, rolled oats, spaghetti, and unpolished rice; string beans and spinach; sardines and kippered herring; Coleman's dry mustard, Snyder's ketchup, paprika, and black pepper; sauerkraut and pickles both sweet and sour; long horn cheese; jams in earthen jars; canned fruit by the gallon, as well as dried apples, peaches, apricots, figs, prunes, raisins, and currants; and ingredients to bake molasses cookies with shredded coconut or cinnamon. (Bananas were already popular in the United States, but this imported fruit had apparently not yet reached Death Valley.) There was lard and Wesson oil. They could have a cup of Newmark's coffee with ginger snaps and soda crackers. On occasion there was that quivering, reflective dessert: Jell-O.[27]

The FWD truck was nicknamed "Death Valley" after a week-long student trip in March 1918. After stopping in a mostly deserted mining town, they reached a town that had been entirely deserted after being stripped of its gold and even of its railroad tracks, though the old railroad building still stood.[28] One boy reported that this trip taught him the skill of "pulling trucks out of the mud."[29]

The poet Scherezade Siobhan recently described the volcanic landscape of Death Valley:

> Here amidst the nightly crepitations of blister beetles, the ice-age lineage of tiny fish giggling in the spasmodic furrows, the hexagonal quatrains of the salt flats, the improbable succulence of pickleweed, I shambled to the tinder of what every root always knows—what is Majestic in nature is also abundantly disobedient and asks no permission for expansion. The stochastic goad of a radical vulnerability: it offers benediction not as stereotype, not as absence-acceptance binary, as Halo Imitation—not these. It ruptures as something that is ensanguined, naked & rapt to the tornado of its own towering chant.[30]

The Student Body, its own self-directed organizational entity, operated under the strong recommendations and veto power of Nunn. Autonomy was intended to be granted as needed and as deserved. In the fall of 1918, four boys, including two sons of the cook, participated in a "roughhouse"; by order of the Student Body, the "Sergeant at arms" confiscated their guns for one month and they were fined fifty cents each, with the money going to the fund to buy new records for the phonograph.[31] Another concern of the Student Body was that records were sometimes not put away in their cases and the phonograph was not always closed. Students agreed to arrive for all meals "properly combed and washed" and wearing a coat, and at the end of dinner they were to exit as a group. Cattle roping was permitted for business but not for sport, bartering in candy was forbidden, and "Mr. Nunn made it emphatic that there is to be no climbing through windows."[32]

This school became Ned's next life chapter. His work on the Deep Springs faculty began in earnest when he was still only seventeen. Though his exact arrival date is uncertain, Dean Thornhill introduced him within the pages of the Telluride News Letter on January 1, 1919. He was described as "a young man who has nearly completed the A.B. course in Harvard University" (again, in actuality, he had completed only his first year at Harvard) and who had just lectured the Deep Springs boys on the novelist Victor Hugo.[33] Teaching alongside Ned was an older married couple. The man, a Lutheran minister, was to teach biographical history, English, and public speaking, and the woman, a high school teacher, to instruct in mathematics and Latin.[34]

By then, the Main Building was well furnished and decorated with tapestries; the Main Room contained copies of the Episcopal *Book of Common Prayer*.[35] There was electrical light for a few hours after dinner, Newell explained, because each night a student would blow-torch the glow plugs of "a diesel-fueled Fairbanks Morse engine and generator" and jump on "the cast-iron spokes of the five-foot-diameter flywheel to set the engine in motion."[36]

Ned was teaching boys who were generally within a year of his own age.[37] The largest age difference was with a young man nearly three years his senior whom he tutored privately in calculus at 7:30 in the morning.[38] Ned spent the rest of the day teaching three levels of French, Cicero in the original Latin, and analytical geometry to "classes" of only two or three students each.[39] If his father had not already taught him a little German, he probably availed himself of the opportunity to study German along with the students, as later, in adulthood, he had reading knowledge of that language.

It is just possible that, here, Ned may have had access to an early copy of *The Elements of Style*. The classic manual of writing advice was privately printed in 1919 by its author, Prof. William Strunk, Jr., for use at Cornell University, with which Deep Springs was affiliated. It was issued by a major publishing house the following year.

The school assessed the boys on their virtues. In the undated "Standings Based on Elements of Character," one of Ned's students, a flu survivor, was ranked at the top of his seventeen-person class for Industry, Thoroughness, and Purpose (and his pontifications on values and standards were soon to be printed in the Telluride Newsletter),[40] while another of Ned's students was ranked dead last on all three.[41]

Nunn composed a pedagogical manifesto that year.[42] He would complain two years later, with some hyperbole, that among these future "trustees of the nation" at Deep Springs, a boy might disappointingly be found "putting his entire heart and soul into playing marbles or jumping around like a monkey on a tennis court." (Construction of the tennis court began in 1920 at the students' initiative.) He was distressed about "average" academic results and "lack of intense earnestness and the spirit of refined selfishness ingrained to the point of saturation."[43]

In the first several years of Deep Springs, Nunn occasionally warned applicants that he opposed "so-called school activities, social functions, athletics, dances, the reading of newspapers and present day trash in the place of absorbing from history and biography the character, earnestness, and purpose" of influential men. His biographer recorded that, if a young man "replied with spirit" he might still be accepted to the school, "but others, especially those whose mothers acted as advocate, were consigned to the outer darkness."[44]

Nunn, having poor eyesight and using his finger to track his place on the page, was limited in the number of books he could read but had a deep understanding of his favorites. He was moved by Herder's *Spirit of Hebrew Poetry*, which said that "dogmas divide and embitter; religion unites" and by Hawthorne's *Great Stone Face*, a short story he was recommending in 1900 and for the rest of his life. As a believer in religious liberalism—an Episcopalian, himself— he had founded Deep Springs as a "theistic institution" independent of any specific creed.

States were ratifying the Constitutional amendment that would eventually enact Prohibition, and both drinking and smoking were forbidden at Deep Springs. The violators of this policy were mostly adults, not students.[45] Thornhill reported to Nunn in 1917 that the previous night "two visitors and three men that hang around here had a fight, and revolvers were drawn, but the haystack was not burned and no one seems to have been much hurt."[46] In 1918, he reported that two men traveling from Los Angeles to Twin Falls had spent six days in idleness at Deep Springs with "several quarts of whiskey" which they shared with the kitchen staff.[47]

≠≠≠≠≠≠≠≠≠

The Thornhills had an accident in late 1919. Their car stalled on the tracks of the Oregon Short Line just as a train, a crouching sphinx with wings of steam, barreled toward them. When their vehicle was struck, Mrs. Lida Thornhill reportedly flew a long distance and broke both shoulders.[48]

There is something that walks on four legs in the morning, two at noon, three in the evening. There is an hour when we have the luxury of contemplating this question and a moment when we need to get off the tracks. If we try to answer the Sphinx at the wrong time in the wrong place, the mortality riddle becomes an increasingly morbid joke.

I have a new riddle. *When train engineers go home and relax with a novel, what do they always see in the book?* Take your time. It will be answered at the end of these pages.

#########

The boys were not allowed to travel to the nearest town nor invite the girls who lived there to visit them on the ranch. On one occasion, Nunn denied the Student Body's request to invite the residents of Owens Valley to dance at their campus, writing that "such an affair is not to be thought of for one moment." On another, he denied the use of the ranch's Ford to drive to parties. "To accept courtesies at the hands of the people of Bishop and Big Pine means that we must extend the same courtesies and hospitality to them. To allow such a system of intercourse to grow up is impossible," he said, and he suggested that the boys enjoy their vacations hundreds of miles away in Los Angeles or San Francisco where it would be harder to form social ties that could be maintained while they were at Deep Springs.⁴⁹ Despite having ordered these restrictions, Nunn found himself paying off the families of pregnant girls in Provo and Claremont, the same situation he had faced in Virginia.⁵⁰

The first Red Scare, the fear of communists and anarchists, may have penetrated their enclave, too, as he obliquely wrote to the student body on March 26, 1920: "The whole national situation is critical. The greater minds are tense with apprehension; the mass hysterical and thoughtless almost to insanity." He said that spending time in the big cities would "best enable them to get a comprehensive view of the situation" and to "prepare for the storm."⁵¹

+++++++++

Nunn never married, and his relationships with some of the young men were odd. We might think so today; the same observation was made at the time and has not been forgotten.⁵² As Dana Goodyear put it recently, this concern

> came to be known among Nunn's followers as the "homosexual problem." Nunn's probable attraction to young men—he was "forever getting crushes on pink-cheeked hotel bellboys," one contemporary said—has been a source of some anxiety at Deep Springs. After Nunn died, his brother P.N. and others seem to have destroyed most of his

correspondence, perhaps because they worried that it would tarnish his reputation, and Deep Springers still joke nervously about Nunn's interest in "the students' bodies."[53]

In 1890, long before he founded Deep Springs, Nunn invited a shoe store clerk, Addison Merrill Wrench—young enough to need his parents' permission, and without a high school diploma—out West. The boy was escorted by an employee of Nunn's. "The last 75 miles to Telluride was by stage coach in real western style, more pleasant to hear about than to endure," a historian wrote. Eventually, Nunn paid for the young man's year of study at Colorado College and then for his wedding to a Connecticut woman. The man died young, and when his son, Merrill, enrolled at Deep Springs, Nunn listed himself as the "parent."[54] Merrill was the official owner of the students' shared phonograph.

At the Nunn train station, there was a dynamo stamped "General Electric Company." In 1901 or 1902, seven teenage boys elaborately posed for a photograph in matching bathrobes, sitting astride the dynamo and tousling each other like nymphs.

A draft version of the Deep Springs application had the typewritten instruction: "Affix here at least one recent photograph of yourself (two or three kodak views, if you have them)." Someone corrected this in black ink, advising him to use the word "camera," as "a

'Kodak' is a single firm's copyrighted name." Also: "Do you wish duplicates?"

Figure 14 – Seven boys on the dynamo.[55]

One historian wrote that Nunn suffered depression and "despaired at the inability to have a relationship" given that he could not reveal his sexual preference.[56] One of the first students at Deep Springs still recalled, sixty-four years later, Nunn's sexual preference for teenage boys: "It was underground, we talked about it among ourselves but we wouldn't talk to strangers about it...it was important that he didn't have any family and kids like the rest of us did—there weren't any distractions. He had this philosophy that he wanted to see preserved because he thought it was saving the world."[57]

This former student remembered that, when he arrived in July 1917, a certain boy named Bruce "was the old man's pet. We all hated him. He wasn't a bad guy, but it was [redacted] enough to put him on our black list."[58] Bruce left Deep Springs before classes began that fall, but he also appears in a Deep Springs photograph a couple years later.[59] His entry and his exit were marked by different privileges: Nunn had appealed to Utah's governor and senator in 1916 to grant the young man a three-day furlough (though the war secretary denied the request);[60] when Bruce's Army service ended, he came to Nunn's school in Virginia, and then to Deep Springs; and when Nunn died in 1925, he left Bruce enough money that he could have bought a house. Another student at Deep Springs' first year quipped of the final gift: "But I think he probably earned it."[61] A third student said that, although Nunn was certainly free to spend his money as he pleased, his favoritism of certain boys "was a sort of weakness in the institution because some of these people didn't really add their weight."[62]

This suggests a new explanation for Nunn's recorded aversion to admitting boys "whose mothers acted as advocate."

TEN PAST NOON

#########

I don't have any "kodak view" that Ned may have sent along with his application to teach. There are many individual portraits of Deep Springs boys in the archives at Cornell University, but none of them look like Ned.

I made a trip to read these archives at Cornell in 2014, leaving Boston late at night and driving five hours west to Ithaca to maximize my time in the library the next day. It is an isolated town, cold and dark in the winter, and the campus is built over gorges. Several years before my visit, within the span of one winter month, shortly before the trees had begun to bud again, three Cornell students had separately jumped to their deaths from bridges. To discourage suicides, the campus subsequently installed netting, which I noticed when I was there. It seems to have worked.[63]

#########

I have shared all my information about Ned's time at Deep Springs, and my conclusion is only that he didn't stay at the school very long. In at least two group photos that include teachers and students, most faces are already identified, and no one looks like Ned.[64] His calculus mentee is still there, but Ned may have already been gone by June 1919.

He liked to track mysteries, but I don't think he was the bear-hunting type. The West wasn't for him. He preferred to track books.

NOTES TO
"INDUSTRY, THOROUGHNESS, PURPOSE"

[1] Jacqueline Rose. *On Not Being Able to Sleep: Psychoanalysis and the Modern World.* Princeton University Press, 2003. p. 109.
[2] Letter from L. L. Nunn to Frank Whitman on June 16, 1909, cited in Orville J. Sweeting's unpublished manuscript, "The Education Experiment of L. L. Nunn," 1970. Sweeting cites this biography of Nunn: Stephen Bailey. *L. L. Nunn: A Memoir.* Ithaca, N.Y.: Printed for Telluride Association, 1933.
Deep Springs College records, Cornell University. Box 25, Folder 3.
[3] George L. Burr's talk "Mr. Nunn's Aims for Telluride Association," delivered at a Telluride Convention on June 16, 1936. Deep Springs College records, Cornell University. Box 25, Folder 22.
[4] "L.L. Nunn Made His Mine Profitable By Running His Mill With AC Power." Jim Pettengill. *Wild West.* April 2014. https://www.historynet.com/l-l-nunn-made-mine-profitable-running-mill-ac-power.htm Accessed Sept. 24, 2019.
L. Jackson Newell. *The Electric Edge of Academe: The Saga of Lucien L. Nunn and Deep Springs College.* Salt Lake City: The University of Utah Press, 2015. pp. 19-22.
[5] "L. L. Nunn." Public domain photograph.
https://en.wikipedia.org/wiki/L._L._Nunn#/media/File:Lucien_Lucius_Nunn.jpg Accessed October 23, 2019.
[6] Newell, *op. cit.,* p. 28.
[7] The line stretched 32 miles downstream, beyond Utah Lake, to the mine in Mercur. The sale was in 1913. "Provo River Parkway Trail – Provo Canyon Utah." http://provo-canyon-on-foot.weebly.com/provo-river-parkway.html

[8] "Chinese Railroad Workers and the US Transcontinental Railroad in Global Perspective," by Gordon H. Chang. *The Chinese and the Iron Road: Building the Transcontinental Railroad.* ed. Gordon H. Chang and Shelley Fisher Fishkin, with Hilton Obenzinger and Roland Hsu. Stanford, Calif.: Stanford University Press, 2019. Chapter 1, p. 40.

[9] Tom Zoellner. *Train: Riding the Rails That Created the Modern World—From the Trans-Siberian to the Southwest Chief.* New York: Viking, 2014. p. 228.

[10] Lucien L. Nunn papers, 1863-1971, Cornell University. Box 2, Folder 36.

[11] Barry Pritzker. *A Native American Encyclopedia: History, Culture, and Peoples.* Oxford University Press, 2000. p. 229.

[12] 47 square miles.

[13] L. Jackson Newell. *The Electric Edge of Academe: The Saga of Lucien L. Nunn and Deep Springs College.* Salt Lake City: The University of Utah Press, 2015. pp. 77-78.

[14] "70 years ago, California ended a type of segregation." Brigid Kelly. KCRW. Feb. 22, 2016. https://www.kcrw.com/news/articles/70-years-ago-california-ended-a-type-of-segregation Accessed Sept. 24, 2019.

[15] Two photos of Charley Walcott with dead animals. Lucien L. Nunn papers, Cornell University. Box 57.

[16] The boy "left to enter the Naval Service."
"A Letter from William L. Burgin, Instructor at Deep Springs Ranch, Big Pine, California." March 12, 1918. Printed in the Telluride News Letter, April 10, 1918. P. 25. https://www.tellurideassociation.org/wp-content/uploads/2017/05/04_8_1918_April.pdf

[17] Of the first year in 1917: "Our one teacher at that time was Burgin. He taught all that was taught. I think literature was taught by Dean Thornhill."
"Herb Reich, DS17, 4/28/82," *ADSTA Oral History Project,* p. 83. Deep Springs College records, Cornell University. Box 16.
Acknowledging an alumni memory, apparently Herb

Reich's, that Thornhill taught English while Paul Cadman "taught pretty much everything else," L. Jackson Newell nonetheless suggests that this "everything else" teacher was Paul Cadman, not William Burgin.

Newell, *op. cit.* p. 111.

This document suggests that Burgin was teaching: "The main courses are Spanish and Social Science, with an emphasis on the latter, which is my specialty."

"A Letter from William L. Burgin, Instructor at Deep Springs Ranch, Big Pine, California." March 12, 1918. Printed in the Telluride News Letter, April 10, 1918. pp. 25-26. https://www.tellurideassociation.org/wp-content/uploads/2017/05/04_8_1918_April.pdf

[18] Deep Springs College records, Cornell University. The same photo is stored in Box 38 and 47.

[19] The man who died was a Greek immigrant working as a carpenter on the campus. "Cabot Coville, DS18 TA19, 4/25/85" *ADSTA Oral History Project,* p. 98. Deep Springs College records, Cornell University. Box 16.

Also: At St. George's in Rhode Island, Micky Harriman, a friend of Felix Kittredge's died of "pneumonia." Letter from Benjamin Kittredge, Jr. to Bessie Kittredge, December 13, 1918. Kittredge family papers, South Carolina Historical Society.

[20] Stephen Bailey. *L. L. Nunn: A Memoir.* Ithaca, N.Y.: Printed for Telluride Association, 1933. p. 103. Deep Springs College records, Cornell University. Box 1 or 2.

[21] "...construction work, followed by a siege of influenza, delayed school work until nearly December 1st..."

F. C. Noon, Chancellor. Los Angeles, Feb. 1, 2019. Printed in the Telluride News Letter, Feb. 1919. p. 10. https://www.tellurideassociation.org/wp-content/uploads/2017/05/05_1_1919_Feb.pdf
Accessed June 27, 2019.

[22] "...about twenty students and a total population of about thirty-five."

Orville Sweeting's research material. Deep Springs College records, Cornell University. Box 23, Folder 11. This material footnotes the information to F. C. Noon, "Chancellor's Report to the Convention," Telluride Association Minutes, 1919, p. 16.

[23] Newell, *op. cit.,* p. 116.

[24] Photos of Whitecotton and Stine, 1918. Cornell collection, Box 57.

[25] Sunday at 11 a.m. was the deadline for laundry. Student Body minutes. February 7, 1920. Deep Springs College records, Cornell University. Box 19, Folder 12.

[26] By 1919, they kept a dozen dairy cows, and they managed several hundred head of beef cattle. Correspondence from Merrill C. Wrench, dated December 12, 1919. Telluride News Letter. December 1919. Deep Springs College records, Cornell University. pp. 14-15. https://www.tellurideassociation.org/wp-content/uploads/2017/05/06_2_1919_Dec.pdf Accessed June 27, 2019.

[27] Mrs. Annie Redhead was in charge of the kitchen. Grocery lists from Sept. 1 and Dec. 8, 1919. Deep Springs College records, Cornell University. Box 18, Folder 19.

[28] The partially deserted town was Lida, and the entirely deserted town was Rhyolite. Deep Springs College records, Cornell University. Box 19, Folder 36.

[29] Herbert Reich, speaking of his own experience; written report in March 1918. Deep Springs College records, Cornell University. Box 19, Folder 36.

[30] "Malpaís / Badlands." Scherezade Siobhan. *Berfrois.* October 22, 2019 https://www.berfrois.com/2019/10/scherezade-siobhan-malpais-badlands/ Accessed October 22, 2019.

[31] The culprits were Leonard and Fred Redhead, Ted Lierly, and Burt Ritter.

[32] Typed version of Student Body meeting minutes. Combed and washed, December 28, 1918; no cattle roping, January 25, 2019; no candy bartering, November 29, 1918; no climbing through windows, November 24, 1918. Deep Springs College records, Cornell University. Box 19, Folder 12.

[33] Dean E. A. Thornhill. Deep Springs, California, Jan. 1, 2019. Printed in the Telluride News Letter, Feb. 1919. pp. 11-12.
https://www.tellurideassociation.org/wp-content/uploads/2017/05/05_1_1919_Feb.pdf
Accessed June 27, 2019.
Also: One of the boys who attended in 1919 recalled much later in life that "they wanted me to learn Latin. They had a staff of great teachers out there. As I remember, every one of them had a Ph.D. from an Ivy League school..." Ned certainly didn't have a Ph.D., but this particular student wasn't his. "Walter Welti, DS17, 7/5/83" *ADSTA Oral History Project,* p. 91. Deep Springs College records, Cornell University. Box 16.

[34] Ludwig Thomsen, a graduate of Oberlin and Yale Divinity, had been a minister in Utah, Idaho, Illinois, Nebraska, and North Carolina. Lottie Thomsen had studied at the University of Michigan.
Eighth General Catalogue of the Yale Divinity School: Centennial Issue, 1822-1922.
http://books.google.com/books?id=kTI4AAAAYAAJ&pg=PA390&lpg=PA390&dq=%22ludwig+thomsen%22+%22deep+springs%22&source=bl&ots=vlsMHxEfpg&sig=Emjbz3cPt2pV0_yNx2xkf1clDJo&hl=en&sa=X&ei=s4tAVNGoMaa1sQTrm4D4DQ&ved=0CCMQ6AEwAQ#v=onepage&q=%22ludwig%20thomsen%22%20%22deep%20springs%22&f=false

[35] Newell, *op. cit.,* pp. 114, 140.

[36] Newell, *ibid.,* p. 109.

[37] From a folder labeled 1918-1919. (Though another schedule in the same folder appears to be from 1919-1920). Deep Springs College records, Cornell University. Box 18, Folder 18.

[38] This student was James Sprint Holmes.

[39] Schedules from Deep Springs College records, Cornell University. Box 18, Folder 19.
The original textbooks—based on a suggested supply list—were Tanner and Allen's *An Elementary Course in Analytic*

TEN PAST NOON

Geometry, Snyder and Hutchinson's *Elementary Textbook of the Calculus*, and Henry C. Pearson's *Latin Prose Composition*. French verb drills were to come from Frazer and Squair's *Shorter French Course*.

[40] Cabot Coville. Untitled letter to the editor. Deep Springs, Dec. 15, 1919. Telluride News Letter. December 1919. pp. 17-19.
https://www.tellurideassociation.org/wp-content/uploads/2017/05/06_2_1919_Dec.pdf
Accessed June 27, 2019.

[41] Deep Springs College records, Cornell University. Box 18, Folder 20

[42] Nunn's manuscript was dated May 1919. From the Sweeting manuscript, Deep Springs College records, Cornell University. Box 25, Folder 23.

[43] "Deep Springs Student Body Minutes: Volume IV. September 27, 1920 – May 28, 1921" Deep Springs College records, Cornell University. Box 19, Folder 13.

[44] Sweeting manuscript, Deep Springs College records, Cornell University. Box 25, Folder 23

[45] Herb Reich, an alum, recalled in his old age that "as far as I know nobody ever smoked...to the best of my knowledge nobody ever drank here except some of the hired help." "Herb Reich, DS17, 4/28/82," *ADSTA Oral History Project,* p. 88. Box 16.

[46] Letter from Thornhill to Nunn, Nov. 11, 1917. Deep Springs College records, Cornell University. Box 18, Folder 17. He also said that "the free use of booze and the sly use of cigarettes is rapidly destroying the morale of the young men here. Some of the offenders are gone and need not be mentioned."

[47] "I don't think any of the boys had any," Thornhill wrote. Letter from Thornhill to Nunn, Feb. 27, 1918. Deep Springs College records, Cornell University. Box 18, Folder 17.

[48] The accident was on November 5, 1919. "Dean Thornhill Suffers Accident," submitted by Jess Hawley, 25 November 1919. Telluride News Letter. December 1919.

pp. 10-11. https://www.tellurideassociation.org/wp-content/uploads/2017/05/06_2_1919_Dec.pdf Accessed June 27, 2019.

[49] In the spring of 1919, Nunn told the boys they couldn't host a dance and invite the Owens Valley girls. In March 1920, he told them they couldn't drive the Ford to parties. Sweeting manuscript, Deep Springs College records, Cornell University. Box 25, Folder 23.

[50] "Chet Dunn, Herb Reich, DS17, Bob Aird, DS21, 5/1/1982," *ADSTA Oral History Project,* p. 154. Deep Springs College records, Cornell University. Box 16.

[51] L. L. Nunn, letter to Student Body, March 26, 1920. Deep Springs College records, Cornell University. Box 18, Folder 20 – DS 1920-1921.

[52] Former student Aaron Jacobson, interviewed in 1999, said, "The whole concept of Deep Springs is homoerotic, and there's a lot of speculation that Nunn was homosexual."

"Boys of Paradise." Denise Dowling. Salon. April 16, 1999. https://www.salon.com/1999/04/16/deep_spring_1/ Accessed Oct. 1, 2019.

[53] "The Searchers: The fate of progressive education at Deep Springs College." Dana Goodyear. *The New Yorker.* August 28, 2006.
https://www.newyorker.com/magazine/2006/09/04/the-searchers-dana-goodyear Accessed Oct. 1, 2019.

See also Parker Bailey's letter to Orville Sweeting:
"...it was during my grade school days in Salt Lake City that I heard scraps of light conversation between my mother and Mrs. J. B. Bailey...to the effect that L.L. was 'forever getting crushes on pink cheeked hotel bellboys.'"

Quoted by Scott McDermott. "Prologue." In Stephen A. Bailey, *L.L. Nunn: A Memoir.* Ithaca, N.Y.: Cayuga Press for Telluride Association, 1933. Rpt., Ithaca, NY: Cayuga Press for Telluride Association, 1993. p. xviii.

Quoted, in turn, by Newell, *op. cit.,* p. 41.

[54] Wrench, the former shoe store clerk, died in 1915.

TEN PAST NOON

[55] Unidentified boys on the dynamo at Nunn's train station, 1901 or 1902. Lucien L. Nunn papers, Cornell University. Box 51, if I recall correctly.

[56] "L. L. Nunn Made His Mine Profitable By Running His Mill With AC Power." Jim Pettengill. *Wild West.* April 2014. https://www.historynet.com/l-l-nunn-made-mine-profitable-running-mill-ac-power.htm Accessed October 1, 2019.

[57] "Chet Dunn, DS17, 9/7/81," *ADSTA Oral History Project,* pp. 73-74. Deep Springs College records, Cornell University. Box 16.

[58] "The old man had got him a [Utah U.S. Senator] Reed Smoot and signed recommendation letters for him to get Bruce [Simmons] in." Chet Dunn oral history transcript. Deep Springs College records, Cornell University. Box 23, Folder 22.

[59] Bruce Simmons left before classes began in the Fall of 1917, according to Newell, *op. cit.,* p. 119. However, he is identified in 1919 photos at Deep Springs.

[60] Nunn was close with Utah's U.S. Senator Reed Smoot. Newell, *ibid.,* pp. 29, 66.

[61] Nunn left $10,000 to Bruce in his will. That sum in 1925 would have resembled about $150,000 in today's 2020 dollars.

"I think he probably earned it."
Carlyle Ashley. "ADSTA Oral History Project: Interviews, Speeches, and Letters 1979-1987)." A spiral-bound book of interview transcripts. Intro paragraph signed by Denis Clark DS69 CB72 TA73, March 5, 2001, Chair, Telluride Association History Committee. Quote from Carlyle Ashley in "Carlyle Ashley, DS17, 3/18/82" on p. 53. Deep Springs College records, Cornell University. Box 16.
(Though Carlyle Ashley returned to Deep Springs in 1920 as a teacher of math and geology, he was not at Deep Springs while Ned Cumming was there.)
Carlyle Ashley also said of Bruce Simmons: he "didn't have anywhere near the qualifications academically that others did" and "was really much closer to L.L. Nunn than most

of the other students...Bruce was very solicitous, let's say, of L.L."

Newell, *op. cit.,* p. 119.

[62] This quote is from Bob Aird. "Chet Dunn, Herb Reich, DS17, Bob Aird, DS21, 5/1/1982", *ADSTA Oral History Project,* p. 155. Deep Springs College records, Cornell University. Box 16.

[63] "A student's suicide jump—are Cornell and Ithaca responsible?" Dave Tobin. Syracuse.com. August 6, 2014. https://www.syracuse.com/news/2014/08/a_students_suicide_jump_-_are_cornell_and_ithaca_responsible.html Accessed October 23, 2019.

[64] These photos are available online at archive.deepsprings.edu. One with 27 people is dated Spring 1919, titled in the archive as "Spring 1919 group" (identifier: 19DEC0056); the other with 31 people is dated more specifically June 25 "Community group on porch with Nunns" (identifier: 18DEC0367). The source is the Kevin West 1989 albums, named after the person who rearranged these the Deep Springs archive photos in albums.

ENTERING
THE GREAT DEPRESSION

Ships bearing molasses from Cuba pumped their product into a two-and-a-half-million-gallon storage tank in Boston's North End.[1] The steel tank was structurally deficient and, on January 15, 1919, it exploded. Pieces of the tank smashed into the supporting structure of the elevated train at Atlantic Avenue, the track collapsed into the molasses, and the next engineer to approach braked hard to avoid the mess. A fifteen-foot wave of syrup, itself traveling as fast as a train, buried the neighborhood. Dozens of people were killed or severely injured.[2] For a week, nothing in the news interested Bostonians as much as this. The Prohibition amendment that had just banned the sale of alcohol nationwide, as well as the Versailles peace talks that ended the war, were relegated to subordinate pages in the local dailies.[3]

TEN PAST NOON

A Pulitzer Prize was posthumously awarded that spring to Henry Adams, the history professor who had taught Ned's father at Harvard, for his autobiography.

Adams had written of the disorientation he felt in an increasingly technological world that was picking up speed. The most relevant knowledge now seemed to belong to scientists. He was conscious that, as a historian, his science questions were naïve: "Did it pull or did it push? Was it a screw or a thrust? Did it flow or vibrate? Was it a wire or a mathematical line?" Humanities scholars like him who found themselves "helpless before a mechanical sequence" could only feel embarrassed for themselves and their society for enabling their ignorance.[4] He was especially impressed with the dynamo, "this huge wheel, revolving within arm's length at some vertiginous speed, and barely murmuring," presenting itself to him as "a symbol of infinity"—which, for him, activated religious ideas and sentiments.[5]

As for the good he acknowledged about Harvard, he described it as imparting "moderation, balance, judgment, restraint, what the French called *mesure*" and aiming to impress young men with "an autobiographical blank, a mind on which only a water-mark had been stamped," or briefly: "a type but not a will."[6]

British investors in American railroads wanted their money back. The war changed their risk tolerance. Shares of the Pennsylvania Railroad, as an example, halved their value between 1902 and 1918.[7] Loss can be a process as well as an event.

While Ned was at Deep Springs, his mother sold her estate on Broadway in Irvington,[8] not a year after Madam C. J. Walker, then the wealthiest African-American woman, completed and moved into her own mansion valued four times more than theirs, essentially next door to them.

Felix, having graduated St. George's that spring, went to Harvard in the fall.[9] Ned came back East but never returned to Harvard, instead rejoining St. George's as a faculty member in the Fall of 1919. They passed in opposite directions.

A descendant (like Ned) of the 18th-century university president Willard, Felix and his Harvard roommate enjoyed "an awfully nice room right on the river," as he reported from Cambridge.[10] This contextualizes his mother's advice when he was thirteen: not "work harder" but simply "stick it out."

In the spring of 1920, Felix was invited to the first of the seven weddings of Cornelius Vanderbilt, Jr. Vanderbilt had driven a Rolls-

TEN PAST NOON

Royce for a British general in France during his wartime enlistment, but he was now honorably discharged. The bride, Rachel Littleton, was graced with over a million dollars' worth of presents, a third of the value of which concentrated in a single diamond tiara.[11] Some of the guests were titled—Ambassador, Governor, Duke, Countess—and their names made the newspaper. Five thousand invitees showed up at a church that held only half that number.[12] (The printed announcements had wisely instructed: "Present this invitation at the church.") Most guests drove automobiles; only three horse-drawn carriages were parked alongside over a hundred motorized cars in one representative area. The groom, however, in a throwback to a rapidly disappearing past, arrived in a carriage "behind a team of spirited animals with purple-coated coachman and footman on the box." Three thousand people squeezed into the church,

> and thousands more filled the sidewalks of Fifth Avenue and adjoining streets, jammed the very stone steps of the church itself, surrounded the red and white canopies on the Fifth Avenue and 53rd Street sides, craned their necks from passing buses and extended their heads from the windows of shops and workrooms up and down the avenue.

Seven hundred guests were received at the bride's parents' home on 57th Street.[13] Felix was not among this elite group (or, at least, this part of the invitation does not survive in his papers). The wedding cake, displayed on a revolving table like some massive Victrola, was a quarter-ton, five-and-a-half-foot tall, seven-tier pyramid capped with candied roses, for which the high-society restaurant Sherry's contracted a baker from the Waldorf and charged the price of a fleet of Model Ts.[14] Some slices were sealed in boxes so the couple could enjoy them on future anniversaries. There was still a whole decade to roar before the Great Depression.

#########

Felix seems to have taken time off from Harvard. That summer, he attended the Evan School in Flagstaff, Arizona before visiting the Grand Canyon and continuing on to Denver to see friends.[15] He disapproved of his Aunt Mary's recommendation of the novel *The Garden of Allah* by Robert Smythe Hichens (1904), a story of an English woman who travels to the Middle East, as he found it "the height of trash—slushy, silly drivel about an impossible woman and her 'soul.'"[16]

He was close with certain cousins. "We are quite a house-party," he wrote at age nineteen. "John and I have my room, and then there are Grandmother and what seem millions of the Canfield family. And Alida, George Dana and Frances come up to-morrow. Where are they to sleep?!...Tucky had the Ford."[17] They played a card game named after the Canfield family.[18]

TEN PAST NOON

Though he was close with the Canfields, it does not seem he was as close with the Cummings. In his surviving letters, there is no mention in his hand of Uncle George, Aunt Lucy, nor cousins Ned and Emily.[19]

#########

American women were allowed, for the first time, to vote in the presidential election. Warren G. Harding won. He had been chosen as the Republican Party's candidate by a handful of cigar-smoking senators in a now-proverbial smoke-filled room.

The Port of New York Authority was founded by the states of New York and New Jersey to build a complex network of rail lines and freight terminals, a plan eventually rejected by the railroads' businessmen.[20]

By this time, three years after the armistice, tens of thousands of veterans across the country had been diagnosed with "shell shock" (post-traumatic stress disorder from proximity to explosions), and, just in New York State, hundreds of veterans had died by suicide.[21]

England had used India's existing railways to move soldiers, weapons, and supplies while focusing railway investment on Africa and the Middle East. India's railways, though having proved useful to England, lay in need of maintenance.[22]

The ancient Greek word *apeiron*, says Frederiek Depoortere, can be translated as 'unbounded', but also as 'infinite', 'indefinite' and 'undefined'. The word had a negative connotation and was used to refer to everything which appeared without rule or regularity: the primeval chaos, an arbitrary curve or even a handkerchief that is dirty and crumpled up; in short, *apeiron* was everything that could not be thought well.[23]

╪╪╪╪╪╪╪╪╪

Felix returned to Harvard but continued to struggle with grades. In December 1921 he wrote home from Harvard's Claverly Hall dormitory: "I am really sick of this place, and very depressed over everything. I feel in every way I'm getting nowhere. It is impossible to get anyone to teach you squash, and there are only too [sic] courses out of which I get a thing intellectually—also the weather is vile....the endless worry over making a false move and being fired, when I ought to be on perfectly good standing is wearisome."[24] Several days later, he added that "this feeling of being watched and that you may be kicked any minute is awful."[25]

After the 1921–1922 academic year, Harvard warned him that he had barely passed his classes. Nevertheless, he successfully completed the following academic year and immediately moved on to Magdalen College at Oxford. There, he received a letter from a Barnard student, reflecting her perception of his

TEN PAST NOON

life back at him: "Your Oxford life sounds simply too charming: panelled rooms, pipe smoke, and beautiful rich colored wines."[26]

For Ned's part, although he taught at St. George's in Fall 1919—as demonstrated by the faculty photo shown earlier—he did not complete the academic year on the faculty. That winter, he and another young man applied for a passport to travel to Cuba "as soon as possible."

Ned was following his father who had gone there the previous year on business for the Barlow Company. Joseph E. Barlow had spent the last fifteen years or so buying up cheap Havana real estate for speculative profit. When a casino didn't pan out, he dreamed of redesigning the city to attract tourists, including an imagined boulevard he called the "Gran Vía" that would join his Havana properties to the suburbs and lead to a proposed park like the Champs-Élysées in Paris. It might be a job for a railroad man and bank president like Ned's father. He traveled there with a longtime acquaintance, George Albert Lee; for the passport office, the Barlow Company wrote them identical letters vouching for their motive of pursuing "some important developments of the resources of the island." (Although developers were interested, the local Cuban politicians in charge of land rights ultimately managed to fence Barlow in.)[27]

Ned's stated motive for going to Cuba was "recreation." His traveling companion was

Walter Hope Mairs, four years his elder, the nephew of his father's friend from the Ardsley Club, George Hope Mairs. (The Cummings and Mairses also happened to be cousins-in-law through two marriages.) Ned and Walter applied for their passports on February 7, and the trip appears to have been quick, as they sailed back from Havana to Key West on February 16.[28]

From an anonymous writer years later, most likely his mother or sister, we are granted the general comments that Ned "loved travel most, and he came to know especially well some of the nations to the south of us that face the Caribbean Sea"; that he "spent a period of time in Mexico"; and that he "worked also in Panama."[29]

Indeed, after his Cuba trip, he sailed for Tampico on Mexico's Gulf Coast, returning in December of the same year.[30] The Mexican revolutionary general Pancho Villa had just surrendered that summer, drawing ten years of civil war to a close.[31]

When he might have gone to Panama is more of a mystery, though he likely had an engineering job there for the firm Stone & Webster.

I don't know what happened on any of these trips: Cuba, Mexico, Panama. How his Latin, French, and German served him in this region is unknown. Later in life, he did not read much, if anything, in Spanish.

TEN PAST NOON

Audre Lorde, too, traveled from New York to Mexico near her nineteenth birthday, according to her story in *Zami*. "I don't know why I was seized with such a desire to go to Mexico," she writes; she had associated it with "color and fantasy and delight, full of sun, music and song." Because it was on the same continent, she reasoned, "I could always walk there."[32]

#########

Apart from this indication of travel and a year of incomplete graduate study in New York, I don't know exactly where Ned was or what he was doing throughout the whole of the 1920s.

His parents no longer had the fancy brick house at Irvington-on-Hudson, but his mother was secretary of the Audubon Society of Irvington in the early part of the decade.

The last Carolina parakeet had recently died in captivity. To this day, no one is sure exactly why the species became extinct.[33]

In the summer of 1919, a twelve-year-old boy who would later become known to history as "The Mad Sculptor" became a ward of the state. His father had deserted his family when he was two. As described by the historian Harold Schechter, the boy had initially appeared to be a gifted student and avid reader; Victor Hugo was one of his favorite novelists. Nonetheless, by age ten, he was distracted and disobedient in school, and, when he turned twelve, his devout Pentecostal mother relinquished her parental rights. It was then discovered that he had been born with syphilis, an infection that can damage the brain over time, but this information did him no good, as he never received treatment. He completed seventh grade but never returned to school. He began to develop a theory according to which, if people could only perfectly memorize and visualize words and images, they could replay them in their minds, rendering libraries obsolete. Moreover, he believed, this activity would somehow connect them to a godlike source of power and make them telepathically omniscient and unbound by the limits of their bodies. He tore color panels out of library books to practice his psychic art. At age nineteen, serving time at a reformatory, he convinced another boy to build him a timer from a Victrola phonograph's motor. He could set the duration between ticking sounds and thereby measure the length of his meditations. The reformatory took the machine away. Upon his release, he traveled cross-country and found apprenticeships with sculptors, though he never held a job so much as a year, usually due to his explosive temper. He started dozens of fistfights in his lifetime; it happened anytime anyone made a comment challenging his heterosexuality.[34] Years later, this man, Robert Irwin, would happen to live in Ned's area.

On January 12, 1920, the *New York Times*

TEN PAST NOON

reported a rocket scientist's claim to have invented a vehicle "for exploring the unknown regions of the upper air...possibly even as far as the moon itself." This was printed together with a statement from the Smithsonian reminding readers that scientists' greatest altitude in air travel so far had been managed with "a free balloon." If a rocket were to escape "the attraction of the earth," the Smithsonian explained, it "would never come back," and we could only observe its progress with a telescope.[35] The next day, the incredulous *Times* editorial board, mocking the physicist's apparent ignorance of our "dreadful slavery" to gravity, declared that a moon landing "will be believed when it is done."[36]

Philippa Ruth Bosanquet, who would grow up to study at Oxford, to change her name through marriage to Foot, and to pose moral questions about trains, was born in England.

At age twenty-one, Ned enrolled for nearly a year in the graduate program in engineering at Columbia University.[37] That sounds like something his father would have wanted him to do.

########

In 1922, *Ulysses,* previously published serially, was released as a complete, 732-page novel on the fortieth birthday of its author, James Joyce. Its namesake, Homer's *Odyssey,* follows a war hero on his ten-year journey home. The entirety of Joyce's *Ulysses,* by contrast, occurs within a single day. (Roughly forty pages, on average, describe each fictional hour.) It's some other chronotope. Mikhail Bakhtin's essay on chronotopes mentions Homer but not Joyce, so we must define Joyce's single-day chronotope for ourselves.[38]

The Ottoman Empire dissolved in 1922 when it abolished the sultanate. Turkey became a republic a year later.

The last Chinese emperor, Pu Yi, awkwardly residing in the Forbidden City in a country that had just become a republic, ejected his eunuchs in the summer of 1923 because he feared they were conspiring against him. He soon lost his own title and was exiled.

Thomas Mann's novel about the tuberculosis patients, *The Magic Mountain,* was published in 1924. Roughly one hundred pages, on average, describe each fictional year. Mikhail Bakhtin's essay mentions Thomas Mann, though not this specific novel.

Among various briefly mentioned characters in *The Magic Mountain* is a trouser-wearing, short-haired, cigarette-smoking, lesbian Egyptian princess. Her attendant, "a Moorish eunuch, a weak and sickly man...clung to life more desperately than most, and was quite inconsolable" over his own respiratory prognosis.[39] For all the characters, the mountain retreat is a place where "they bring you your

TEN PAST NOON

midday broth, as they brought it yesterday and will bring it to-morrow; and it comes over you...the true content of time is merely a dimensionless present in which they eternally bring you the broth." The bored sanatorium residents flip through decks of playing cards to contemplate randomness. They let their books lie closed in their laps.[40]

As the author later explained, *The Magic Mountain's* protagonist develops the wisdom "that one must go through the deep experience of sickness and death to arrive at a higher sanity and health; in just the same way that one must have a knowledge of sin in order to find redemption."[41] While writing, Mann says, he did not consciously realize that his character "is a searcher after the Holy Grail." But indeed the sanatorium, too, "is a variant of the shrine of the initiatory rites, a place of adventurous investigation into the mystery of life."[42]

≠≠≠≠≠≠≠≠≠

Fantasies of ancient Egypt inspired Americans in the year 1923. King Tut's tomb, the stories of which more likely appealed to Ned's natural interests than modern mechanical engineering, had just been discovered. In the winter, theaters carried the film *Dancer of the Nile,* "a lively piece of design," as Matthew Coniam described it, "that captures the fun and energy of Tutmania at its youthful height."[43]

Though Ned did not graduate from the Columbia program, he was hired by the engineering firm Stone & Webster. The firm operated streetcar systems in the early 20th century and built power infrastructure. In 1920, it began work on an 18-mile tunnel that brought water from the Catskills to Manhattan.[44] In 1922, it completed a plant in Fall River, Massachusetts to convert heavy oil into gas.[45] In 1924, with the El Paso Electric Railway Company, it began to update the international bridge between Ciudad Juárez and El Paso.[46]

For a dollar per year, one could subscribe to Stone & Webster's monthly journal, each issue delivering a hundred pages of philosophical reflections and business reports. The January 1923 issue began with a long rebuttal of an insult against the editors. A reader had called them "spiritually barren." In response, the editors first aroused suspicion of the anonymous critic's gender. They could not exclude the possibility that the handwriting, though they deemed it masculine, belonged to a modern woman who had usurped a "mannish and swashing" style. They asserted that, as men, they were inherently more spiritual than women.[47] Broadening their sermon, they said that free will enables human dignity, despite the otherwise undignified constraint on human life by which we realize that we are "here in time and space, but we made neither time nor space."[48] An engineer's envious complaint.

TEN PAST NOON

Ned was based out of Boston, where Stone & Webster counted hundreds of employees, and he worked elsewhere. I don't know where. Maybe Panama.[49] Meanwhile, his parents lived alone in the Bronx.[50]

Benjamin Kittredge, Sr., who, again, was Ned's uncle and Felix's father, had purchased 170 acres of a former rice plantation outside Charleston, South Carolina to have a place to shoot ducks.

━━━━━━━━━━

Here is how the book works. The reader assumes they are going to eat roast duck. This is due to "Chekhov's gun," the rule of dramatic storywriting that dictates that a playwright must not hang a duck-hunt shotgun over the fireplace at the beginning of the play if they do not intend for a duck to be shot by the end of the play.

━━━━━━━━━━

Benjamin was responsible for the first known use of the phrase "plantation life" which in the 1930s became an accepted way of describing the recreation of wealthy Northerners vacationing in the South.[51] "Plantation life melded visions of a romantic South with upper-class sporting pursuits and the physical space of remade plantations...[and] supplied owners and guests with characteristically 'southern' experiences," as the historian Daniel J. Vivian explains the term. In many locations, "vestiges of a majestic past and throngs of 'plantation Negroes' imparted exoticism and a sense of racial privilege."[52] The Kittredges called their tract of land "Cypress Gardens."

⧗⧗⧗⧗⧗⧗⧗⧗⧗

Zora Neale Hurston transferred to Barnard in 1925 and several years later became the first black person to graduate from that college.[53]

Ernest Hemingway published *The Sun Also Rises*. The novel's narrator was an American pilot who recovered in a special ward for men with—it is implied—genital injuries. "In the Italian hospital," he recalls, "we were going to form a society. It had a funny name in Italian. I wonder what became of the others, the Italians." He remembers that a visiting officer lauded him, while he was still bandaged, for having "given more than your life," but the narrator himself expresses only understated dismay about his injury. ("My head started to work. The old grievance.") Most of the novel deals with his banter with his girlfriend. She has sexual needs and reluctantly decides that she cannot commit to a romance with the wounded man because she imagines it will quickly frustrate both of them. "I don't want to go through that hell again," she insists by way of explanation for why she cannot take up with him again, yet she cannot stay away from him, either. He tries to keep the discussion light, assuring her that "what happened to me is supposed to be funny. I never think about it." Privately, however, he reflects "that certain injuries or imperfections are a subject of merriment while remaining quite serious for the person possessing them" and that the girlfriend "only wanted what she couldn't have. Well, people were that way. To hell with people." A male friend advises him that his injury is "the sort of thing that can't be spoken of. That's what you ought to work up into a mystery. Like Henry's bicycle." He corrects his friend: "It wasn't a bicycle…He was riding horseback." (This is a jab at a fellow novelist, the late Henry James, whose vaguely worded memoir of a horseback riding accident had previously been published by the same press, Scribner's.[54] Scribner's agreed to publish Hemingway's joke using only James' first name.[55] The exact nature of James' injury remains a mystery to this day.) In any case, the narrator of *The Sun Also Rises,* while maintaining his detached attitude toward his own sexual disability and the social drama that surrounds him because of it, is passionately interested in something else entirely: watching the bullfights in Spain.

Robert Goddard launched the first liquid-fueled rocket in Massachusetts. He used gasoline, having lacked access to liquid hydrogen. The rocket "rose, slowly until it cleared the frame, and then at express train speed," he journaled.[56]

Indeed, it rose about three stories before coming home to Earth. That distance times thirty million will get you to the moon.

Harry Houdini died.

≠≠≠≠≠≠≠≠≠

Walter Mairs, the older cousin with whom Ned had once traveled to Cuba, buried his father Edwin Mairs in Irvington and began a tumultuous marriage to the Russian Baroness Helene Tartartinzoff Bistrom.

In 1927, Cornelius Vanderbilt Jr. and Rachel Littleton divorced. Felix would never get that piece of cake.

Nellie Duryea, the old family friend of Benjamin and Bessie Kittredge, died, her husband having preceded her.

Ned's father, George Miller Cumming, "the superintendent who is not likely to be deceived," died at age 72.[57] His Harvard obituary says he died in New York City, but the city does not have his death certificate, nor have I found a newspaper obituary. He was buried at his wife's family plot at Hillside Cemetery with a simple white cross-shaped plaque lying horizontally in the dirt and engraved with his initials.

He had left a nation full of trains. The *New York Times* warned in 1927:

> the number of suicides from the 110th Street Station of the Sixth Avenue

TEN PAST NOON

> elevated [today, this would be Lenox Ave, near today's Central Park North station] is ruining the business of the merchants with shops below, according to [the merchants]... According to [a spokesperson] there were eleven suicides from that station in the past year, and the effect has been such that potential customers prefer to walk a little farther rather than risk seeing a person hurtle from above.[58]

If he left behind invested assets from his decades as an executive for railroads and banks—and if his wife Lucy had likewise invested anything from the sixty-thousand-dollar proceeds of the Irvington estate ten years earlier—the stock was not worth very much anymore. Stocks are derivatives; they pull their value from something else. Imagine that you are playing Monopoly, you roll the dice, you land on someone else's property, and you owe everything you have to the other player. When this happens to everyone and only one player is left standing, the game ends. The money is all fake, it always was, and anyway you don't have it anymore.

In 1928, the Colombian military massacred workers for the United Fruit Company. The workers were participating in a left-wing labor strike for better working conditions. As families waited for the governor's address in a town square after Sunday mass, soldiers opened fire with machine guns. It was known as "la masacre de las bananeras" (the Banana Massacre).

For different reasons, on October 24, 1929, New York Stock Exchange share prices collapsed.

Over the next two months, the *New York Times* reported on a hundred suicide attempts, including a bond clerk and a produce salesman who jumped to their deaths from tall buildings on Wall Street weeks after the market crash.[59] It is an urban legend that investors jumped from their office windows on the very day of the crash, though the image of an indistinct human figure hurtling through the sky, this emblem of an American banker's despair, is now stored in the collective unconscious. The image sticks, I think, because of our intuitions that someone's fate is determined by what they have been tied to, and that how someone has lived is how they will die.

In the long term, the era of financial stress did correlate with a higher suicide rate in the general population.[60] It so happens that, in 1928, the Episcopal Church had released a revision to its Book of Common Prayer that lifted the restriction on funeral prayers for suicides.

The Boston-based Stone & Webster engineering firm made its first stock offering to the public just before the market crashed. After its existing contracts dried up, it cut staff in 1934.[61] By then, Ned's days as an employee were probably long gone, as he was back with his mother and sister in New York.

TEN PAST NOON

The Cummings' money wasn't going to rematerialize. Ned might have needed to work some magic on the trains if there was even a chance of that happening. (Why would anyone have expected the money to rematerialize by any method other than the train it first rode in on?) But Ned only wanted to ride the trains, not work the trains.

The family's standard of living apparently having changed with their patriarch's death in 1927 and the subsequent market crash, by 1930 they had more modest arrangements: Lucy, Emily, and Ned were lodging for sixty dollars per month in a three-bedroom house owned by newlywed Swedish immigrants Rudolph and Alida Johnson, twenty miles north of the city in the suburb of Scarsdale. Rudolph was the same age as Ned, and Alida was fifteen years older. The suburb's population had doubled during the previous decade and there were many new subdivisions. From the train station,[62] it was less than a mile's walk uphill to the house on Alkamont Avenue, newly built and situated in one of Scarsdale's cheaper neighborhoods. The Johnsons' house was valued at just fifteen percent of what the Cummings' income property in Irvington had sold for a decade earlier.[63] Probably the Johnsons slept in one room, Ned's mother and sister in another, and Ned in the third.

Everything was more compact. It wasn't the vast American West where someone could mine gold and claim to have found a priceless artifact with a graven image of the first modern human (as his father's colleagues had done with the Nampa figurine). It wasn't New York City, either. Ned didn't have to go to St. George's, Phillips Exeter, the Royal Flying Corps, Harvard, Deep Springs, or Columbia anymore, and he didn't have to be an engineer. His world was now a suburb with a wall separating him from his mother's voice.

Silently, elm bark beetles were making their way toward New York. They had recently arrived in the United States on a Netherlands timber shipment. They would spread a lethal fungus to tens of millions of elm trees.

"Ickira, trecketre, stedenthal, said the train," wending back and forth between the station downhill and the big city, to cite the rhythm captured by the South African poet Katharine Kilalea.[64] Cycle of cycles, *in sæcula sæculorum.*

His father gone, his money gone, his environs quieter, Ned began to write about what really interested him.

NOTES TO
"ENTERING THE GREAT DEPRESSION"

[1] "Remembering Boston's Deadly Molasses Flood, 100 Years Later." Julia Press, WNPR. January 15, 2019. https://www.wbur.org/news/2019/01/15/boston-molasses-flood-100-years-later Accessed Nov. 10, 2019.

TEN PAST NOON

[2] "Without Warning, Molasses in January Surged Over Boston." Edwards Park. Originally appeared in *Smithsonian* 14 No. 8 (November 1983), pp. 213-230. https://edp.org/molpark.htm Accessed Nov. 10, 2019.

[3] Stephen Puleo, author of *Dark Tide: The Great Boston Molasses Flood of 1919*, quoted in "Remembering Boston's Deadly Molasses Flood, 100 Years Later," *op. cit.*

[4] Henry Adams. *The Education of Henry Adams.* The Massachusetts Historical Society, 1918. "Chapter XXII: Chicago (1893)."

[5] Adams, *ibid.* "Chapter XXV: The Dynamo and the Virgin (1900)"

[6] Adams, *ibid.* "Chapter IV: Harvard College (1854-1858)."

[7] Albert J. Churella. *The Pennsylvania Railroad: Building an Empire, 1846-1917.* Vol. 1. University of Pennsylvania Press, 2013. pp. 716, 721.

[8] "Cumming Huntington Estate, Valued at $60,000, Sold." *New York Tribune,* April 28, 1919.

[9] Felix graduated St. George's in 1919 (according to the St. George's School Archives) and went to Harvard's campus that fall (Kittredge family papers, South Carolina Historical Society).

[10] Willard was the maternal grandfather of their grandmother, Lucy (Dana) Kittredge. Lucy was Felix's paternal grandmother and Ned's maternal grandmother. Felix identified his roommate as "Wain."

Letter from Benjamin Kittredge, Jr., undated, 1919. Kittredge family papers, South Carolina Historical Society.

[11] "$1,000,000 in Gifts for Vanderbilt's Bride: Miss Rachel Littleton Who Marries Financier Showered With Costly Presents." *The Washington Times.* April 29, 1920. p. 2. https://chroniclingamerica.loc.gov/lccn/sn84026749/1920-04-29/ed-1/seq-2/

Accessed August 5, 2019.

The tiara had "one huge stone surrounded by eighteen square diamonds and 200 smaller ones."

"C Vanderbilt Jr. Weds Rachel Littleton." *New York*

Tribune. April 30, 1920. p. 13.
chroniclingamerica.loc.gov Accessed August 5, 2019.
[12] "C Vanderbilt Jr. Weds Rachel Littleton." *ibid.*
[13] "Vanderbilt Jr. and Bride Start Honeymoon Trip: Will Tour Across Country—Usher at Their Wedding is Engaged." *The Evening World.* April 30, 1920. p. 3. chroniclingamerica.loc.gov Accessed August 5, 2019.
[14] Sherry's had operated at several locations in the city, and it had recently moved to a hotel a few blocks from the church.
The following articles were accessed in 2019 at chroniclingamerica.loc.gov.
    "Vanderbilt weds Miss Littleton." *The Sun and New York Herald,* April 30, 1920. p. 4.
    "C Vanderbilt Jr. Weds Rachel Littleton." *New York Tribune.* April 30, 1920. P. 13.
    "Vanderbilt's Guests Eat Sky-Scraper Wedding Cake." *Bismarck Daily Tribune.* May 4, 1920. p. 5.
    "5-Foot Cake for Vanderbilt Wedding." *The Washington Times.* April 29, 1920. p. 2.
    "Vanderbilt's Guests Eat Sky-Scraper Wedding Cake." *Bismarck Daily Tribune.* May 4, 1920. p. 5.
The price of a Ford Model T dropped to $300 in the early 1920s.
"1920 Ford Model T." Daniel Vaughan. *Conceptcarz.* March 2006. https://www.conceptcarz.com/vehicle/z12499/ford-model-t.aspx Accessed August 5, 2019.
[15] A newspaper clipping from Summer 1920. Kittredge family papers, South Carolina Historical Society.
[16] Letter from Benjamin Kittredge, Jr. August 1, 1920. He had previously mentioned the book in a July 17, 1920 letter as "rather interesting. But the style is somewhat trashy." Kittredge family papers, South Carolina Historical Society.
[17] Letter from Benjamin Kittredge, Jr., undated, 1920. Kittredge family papers, South Carolina Historical Society.
[18] Letter from Benjamin Kittredge, Jr., undated, 1918. Kittredge family papers, South Carolina Historical Society.

TEN PAST NOON

[19] Not even in 1927, the year Uncle George died, nor 1940, the year Cousin Ned died.

[20] It was founded in 1921 with the initial intention to build "fifteen rail lines and twelve freight terminals."
Ted Steinberg. *Gotham Unbound: The Ecological History of Greater New York.* New York: Simon and Schuster, 2014. p. 187.

[21] "The Army's Message to Returning World War I Troops? Behave Yourselves." David Chrisinger. *New York Times.* July 31, 2019.
https://www.nytimes.com/2019/07/31/magazine/world-war-i-veterans-treatment.html February 16, 2020.

[22] Rajendra B. Aklekar. *A Short History of Indian Railways.* New Delhi: Rupa, 2019. pp. 105-106.

[23] Frederiek Depoortere. *Badiou and Theology.* New York: T&T Clark, 2009. pp. 12-13.

[24] Letter from Benjamin Kittredge, Jr., December 13, 1921. Kittredge family papers, South Carolina Historical Society.

[25] Letter from Benjamin Kittredge, Jr., December 16, 1921. Kittredge family papers, South Carolina Historical Society.

[26] Letter from Mabel at Barnard College in New York City to Benjamin Kittredge, Jr., 1923. Kittredge family papers, South Carolina Historical Society.

[27] Rosalie Schwartz. *Pleasure Island: Tourism and Temptation in Cuba.* Lincoln and London: University of Nebraska Press, 1997. pp. 27-30.

[28] Manifest for the S. S. Governor Cobb sailing from Havana, Cuba to Key West, Florida on February 16, 1920. "List of United States Citizens."
"Florida, Passenger Lists, 1898-1963 for Edward D. Cumming." A3618: Arriving at Key West, Florida, 1907-1949: 03.
https://www.ancestry.com/interactive/8842/41256_b126415-00484/2700993 Accessed February 21, 2020.

[29] *Harvard '21. A collective biography.* Printed for the 20th anniversary. Cambridge, Mass. 1941, p. 143. Housed with MS Cumming, *Eunuchry.*

[30] "New York, Passenger and Crew Lists (including Castle Garden and Ellis Island), 1820-1957." Roll T715, 1897-1957: 2001-3000: Roll 2902. S. S. Esperanza sailing from Tampico, Mexico on December 19, 1920, arriving at New York City, December 31, 1920. "List of United States Citizens."
https://www.ancestry.com/interactive/7488/NYT715_2902-0029/4024888108 Accessed February 21, 2020.
[31] "Francisco 'Pancho' Villa surrenders to Mexican authorities." R. H. Turner. United Press. August 10, 1920. https://www.upi.com/Archives/1920/08/10/Francisco-Pancho-Villa-surrenders-to-Mexican-authorities/6847113188140/ Accessed February 22, 2020.
[32] Audre Lorde. *Zami: A New Spelling of My Name.* Berkeley: Crossing Press, 1982. Chapter 20.
[33] "Why did the Carolina parakeet go extinct?" Ben Crair. *Smithsonian.* May 2018.
https://www.smithsonianmag.com/science-nature/why-carolina-parakeet-go-extinct-180968740/ Accessed August 5, 2019.
[34] Harold Schechter. *The Mad Sculptor: The Maniac, The Model, and the Murder that Shook the Nation.* Seattle: Amazon Publishing, 2014. pp. 59-90.
[35] "Believes Rocket Can Reach Moon: Smithsonian Institution Tells of Prof. Goddard's Invention to Explore Upper Air." *New York Times.* January 12, 2020.
https://timesmachine.nytimes.com/timesmachine/1920/01/12/96871388.html?pageNumber=1
Accessed August 7, 2019.
[36] "Topics of the Times: A Severe Strain on Credulity." Editorial. *New York Times.* January 13, 1920.
https://timesmachine.nytimes.com/timesmachine/1920/01/13/102738081.html
Accessed August 7, 2019.
[37] According to the Registrar's office at Columbia University, he was enrolled Feb. 1923–Jan. 1924 and did not graduate as expected with the Class of 1925.

[38] For an endeavor in this area, see "Times in the Novel." John Hunt. *The Joyce Project.* http://m.joyceproject.com/info/times.html Accessed January 16, 2020.

[39] Thomas Mann. *The Magic Mountain* (originally S. Fischer Verlagberlin, 1924). Translated from the German by H. T. Lowe-Porter. England: A. Wehaten and Co., Exeter, 1971. p. 548.

[40] Mann, *ibid.* pp. 183-184, 633, 272.

[41] "The Making of *The Magic Mountain.*" Thomas Mann. *The Atlantic,* January 1953. Reprinted in Mann, *ibid.,* pp. 726-7.

[42] "The Making of *The Magic Mountain.*" *ibid.,* p. 728.

[43] Matthew Coniam. *Egyptomania Goes to the Movies: From Archaeology to Popular Craze to Hollywood Fantasy.* McFarland, 2017. p. 49.

[44] "Stone & Webster, Inc. History."
http://www.fundinguniverse.com/company-histories/stone-webster-inc-history/ Accessed June 1, 2014.

[45] "Engineering and Construction Activities: Formal Opening of Water Gas Plant at Fall River." *Stone & Webster Journal.* v. 32, no. 1 (January 1923) p. 46.

[46] "Stone & Webster, Inc. records, 1921-1928, bulk 1923-1924."
http://encore.utep.edu/iii/encore/record/C__Rb1748304__Sstone%20and%20webster__Orightresult__X5;jsessionid=D6D54469F6584CB126C1EF57C7087162?lang=eng&suite=cobalt

[47] "On Spiritual Barrenness." Editorial comment. *Stone & Webster Journal.* v. 32, no. 1 (January 1923) p. 5.
https://babel.hathitrust.org/cgi/pt?id=njp.32101048991424&view=1up&seq=27 Accessed January 30, 2020.

[48] "On Spiritual Barrenness." *ibid.,* pp. 6, 8.

[49] "In the Boston office of Stone & Webster there are six hundred individuals at work."
"Rainy Days." Henry B. Sawyer. *Stone & Webster Journal.* v. 32, no. 1 (January 1923) p. 20.
https://babel.hathitrust.org/cgi/pt?id=njp.32101048991424&view=1up&seq=42

Accessed January 30, 2020.
Ned's obituary says that he worked in Panama and separately comments that, while employed at Stone & Webster's Boston headquarters, "he served them also in the field." The obituary does not conclusively state that Stone & Webster is the same employer for whom he worked in Panama.
Source: *Harvard '21. A collective biography.* Printed for the 20th anniversary. Cambridge, Mass. 1941, p. 143.
The engineering firm Stone & Webster was acquired by Westinghouse Electric Company on Jan. 1, 2016. All Stone & Webster company history prior to that date was to be accessible under Chicago Bridge & Iron, but Chicago Bridge & Iron soon afterward merged into McDermott, and McDermott told me in April 2019 that they could not assist with inquiries about Stone & Webster personnel records in the '20s and '30s.

[50] In 1925, they lived at 2268 Sedgwick Ave.

[51] Daniel Vivian, author of *A New Plantation World,* attributes this to a letter from Benjamin R. Kittredge, Sr. to S. Dana Kittredge, n.d. [ca. 1927] Kittredge Family Papers, South Carolina Historical Society, Box 15, Folder 4. He writes this in a footnote. Daniel J. Vivian, *A New Plantation World: Sporting Estates in the South Carolina Lowcountry, 1900-1940.* Cambridge, U.K.: Cambridge University Press, 2018. p. 253.

[52] Vivian, *ibid.*, p. 21.

[53] "Documents on Zora Neale Hurston from the Barnard College Archives" in "Jumpin' at the Sun: Reassessing the Life and Work of Zora Neale Hurston," ed. Janet Jakobsen and David Hopson. *S&F Online* (3:2). Winter 2005. http://sfonline.barnard.edu/hurston/archives_01.htm
Accessed August 13, 2019.

[54] Henry James. *Notes Of A Son and Brother.* New York, Charles Scribner's Sons: 1914. p. 297-8. Quoted in "The Mystery of Henry's Bicycle." Michael Wood.
http://www.jonathanames.com/james/james.html
Accessed August 25, 2005.

TEN PAST NOON

Archived at
https://web.archive.org/web/20050518081223/http://www.jonathanames.com/james/james.html
Accessed February 22, 2020.

[55] Scott Donaldson. "Humor in *The Sun Also Rises.*" Linda Wagner-Martin, ed. *New Essays on* The Sun Also Rises. Cambridge University Press, 1987. p 27.

[56] Diary of Robert H. Goddard. March 17, 1926. Quoted by Stephen Corda. *Introduction to Aerospace Engineering with a Flight Test Perspective.* UK: Wiley, 2017. p. 85.
https://books.google.com.co/books?id=frfBDQAAQBAJ&pg=PA85&lpg=PA85
Accessed January 16, 2020.

[57] According to his obituary, he died in New York City on July 2, 1927. However, the five boroughs of New York City cannot find a copy of his death certificate.

[58] "Merchants Complain Suicides Hurt Business; Seek Way to Guard 110th St. Elevated Station." *New York Times.* January 31, 1927. p. 19.

[59] "Death on Wall Street, Fact and Rumor." Derek Kravitz. *Washington Post.* January 22, 2009.
http://voices.washingtonpost.com/washingtonpostinvestigations/2009/01/the_wall_street_leap.html Accessed February 2, 2020.

[60] "1929 Stock Market Crash: Did Panicked Investors Really Jump from Windows?" Christopher Klein. History.com. Feb. 25, 2019.
https://www.history.com/news/stock-market-crash-suicides-wall-street-1929-great-depression
See also: Harold Schechter. *The Mad Sculptor: The Maniac, The Model, and the Murder that Shook the Nation.* Seattle: Amazon Publishing, 2014. p. 103.

[61] "…the Rock Island Dam (the first to cross Washington's Columbia River), the 50-story RCA building in New York City, and a natural gas pipeline in Texas and New Mexico…" http://www.fundinguniverse.com/company-histories/stone-webster-inc-history/

[62] There were three train stations in the town as of 1917: Scarsdale, Hartsdale, and Heathcote. The nearest one to the house on Alkamont Ave. was Scarsdale.
"Village of Scarsdale, New York: Reconnaissance Level Cultural Resource Survey Report." Li-Saltzman Architects, P.C. and Andrew S. Dolkart. July 12, 2012.
https://s3.amazonaws.com/scarsdale/120712+Scarsdale+Cult+Resc+Survey+Rpt.pdf Accessed Sept. 27, 2019.
The New York, Westchester, and Boston Railway was in service 1912-1937. It traveled between White Plains (stopping at the Heathcote Station in Scarsdale) and 113rd St at the Harlem River in the Bronx.
"New York, Westchester, and Boston Railway."
http://www.nycsubway.org/wiki/New_York,_Westchester,_and_Boston_Railway Accessed May 16, 2014.
[63] Ned is not mentioned on the 1930 census along with the other four occupants of this address, but he used this as a correspondence address for his work on *Eunuchry*.
1930 United States Federal Census. New York: Westchester: Eastchester: Enumeration District 0126, Supervisor's District 20.
https://www.ancestry.com/interactive/6224/4638873_00869#?imageId=4638873_00870
Accessed February 21, 2020.
[64] Katharine Kilalea. "Hennecker's Ditch." *PN Review* 195, Volume 37 Number 1, September–October 2010.
https://www.pnreview.co.uk/cgi-bin/scribe?item_id=8078 Accessed February 16, 2020.

TRACKS 29-36
THE CART

BY SUBJECT
NOT ALPHABETICAL

How infuriating it must have been for Ned that his cousin, who was almost a year older than he and yet years behind him in school, had found a publisher for his novel, *Crowded Solitude,* while Ned, who had traveled across the country by train at age seventeen to lecture on Victor Hugo, could not finish his own intended *magnum opus* of *Eunuchry.*

Felix had complained in a letter to his mother in October 1928 that, although a friend had promised to seek feedback from the important editors at Harpers, he had low hopes for his novel's marketability.[1] *Crowded Solitude* was nonetheless published by Coward-McCann in 1930.

Meanwhile, Ned handwrote the title of his own intended book on a sheet of paper:

TEN PAST NOON

Eunuchry
The History of Human Castration
With Notes on the Personalities of Eunuchs

At the outset, he defines his terms: "the complete destruction of the functional organization of that part of the male genital organs called the testicles is always known as castration and a human male in whom no function is performed by these glands is always termed a eunuch."[2]

In other words: A eunuch is someone whose testicles don't produce testosterone, have been entirely removed, or perhaps have been "missing" from birth. A eunuch is not female, but isn't quite male in all respects, either. He may have once been seen as unambiguously male, but he is no longer so. Once he is a eunuch, he cannot go back to being male—at least, this was not possible when Ned began to write in the early 1930s, several years before testosterone was synthesized. For most of human history, testosterone was not understood and certainly was not available to inject into human bodies. Many languages had a word for "eunuch," and this is the context in which those words were used for millennia.

In some cultures, eunuchs had separate gender roles, while in other cultures they were simply seen as disabled, injured, or damaged men, but we are getting ahead of ourselves if we discuss that right now. Physical castration—minus the layers of personal and cultural interpretation—is easy enough to identify. Even if the physical generalization is ultimately insufficient, it is a clear starting point.

That is where Ned begins his project. He will write about castration. Specifically, he wants to learn about the castration of boys and men, not the mutilation or sterilization of girls and women. The former group are the "eunuchs." He will not write about women or men unless he can use them to make a point about eunuchs. He has chosen a focus.

#########

Ned acknowledged the New York Academy of Medicine for helping with his research, but he was not affiliated with the institution, and it has no record of how his papers ended up in their collection.

On that point, all I can contribute is my observation that Ned was distantly related to a former president of the New York Academy of Medicine, the neurologist Charles Loomis Dana. They may not have known exactly how they were related, but they clearly shared a family name. Their common ancestor was Richard Dana. He was born in England or France around the time the Mayflower departed; came to Cambridge, Massachusetts as a young man; and had many children in the Massachusetts Bay Colony.[3] Six generations later, there was Ned's maternal grandmother Lucy (Dana) Kittredge, and, through a different line, her fifth cousin Charles Loomis Dana. Perhaps that is how Ned found his way into the library—the newly completed Romanesque building on Fifth Avenue that had recently opened in 1927—just as his Dana heritage was part of the reason he found his way into Harvard.

Figure 15 – Charles Loomis Dana.[4]

Dr. Dana could not have helped Ned for very long. He retired in 1933 to a convalescent home in Harmon-on-Hudson where he died of a cerebral hemorrhage in 1935.

In the library's catalog, Ned's manuscript is

dated 1931–1937, as that seems when he was most active. As a reminder, his rough draft looks like this:

Figure 16 – The manuscript (most of it, anyway) on the cart at the New York Academy of Medicine.

The light blue folders on the top shelf are what he called the "preliminary text." The black folders on the lower shelves are the supposedly more mature "text."

Then, what seems to be a third draft of the same material:

TEN PAST NOON

Figure 17 – The third draft of the manuscript, kept in boxes.

There is a table of contents, but it doesn't quite correspond to the chapters that were actually written.

He hand-copied passages in Latin, French, and German. He often numbered the sources in red ink, like "40 Millant," "201 Davenport," "816 Jewish Encyclopedia," "1109 Ramamurthi." The full references are in a folder he called "Abstracts."

The full bibliographical information for the twelve hundred numbered sources was recorded on index cards. (They are not pictured here. Just imagine a box of more index cards than you've ever dreamed could be necessary for any purpose.)

It's like a wheeling memorial, or, better, a haunting. Bad dreams bound in a nutshell, as Hamlet would describe it. I bet it rolls down the library hall by itself at night with a squeaky wheel like a renegade train car. The material by which he wants to be remembered *is on that cart.*

I imagine him saying, in a demon child's falsely pleading voice, *"Did I make something bad?"*

"Yes, yes, this thing you made is bad and—"

—and? How will *I* be remembered? I criticize what I fear. If my files weren't mostly in digital format, I, too, would glue a similar geological concretion of ink and paper onto a cart. I admit that. I am not showing you my digital files, which are vast and intimidating in their own way.

How is it organized? Frankly, it's not. Here is one version of his *intended* organization.

> A. Preface
> B. Analytical Table of Contents
> > I Origin of Castration
> > II Effects of Castration
> > III Crime and Strife
> > IV Disease
> > V Insanity and Religion
>
> C. Excursus on Unilateral castration
> > VI Employment of Eunuchs
> > VII Eunuch Trade and Manufacture
> > VIII Behaviour of Eunuchs
>
> D. Biographies
> E. Critical Review of the Sources
> F. List of works cited in the Text and Notes
> G. List of Plates
> H. Index

TEN PAST NOON

A funny thing, that organization. It has a way of changing. He suggested a revision, replacing II-IV with:

> II Anat and Phys of Eunuchs
> III Therapy
> IV Victor and Vanquished
> V Punishment

and D-H with:

> B. [Notes]
> Biographical Table of Eunuchs
> Critical Review of the Principal
>   Bibliographical Works
> Works Cited in the Text and Notes

In the second draft (called the "Text" in the black folders), the first volume does not appear to be about "Origin of Castration" after all, but is now labeled "Eunuchry by subject not alphabetical," and it seems to deal mainly with castration's use as a punishment. The tabs in the folder (Ned called them "guides") refer to the further breakdown of subjects:

> 1 – Natural eunuchs
> 2 – Trophies in war; torture
> 3 – Castration as punishment
> 4 – Sterilization
> 5 – Legislation

The third volume was to be

> 1 – Accident
> 2 – Punitive
> 3 – Therapeutic

4 – Religious
5 – Miscellaneous

The blank paper sheets were stamped by the manufacturer, "HAMMERMILL BOND Made in U.S.A." When I saw it, I noted it carefully, as if I might gain forensic information from it. It felt just as informative as the table of contents.

NOTES TO
"BY SUBJECT NOT ALPHABETICAL"

[1] Letter from Benjamin Kittredge, Jr. to Bessie Kittredge, October 11, 1928. Kittredge family papers, South Carolina Historical Society.
[2] MS Cumming, *Eunuchry.* Vol. 1.
[3] "Hinsdale New Hampshire Journalist, Editor, and Publisher: Charles Anderson Dana (1819-1897)." Janice Brown. *New Hampshire's History Blog.* October 26, 2007.
http://www.cowhampshireblog.com/2007/10/26/hinsdale-new-hampshire-journalist-editor-and-publisher-charles-anderson-dana-1819-1897/ Accessed February 19, 2020.
[4] Public domain photo of Charles Loomis Dana, M.D. HMD. No year given. Courtesy of the National Library of Medicine. Alman (photographer). From the Images from the History of Medicine (IHM).
http://ihm.nlm.nih.gov/images/B05041
Accessed October 23, 2019.

DAMN THE SURGEONS!

Ned's papers are a continuous brainstorm, and, as often happens for writers, the better material comes later. (This is true almost by definition, since, once you get your ideas correct, you can stop writing. Your missing car keys are always in the last place you look because once you find them you stop searching.) I want to pull some highlights, but I won't start with the diffuse notes at the beginning. I'll pull some of the harder-hitting pieces, which may mean starting from the end. I am the one who is alive to give order to his manuscript, and I have decided that this is the order.

This paragraph is key for Ned:

> Surgeons are today wholly uneducated outside their limited sphere. Engineers are if anything worse but they rarely intrude on affairs outside their own field except perhaps regarding economic questions. The military are the most ignorant of all.

TEN PAST NOON

> Who would approach a colonel of infantry as a guide to the good life.[1]

The face value of these sentences can be set aside. What's important here is between the lines. Ned would have participated in military exercises at St. George's, where he had formed an intention to train in an early version of Canada's air force. He studied engineering for a couple semesters and worked for an engineering firm. Thus, his mention of "the military" and "engineers." This corresponds to his real life experience. Surgeons, then? From where did he gain his experience interacting with any surgeons?

Among his first fourteen volumes (the ones that aren't "supplementary," i.e. are primarily about history and biology rather than psychology), *three* end with a pointed comment about surgeons. It is as if, when he spoke out to curtail the power of surgeons, he felt he had accomplished what he set out to do in each of those chapters and so he ended them. The end of Vol. 4 notes that many surgeons past and present use the maxim "When in doubt, castrate!" The end of Vol. 13 mentions two surgeons who were subsequently murdered by patients they had castrated (even though one patient had given consent and the other's castration was only accidental). At the end of Vol. 14, he opines:

> Surgeons in so far as they are surgeons are merely artisans. They may judge of surgery as surgery not however of its

social or ethical implications. Their responsibility in regard to these aspects of their work never transcends that of the executioner who raises the axe at the bidding of the state. As citizens they are on the whole less qualified to pass on these implications of their work than many other groups. It is in regard to social therapy that physicians are hopelessly beyond their depth. They are technicians—nothing more.

If the government wants to build a canal, he argues, it consults engineers, but it doesn't ask engineers to decide whether the project happens. Similarly, surgeons should be relieved of such strategic power. "Society must enforce the dictum on surgeons: When in doubt, don't castrate!!"[2] His Vol. 1 additionally claims that surgeons more readily recognize the "outrage" of the removal of ovaries but are more tolerant when the offense concerns the male "glands of internal secretion."

Since *someone* needs to be held accountable for castration, he says that "society at large must take the blame for the the [sic] abuses which it tolerates," as no one expects surgeons to have the discernment or the courage to fight social mores. Where there was social demand for eunuchs, "all participated in the benefits and none protested loudly the wrong."[3] If change is to happen, there must be a collective movement.

"The burden of proof in every case rests with

those advocating castration," he wrote. Allowing for a more utilitarian approach to ethics, he notes that the procedure's costs need to be considered alongside its benefits. "All must concede that the eunuch is in many respects both individually and socially inferior to the uncastrated. Thus the benefit derived from the operation must be real and must exceed by a certain margin the loss entailed to the individual and to society."[4]

Hypothetically entertaining the possibility that castration could be appropriate in some cases, Ned still refers to the patient as a "proposed victim"[5] even when he apparently consents to the operation. Children and slaves can't consent, he points out. Furthermore, sometimes the treatment doesn't provide any benefit. If you can't sing soprano now, you won't do so after the operation, either.

He also opposes castration as punishment (e.g. for sex offenses) on the general principle that retribution is a race to the bottom. He fears that castration could be a slippery slope toward other judicial mutilations and beatings. He knows that the first Norman king of England, William the Conqueror in the 11th century, codified amputation of all extremities (feet, hands, scrotum, and eyes) in place of capital punishment, and that, by the early 18th century, for a case of high treason, castration was recommended as a concurrent enhancement to a grisly death sentence.[6] It is often just one corporal punishment among others. When it is used to shame and torture, there is nothing essentially humane about it. It reappears throughout history as "an atavistic policy,"[7] meaning something we just can't seem to get rid of.

The new scientific awareness of sex hormones introduced bioethical complexities. In the 1920s, the American dairy industry sought to maximize the productivity of cows[8] and, by the 1930s, gonadal hormone treatment was available for humans. This upended humanity's operating assumption since time immemorial that all the effects of castration are irreversible.

The train could roll in the opposite direction; it was now a switchback, and this feature enabled it to climb a zig-zag track up a steep hill.

This introduced a loophole, "an entirely new element" to punitive castration.[9] If criminals punished with the knife simply took an androgen, they'd still be infertile but wouldn't be eunuchs in the full sense of the word, not as the idea had always been known. They would thereby circumvent the androgen-deprivation part of their punishment.[10]

Ned was also concerned that therapeutic and punitive motives are often muddled, as when "epileptics and the feeble minded" are castrated to protect the public from "their uncontrolled sexual impulses," a power play on the part of the medical establishment that seemed wrong to him.[11] Other therapeutic motives he perceived as simply ill-conceived, such as the treatment of an imprecisely defined "mania" or the encouragement of weight gain for tuberculosis patients.[12] This last notion may have been emotionally resonant for him, as he may have remembered that the director of Deep Springs had suffered weight loss due to tuberculosis and had also struggled with sexual impulses.

We are not going to get any closer to hearing from Ned directly why he filled a cart with notes on eunuchs.

We can speculate. He was mad at surgeons, so perhaps he'd had a hernia repair? Inguinal hernias, in which part of the intestine may descend into the scrotum, were often misunderstood and addressed by surgeries that physicians today would not advise.[13] Ned was aware that the idea that eunuchs were less likely to suffer hernia had been around since the Middle Ages.[14] He provides Celsus' contemporary description of a second-century hernia operation and annotated it in pencil: "wrong!!" He brings up a passage from George Medicus Amaud's 1748 *Dissertation on Hernias, or Ruptures* that refers to a "Mr. Heister" (probably Lorenz Heister) who argues, in Amaud's paraphrase, that "strolling surgeons…ought to be put to death for such practices."[15] Such a surgical mishap could have befallen Ned, but I have no evidence.

If I were to make up a story and if a hernia story didn't feel dramatic enough, I could place him next to a moving airplane propeller in Canada and then in the office of a military surgeon whom he later blamed for his outcome, but I am not sure how a fictionalization would illuminate this matter.

I do not have the sense that he identified as a woman or that he felt like a woman in any particular way, nor that he aspired to change his body, nor that he was sexually interested in men or eunuchs. Nothing I found seems like evidence of that. On the other hand, nothing I found confirms that he identified as a man and was sexually interested in women, either.

It is this particular kind of silence that binds us: unending words troubling the surface of still, deep water, none of them ever reaching what's underneath.

There are other possible reasons for his academic fascination. Many men are drawn to the idea of being castrated, often because they desire a long-term solution for the distress caused by their sexual urges or because they sexually fantasize about castration itself. Today, there are thousands of active members on a single website dedicated to this topic. Most identify as men. Some pursue castration in reality, while others are content to live with an intense, private interest in the idea alone. Either way, they may research the subject matter for years or even decades, perhaps as a tactic for exploring and containing their feelings.[16] Maybe that's what powered Ned's papers: anxiety management.

But I cannot let go of my intuition that his anger about "the surgeons" is meaningful. Why would an author spend energy trying to tell engineers, military officers, and surgeons what to think about castration if he also believes that these people do not care and that their disciplines cannot help? Why would he waste breath on something he admits to be fruitless? Only because he has a personal score to settle. He is still mad about engineers even though his railroad president father has been dead for years, he is dismissive of military officers even though he only *almost* went to war, but his most pointed comments are about surgeons.

If he is not castrated, he nevertheless somehow "identifies with" eunuchs. He has a certain kind of sympathy for them; he takes their side in history. Regarding this identification, I don't know how much is literal and how much is figurative. It could be both. There is the fact of the matter, and there is how one feels about it.

⧸⧸⧸⧸⧸⧸⧸⧸⧸

What one sweeps under the rug may grow larger in the imagination. To use the jargon: "Psychological compartmentalization" may lead to "psychic splitting." A phrase that often makes better sense to me, as popularized by the psychoanalyst Stephen Grosz, is "the bigger the front, the bigger the back."[17] After all, compartmentalizing or splitting physical substances make them *smaller* or *thinner,* but ideas that you hide from yourself become *bigger.* Unaddressed fear makes a copy of you. The copy can balloon out of control, eclipsing your former self.

#########

In the 5th-century B.C.E. play *Oedipus Tyrannus,* the author used different words to describe what happened to the infant Oedipus' feet when he was exposed and left to die: *yoked, pierced, fettered.* Sophocles didn't need to be precise and consistent, as one critic argued, because the mutilation's meaning wasn't literal anyway. As a newborn, Oedipus couldn't have crawled away. More likely, we are supposed to understand that his birth inspired such fear that, not only did someone attempt infanticide, but they practiced sorcery on his feet to block his tiny vengeful spirit from returning. The magical footbinding may also represent how each of us is held to our own spot. While "fate" may be used to describe a parlor-trick prophecy in which we pick the card upon which we mentally concentrate, to the Greek mind it implied a deeper recognition that each of us has our own limit.[18] We are held by forces we cannot see: by ancestry, by liquid asphalt, by gravity.

We don't like to hear about limits. We like to hear about freedom. We'd like to hear that each of us has an immaterial soul that makes our

TEN PAST NOON

choices, or at least that there is a god who transcends the world and who decides on our behalf. But the idea is incoherent. If a thoroughly unbound soul or god came into being by "an undetermined accident," explains secular activist Dan Barker,

> it would be random, chaotic, undefined, and unreliable. Whatever it is, in order for "it" to be able to make judgments— in order for "you" to be a "self"—it must be defined. To be defined is to be limited. … You cannot be a "you," biological or not, without having been determined to be a "you."[19]

The world is determined. To be able to operate in the world, we, too, are determined.

There is so much of who we are that we have not yet learned to see, or are not prepared to see.

NOTES TO "DAMN THE SURGEONS!"

[1] MS Cumming, *Eunuchry*. Vol. 14.
[2] MS Cumming, *Eunuchry*. Vol. 14.
[3] MS Cumming, *Eunuchry*. Vol. 14.
[4] MS Cumming, *Eunuchry*. Vol. 14.
[5] MS Cumming, *Eunuchry*. Vol. 14.
[6] MS Cumming, *Eunuchry*. "Text" in black folder, Vol. 1. He quotes the punishment for high treason: "…you are to be hanged by the Neck, and being alive to be cut down, and your Privy-Members to be cut off, and your Bowels to be taken out of your Belly, and there burnt, you being alive:

and your Head to be cut off..." (1709)

[7] MS Cumming, *Eunuchry,* "Text" in black folder, Vol. 1.

[8] "Permit me to congratulate you and Dr. McGee on your biological test for the male hormone...Recently Dr. W. W. Swett called on me regarding a man to fill a new research position in the Bureau of Dairy Industry, Washington, D.C....The projects especially desired are concerned with fertilization and sterility; resorption of foetuses and lactation problems."
A unsigned letter to be sent from Errol T. Engle (probably) to Dr. Carl R. Moore, January 14, 1928.
Errol [Earl] T. Engle papers, 1896-1970 (bulk 1922-1930), Health Sciences Library Archives and Special Collections, Columbia University.

[9] MS Cumming, *Eunuchry*, Vol. 14.

[10] MS Cumming, *Eunuchry*, Vol. 3.

[11] MS Cumming, *Eunuchry*, Vol. 14.

[12] MS Cumming, *Eunuchry*, Vol. 4.

[13] Andrzej L. Komorowski (June 4th 2014). History of the Inguinal Hernia Repair, Inguinal Hernia, Silvestro Canonico, IntechOpen, DOI: 10.5772/58533. https://www.intechopen.com/books/inguinal-hernia/history-of-the-inguinal-hernia-repair

[14] MS Cumming, *Eunuchry,* "Text" in black folder, Vol. 1.

[15] MS Cumming, *Eunuchry*, "preliminary text" folder for Vol. 3, in a section marked "Castration for Medical Purposes," three-quarters of the way to the end. He cites this in red to 905 Arnaud.

[16] "A Passion for Castration: Characterizing Men Who Are Fascinated with Castration, but Have Not Been Castrated." Lesley F. Roberts, Michelle A. Brett, Thomas W. Johnson, PhD, and Richard J. Wassersug, PhD. Journal of Sexual Medicine, 2007. DOI: 10.1111/j.1743-6109.2007.00636.x

[17] "The Examined Life by Stephen Grosz – Review." Alexander Linklater. *The Guardian.* January 27, 2013. https://www.theguardian.com/books/2013/jan/27/examined-life-stephen-grosz-review Accessed August 6, 2019.

[18] Jules Brody. *'Fate' in* Oedipus Tyrannus: *A Textual Approach.* (Arethusa Monographs, XI.) Buffalo, N.Y.: State University of New York at Buffalo, 1985. pp. 28-32. The words translated as "yoked," "pierced," and "fettered" may be found in *Oedipus Tyrannus* at lines 718, 1034, and 1349.

[19] Dan Barker. *Free Will Explained: How Science and Philosophy Converge to Create a Beautiful Illusion.* New York: Sterling, 2018. p. 41.

THOUGHT PROCESSES

Ned especially admired three books. They were written in Arabic, French, and German. Understanding the works he most appreciated helps me understand the work he was trying to create.

※※※※※※※※※

Abu-Uthman Amr ibn Bahr, known as al-Jāḥiẓ, born at the end of the 8th century in Basra, "wrote the first comprehensive treatise on the subject which has been preserved," better than anything the classicists produced, Ned claimed. It was *Kitāb al-Ḥayawān [The Book of Living Beings]*, supposedly unequalled anywhere in the world for a millennium.

Al-Jāḥiẓ believed that eunuchs were masculine, smelly, energetic horseback riders, voracious eaters, and exceptionally passionate about women. He said they inclined toward domestic housework and frivolous activities. Should a slave be castrated, al-Jāḥiẓ said, the master should not be permitted to sell him for profit, which he hoped would reduce a slave owner's incentive to castrate numerous slaves. Though writers like Bachari and Ibn Kutaibah would criticize him and though Maçoudi disagreed about the body odor, al-Jāḥiẓ aimed for accuracy, and his work is notable to Ned because, he said, "no Islamic author after Jahiz wrote of the effects of castration at any length."[1]

Some of Ned's information came from a 1930 journal article, "El Libro de los Animales," that he received through correspondence with the author, Miguel Asín Palacios, who wrote to him briefly in Spanish from Madrid. (This is a rare instance of Spanish material in Ned's sources; there is no indication of whether he was able to read it unassisted.)

Al-Jāḥiẓ admired Aristotle, Jeanne Miller says, for what he saw as a "firmly clinical and affectively neutral approach" to identifying categories of beings. Al-Jāḥiẓ sensed that popular understandings of "intercategory" beings (including eunuchs) were "the key to understanding a cultural divide present in his society."[2]

#########

Next was Dr. Richard Millant's *Les Eunuques à Travers les Ages [Eunuchs Through the Ages]* (Paris, 1908). Ned may have first learned about it through his 1932 correspondence with the Welch Medical Library at Johns Hopkins University. He calls it the sole work devoted to eunuchs that "possesses any considerable merits," and he explains the author's background:

> Even as a student at the university, Millant seems to have been interested in eunuchry, for he selected the performance of castration by criminals and by the insane as the subject of the theses presented for his degree in medicine. His interest continued throughout his life and besides this work on the history of the operation he wrote several articles on the effects of castration on the development of the body and on the Skoptzi, his last article appearing posthumously, Millant having been killed in the War.[3]

Here is an example of how Millant writes about a goddess-worship cult in ancient Rome:

> Bientôt les derniers desservants d'un culte dont on avait abandonné les autels durent se résigner à parcourir le monde en parias, toujours coiffés de la mitre, mais une simple robe de lin ayant remplacé la pourpre et l'or.
>
> Ils allaient, sortes de jongleurs ambulants, mendiant de lieu en lieu, remettant pour quelque menue monnaie les péchés de toute nature, et «vendant, avec un égal cynisme, prières et philtres amoureux». Apulée nous apprend qu'un certain nombre des leurs, les Métrargyrtes,

promenaient à travers le monde grec des statues de la déesse syrienne, en prédisant l'avenir.⁴

[Soon the last servants of a cult whose altars had been abandoned had to resign themselves to traveling the world as pariahs, always wearing the miter, but a simple linen dress replaced the purple and the gold.

They went, like itinerant jugglers, begging from place to place, remitting for some small change the sins of all kinds, and "selling, with equal cynicism, prayers and love potions." Apuleius informs us that a number of them, the Metargyrtes, roamed the Greek world with statues of the Syrian goddess, predicting the future.]

Millant's anecdotes of history and religious ideas span nearly three hundred pages, and, though the book is disorganized and "casual," Ned judged it to be "throughout entertaining." This is what Ned aspired to do. "As a labor in the same field," he intoned about his own handwritten draft of *Eunuchry*, addressing his still-imaginary publisher and audience, "the present volume is with some diffidence submitted."⁵

#########

Then came Dr. Johannes Lange's *Die Folgen der Entmannung Erwachsener [The Consequences of Adult*

TUCKER LIEBERMAN

Emasculation] (Leipzig, 1934). This was a monograph in the "Arbeit und Gesundheit" Sozialmedizinische Schriftenreihe ["Work and Health" socio-medical series] of the Reichsarbeitsministerium [the German Reich Ministry of Labor]. That ministry was established in 1919, and it was connected to the rising Nazi government.[6] The study in question physically examined a number of war veterans who had experienced genital injury some fifteen years previously, noting changes in their skin, hair, fat distribution, and sexuality, occasionally referencing words like *"Epilepsie"* and *"Schizoid."*

The Foreword said:

> Für viele dieser Verstümmelten bedeutet jede Untersuchung eine neue seelische Wunde. Nur, wo es unumgänglich nötig ist, dürfen schmerzende Narben berührt werden. Dies war es im späteren Verlauf der Erhebungen, was mich darin bestärkte, die persönliche Nachuntersuchung auch der räumlich erreichbaren Verstümmelten zu vermeiden.[7]

> *[For many of these mutilated men, every examination means a new emotional wound. Only where absolutely necessary can painful scars be touched. This was later in the surveys, and it encouraged me to avoid the personal follow-up*

examination of those mutilated men I could physically reach.]

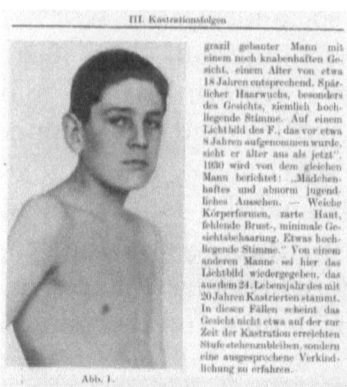

Figure 18 – The monograph included the shirtless portrait of a 24-year-old man reportedly castrated at age four. The author commented:

"In diesen Fällen scheint das Gesicht nicht etwa auf der zur Zeit der Kastration erreichten Stufe stehenzubleiben, sondern eine ausgesprochene Verkindlichung zu erfahren."[8]

["In these cases, it appears that the face does not remain at the stage attained at the time of castration, but rather becomes notably more childlike."]

Though cases of castration in childhood were mentioned anecdotally, the study included only men who were of military age at the time of their castration, and this was, in Ned's view, a limitation. He also expressed doubt about the study's findings about the rates of disruption to sexuality. What Ned seemed to like so much about this book, however, is that someone had bothered to investigate the question scientifically. The researcher had made a thorough questionnaire asking for medical data (e.g. blood sugar, thyroid, galvanic excitability), emotions, sexuality, and hobbies. He had even found the empathy, sensitivity, or curiosity to investigate the men's attention spans. Ned described it:

> The thought processes of eunuchs have received very little study and they have miraculously escaped the notice of the mental testers even the "intelligence" testers. Many of Lange's late castrated eunuchs who complained of sensations of somatic fatigue also reported "mental fatigue," "difficulty in concentrating" and a "tendency to forget." That certain of the conditions described as "depression" entailed retardation in the thought processes seems probable but is not mentioned in the records.[9]

Ned called it "the most important modern work" on the subject and "the most important single contribution to the knowledge of the effects of castration ever published," as well as "the only comprehensive study"[10] on post-pubertal castration that "might well serve as a model and standard" for future studies. "Nothing at all comparable to this volume had previously been published."[11]

TEN PAST NOON

Today, war continues to cause this sort of damage to human bodies. During the first decade of war in Afghanistan and Iraq, for example, improvised explosive devices (IEDs) left over 1,800 U.S. soldiers with severe genital injuries.[12] The problem still needs attention. We need science, psychology, foreign policy. We need to have lots of better thought processes.

✂✂✂✂✂✂✂✂✂

Ned did not explain why, if these three books were so good, they needed to be repeated. Why did he sit down to write his own *Eunuchry*? What did he plan to do differently? It seems he wanted to begin with the classical sensibilities and folksiness of al-Jāḥiẓ and Millant and update them with 20th-century attention to scientific method like Lange. Or, perhaps—not being a scientist himself—he hoped to somehow inspire others to do that.

NOTES TO "THOUGHT PROCESSES"

[1] MS Cumming, *Eunuchry*. Vol. 1.
[2] Jeanne Miller. "More Than the Sum of Its Parts: Animal Categories and Accretive Logic in Volume One of al-Jāḥiẓ's *Kitāb al-Ḥayawān*." Dissertation, New York University, January 2013. pp. 13, 10.
https://www.scribd.com/document/282731660/Kitab-al-Hayawan-de-Al-Jariz Accessed October 23, 2019.

TUCKER LIEBERMAN

[3] MS Cumming, *Eunuchry.* Vol. 14.
[4] Richard Millant. *Les Eunuques à travers les ages.* Paris: Vigot Frères, 1908. p. 30.
https://ia802701.us.archive.org/16/items/leseunuquestra00mill/leseunuquestra00mill.pdf Accessed October 22, 2019.
[5] MS Cumming, *Eunuchry.* Vol. 14.
[6] "Historikerkommission stellt Bericht zur Geschichte des Reichsarbeitsministeriums vor." 27. Juni 2017.
https://www.bmas.de/DE/Presse/Pressemitteilungen/2017/historikerkommission-symposium-2017.html
[7] Johannes Lange. "Vorwort" [Foreword] to *Die Folgen der Entmannung Erwachsener.* Leipzig: Georg Thieme/Verlag, 1934. p. 7.
[8] Johannes Lange. *Die Folgen der Entmannung Erwachsener.* Leipzig: Georg Thieme/Verlag, 1934. p. 24.
[9] MS Cumming, *Eunuchry.* Vol. A-2.
[10] MS Cumming, *Eunuchry.* Vol. 2.
[11] MS Cumming, *Eunuchry.* Vol. 14.
[12] Ann Jones. *They Were Soldiers: How the Wounded Return from America's Wars—The Untold Story.* Haymarket/Dispatch, 2013. Excerpted as "We Sent Them to Brutal Wars: Now, the Untold Story Of What Happens When Soldiers Come Home." *AlterNet.* November 6, 2013. https://www.alternet.org/2013/11/how-wounded-return-americas-wars-afghan-bomb/ Accessed February 16, 2020.

HYPOTHETICS AND HOARDING

Edward Gibbon, notable for his sweeping *History of the Decline and Fall of the Roman Empire* written in the late 18th century, portrays eunuchs as malign influences in ancient Rome and also scapegoats them for the ends of dynasties in Persia, India, and China. Ned counters this portrayal by noting that eunuchs also supported the rise of dynasties. Furthermore, Ned asks, how do we know that any activity by eunuchs—whether negative or positive—occurs *because* they were eunuchs?

I can pose the same question in several different ways:

How much of the historical status and influence of eunuchs can be attributed to their castration?

Which social conventions or power dynamics had some kind of grounding in what eunuchs actually were, and which were wholly irrational superstitions or customs?

What did eunuchs' beliefs, feelings, and

agency have to do with their genders and bodies?

When did others treat them primarily as stereotypical instances of a gender, and when were they treated more empathetically as individuals?

Ned, echoing Theodorus, asks: Why is a man judged on his merits, while eunuchs "are always judged as eunuchs"?[1] It is surely unfair that "actions which would have been accounted virtuous if performed by an entire man were condemned when performed by eunuchs."[2]

It is hard for anyone to answer. In a rare moment of humor, Ned says that it may require "the Science of Hypothetics described by Sir Henry Maine as 'the science of what might have happened but didn't,'"[3] i.e. knowledge of whether things would have been different for any given man if he hadn't been castrated. Who knows how opera would have developed without the male soprano, the distinctive castrato voice? Would the seclusion of women have been possible without eunuch liaisons who conveyed information to and from the public society of men? Would men whose sexual interests were directed at castrated boys have given up on sex with children entirely if they had found none of their preferred type, or would they have transferred their attention to uncastrated boys?

If things were different, something else might have happened. But, of course, it didn't. This is the science of non-events.

It isn't even his joke.

I don't know if he even recognized it as a joke.

Ned had no methodology for addressing these so-called hypothetics. His strategy seemed more simply to involve hoarding any and all information about eunuchs. When he found a eunuch, he put him on the library cart. There are extensive lists: over two hundred years of "the Sultans of Ironium (Rûm)" as well as "the Fatimide Caliphs of Africa,"[4] and a penciled note-to-self that "each Turkish tribe should then be traced ending with the Ottomans."[5] These lists were important only insofar as these kingdoms might be tied to the existence of a sort of person he cared about.

He was not inherently interested in men or women. If the sentence was not about eunuchs, it did not go in his manuscript.

Despite this focus, we are making quite a lot of stops. *This is the local train. Doors will open at every stop.* Each stop has a eunuch.

✂✂✂✂✂✂✂✂✂

Character dialogue in Richard Powers' novel *Galatea 2.2*:

"Our matrix is bumping up against you. It's bumping up against the lines you feed it."

"It could bump up against word lists forever and never have more than a collection of arbitrary, differentiated markers."

"And what do we humans have?" Lentz removed his glasses to wipe them. As monstrous as he looked with them on, he was even worse without.

"More." I didn't know what, at the moment. But there had to be more. "We take in the world continuously. It presses against us. It burns and freezes."[6]

++++++++++

In Vol. 3, Ned restates his plan to structure his text according to the reasons for castration: "accident," "punitive," "therapeutic," "religious," and "miscellaneous." This convention, he admits, is only to make his book easier to read. It is explicitly "not to serve as a scheme for interpretation" of actual eunuchs, and he will try to avoid establishing "a set of arbitrary definitions by which these classes could be made mutually exclusive."[7] In other words, he admits he has no accurate or meaningful way of grouping eunuchs and cannot tell us which contexts of castration are the most important for us to understand nor whether different kinds of castration produce particular effects. He is still in conceptual chaos. He just knows that a book needs to be divided into chapters. Despite his best intentions, his book unfortunately remains in structural chaos, insofar as he never carried through with the announced structure.

"Social categories," the biologist Joan Roughgarden wrote in 2004, "can't be made to coincide with biological categories except by fiat."[8]

Another manuscript page toys with the idea of a totally different structure:

> Angelic castration
>
> Witchcraft, restoration of genitals
>
> Castration and Emasculation by Jewish notions of the cause of Congenital Eunuchry.
>
> Diet makes Eunuchs[9]

This does not make sense.

Why not instead the Deep Springs list of values: *Industry, Thoroughness, Purpose?*

~~~~~~~~~~

Ned ultimately spent far more time cataloging the eunuchs than successfully organizing them. He doesn't provide insight into why he works this way, but comments from others can shed light on his personality type. After all, "people actually collect bad poetry, barbed wire, knock-knock jokes, wax paper liners out of cereal boxes, swizzle sticks, string, mouse pads, phone books, type fonts, clothing of famous people or Mersenne primes (prime numbers)," writes Mark B. McKinley in the 21st century.

Collectors may aim to comfortably organize the world, fill an inner emptiness, or gain prestige. "For some people collecting is simply the quest, in some cases a life-long pursuit that is never complete."[10] Since humans cannot remember many pieces of information in our short-term memory, we tend to classify them; it is easier to remember the groups than the individual items within the groups.[11]

If we notice that we are classifying, we might take a step back and ask why. "Classical understanding is concerned with the piles and the basis for sorting and interrelating them. Romantic understanding is directed toward the handful of sand before the sorting begins," Robert M. Pirsig suggested in *Zen and the Art of Motorcycle Maintenance.* A unitive approach "will not reject sand-sorting *or* contemplation of unsorted sand" but "will instead seek to direct attention to the endless landscape from which the sand is taken."[12]

One can derive a great deal of satisfying music from brief riffs on three chords because, says the novelist Ian McEwan, of "absorbing variation on an unchanging theme," "a microcosm giving you the whole world."[13]

The neurologist Jean-Martin Charcot wrote in 1872:

> How is it that one fine morning Duchenne discovered a disease that probably existed in the time of

Hippocrates?...Why do we perceive things so late, so poorly, with such difficulty? Why do we have to go over the same set of symptoms twenty times before we understand it? Why does the first statement of what seems a new fact always leave us cold?

Because our minds have to take in something that deranges our original set of ideas, but we are all of us like that in this miserable world.[14]

Close readers of *Oedipus Tyrannus* pay much attention to the details of the infant's foot mutilation, that being the source of the character's very name. There might be a hundred ways of expressing that question. It's really just one question, said the critic Jules Brody.

The answers to these questions, in whatever alternative ways we choose to rephrase them, must all revert sooner or later to the composite *Ur*-question, the very last one that at the end of his quest Oedipus will ever have or want to ask: how, when and why he had been left as an infant to die on Mount Cithaeron with his feet "bound" together.[15]

And if one has to revert to classifying, one might ask what's at the root of all these seemingly different objects and events and their variations, as well as the varied ways that we perceive them. Are they, at base, the same? H. Sperling wrote in 1910 that "the human mind cannot hold isolated

TEN PAST NOON

facts for long. At a definite stage of man's development he puts himself seriously to the task of arranging facts and fancies, dreams and realities, into tribes, classes, families, until he arrives at what he thinks the first parent out of which the whole universe proceeded."[16]

For some ancient Greeks, as Sperling noted, that universal core was water, fire, or air.

For Ned, it was eunuchs. The universe was made of eunuchs.

"Recently some books have appeared in which the history of the world is presented in relation to the women rather than the men of each generation," he wrote, his only nod to feminism in his entire doorstop manuscript being this simple acknowledgment that others have told stories from women's points of view. "If such a *tour de force* were desired"—that is, a similar effort on his preferred gender topic—"the history of the world might with much more reason be written in terms of eunuchs."[17] In his imagination, the history of the world hangs on men deprived of testosterone.

His manuscript—its words, and the fact that he wrote it—does not make any psychological sense if he did not somehow personally identify with eunuchs. "A man is what he thinks about all day long," said Ralph Waldo Emerson.

I don't have any external proof of his sexual biology, gender identity, or sexuality. I probably will not find it. I don't need it.

TUCKER LIEBERMAN

NOTES TO "HYPOTHETICS AND HOARDING"

[1] MS Cumming, *Eunuchry*. Vol. 12.
[2] MS Cumming, *Eunuchry*. Vol. A-3.
[3] MS Cumming, *Eunuchry*. Vol. 14.
[4] MS Cumming, *Eunuchry*. "Text," black folders, Vol. 15.
[5] MS Cumming, *Eunuchry*. "Text," black folder, Vol. 8.
[6] Richard Powers. *Galatea 2.2.* New York: Farrar Straus Giroux, 1995. p. 148.
[7] MS Cumming, *Eunuchry*. Vol 3.
[8] Joan Roughgarden. *Evolution's Rainbow: Diversity, Gender, and Sexuality in Nature and People.* (uncorrected page proof) University of California Press, 2004. p 14, 23.
[9] MS Cumming, *Eunuchry*. Vol. 3.
[10] "The psychology of collecting." Mark B. McKinley. *The National Psychologist: The independent newspaper for practitioners.* Jan. 1, 2007.
http://nationalpsychologist.com/2007/01/the-psychology-of-collecting/10904.html
[11] "Taxonomy: Why do we have this whole branch of science?" Gwen Nicodemus. *Ezine Articles.* October 6, 2010.
http://ezinearticles.com/?Taxonomy:-Why-Do-We-Have-This-Whole-Branch-of-Science?&id=5156594
Accessed February 22, 2020.
[12] Robert M. Pirsig. *Zen and the Art of Motorcycle Maintenance.* (1974) New York: Bantam, 1975. p. 76.
[13] Ian McEwan. *Saturday.* (2005) New York: Anchor, 2006. p. 27.
[14] J. M. Charcot (1872) Quoted in Harold L. Klawans, M.D. *Toscanini's Fumble, And Other Tales of Clinical Neurology.* Chicago: Contemporary Books, 1988. p. 73.

TEN PAST NOON

---

[15] Jules Brody. *'Fate' in* Oedipus Tyrannus: *A Textual Approach.* (Arethusa Monographs, XI.) Buffalo, N.Y.: State University of New York at Buffalo, 1985. p. 20.

[16] "Jewish Mysticism." H. Sperling. *Aspects of the Hebrew Genius.* ed. Leon Simon. London: George Routledge & Sons, Limited. New York: Block Publishing Co. 1910. p. 156.

[17] MS Cumming, *Eunuchry.* Vol. 11.

CORRESPONDENCE

Ned's papers at the New York Academy of Medicine include not only his attempt at a book manuscript but also a few letters that he saved while reaching out to scholars. This correspondence was necessary because finding material on such a specific topic was rarely a matter of walking to a local library and flipping through a card catalog. A library might catalog one or two books under "eunuchs." He managed to obtain over twelve hundred sources.

> He never went out without a book under his arm, and he often came back with two.
>
> —Victor Hugo, *Les Misérables*

For a while, Ned was in search of Col. Raoul Du Bisson's work *Les femmes, les eunuques et les guerriers du Soudan [The women, eunuchs, and warriors of the Sudan]*, published in Paris in 1868. Written responses from Harvard College Library and Boston Public Library in October

TEN PAST NOON

1932 indicated they did not have this book. The following summer, Charles F. McCombs, writing from London, said the British Museum had a copy.[1]

A handwritten letter from Prof. Philip Hitti of Princeton University dated December 28, 1932 advised, regarding Al-Suyuti's manuscript on *Fi'l-Tahrimi Khidmati'l-Khisyan,* that Ned should write to Mr. Tewfic Iscarous, Sharia Saidliz Sakakini, Cairo, a retired official formerly of the Khedivial Library.[2]

The Library of Congress in Washington replied to him on September 5, 1933 that they had located only one copy of the Epigrams of Joannes Vulteius, *Ioannis Vulteii Remensis eiusdem Xenia Lugduni, apud M. Parmanterium,* 1537, kept at the University of Chicago.[3]

The Smithsonian Institution, Bureau of American Ethnology, on November 23, 1933 said they had "no data concerning castration among the Pueblo Indians," but referred him to Dr. Leslie A. White of the University of Michigan at Ann Arbor.[4] White's letter two weeks later said he was aware of terms like *mujerados, berdache, koquimo,* who are "men who dress and live as women...But I know of no instance where castration or self-mutilation has been practiced in the Pueblos or anywhere else among the North American Indians."[5] (As a note to today's readers: None of these words are good to apply to other people. *Berdache* is not in favor, while *mujerado* and *kokwimu* are terms belonging to Pueblo people.)[6] Later, White responded to Ned's recommendation of Hammond's 1883 *Sexual Impotence:*

> I know, also, that during the past 50 or 75 years the Indians have in some instances withdrawn phallic rituals from their public ceremonies or have abandoned them entirely. Due to the disapproval of white people, especially the Americans after 1846, the Indians have "expurgated" their ceremonies to a considerable extent, or have relegated the "obscene" parts to the secrecy of their private chambers.[7]

In 1933, A. Kaiming Chiu, the librarian at the Chinese-Japanese Library at Harvard, wrote that the *Kuo ch'ao kung shih [History of the Palace]* "should be the first source of authority of a study of the employment of eunuchs in China."[8]

That same year, Eldon R. James, librarian for Harvard Law: "We have the Decisions of the Nizamut Adawlut, North Western Provinces, for 1852, which contains on page 1314 the case of the Government against Ali Buksh. This decision was made November 6, 1852, and I suppose is the one you want."[9] (This sort of case law was far more interesting to Ned than his father's 19th-century classroom handout of American corporate lawsuits. Or, at least, the idea of it was interesting.)

The New York Public Library issued him a

card for research in late 1933 through mid-1934, indicating that "Mr Edward D Cumming is hereby admitted to the Reserve Room (303) for the purpose of ____" The blank line is filled out: "Eunuchs."[10] He did not want a methodology. He wanted anything and everything about eunuchs. From this library, Ned requested George W. Crile's 1915 *Origin and Nature of the Emotions*. He wanted to know how his own brain worked, and he wanted to relate it to his study of eunuchs. Feelings themselves would have to connect to eunuchs in the end. He had a similar library card for Columbia University.[11]

He wrote the Library of Congress in Washington on Feb. 20, 1934 asking about Benoit, Guillaume, *Repetitio admodum solennis o. Raynutius extra de testamentis, etc.,* (1530). His question was about a chapter "qui cum alia, numbers 16 and 17, referring to a crime committed in the Prefecture of Cadurcensus in 1482." They replied on March 10, saying that their Superintendent of the Reading Room "has not found any chapter heading 'qui cum alia'. There are a large number of chapters in this work, and nearly all of them have numbers 16 and 17, thus making considerable search necessary to identify the passage you are seeking." Would he pay someone to read the book? He affirmed this request on April 15 and canceled it on May 14. The library replied a week later: "Although Mr. Vladimir Gsovaki, a foreign law assistant in our Law Division, spent several hours of his own time in searching for the passage to which you referred, no charge will be made by him for his services."

He received two letters from Prof. Barnette Miller at Wellesley College in early 1934, saying that publication of her monograph on the Palace School was held up by the financial depression. Miller had traveled to see the Turkish harem shortly after the Ottoman Empire fell. She said, "I should be interested to know what your interest is in the subject," and, when Ned confirmed his curiosity about the white eunuchs in Turkey, she replied briefly:

> ...it is always interesting to learn of some one else's interest in the field of one's own work.
>
> Unfortunately I am unable to give you any references in regard to the specific matter in which you are interested. The material on the white eunuchs, as indeed the entire material on the Palace School, was obtained in *scattered bits* from a variety of sources, all of which are given in the bibliography of my [1931] book, *The Sublime Porte*.[12]

In October, the Egyptian Library at Midan Bab el Khalq in Cairo mailed him a copy of a 1913 journal article: "photostat, negative only." White text on a black background.[13]

In 1935, Lionel Giles at the British Museum twice charged him ten dollars for advice about

TEN PAST NOON

sources on Chinese eunuchs.[14]

On an index card, he wrote a note to himself: "I should look up histories of Spanish Medicine and Surgery for 16th century references to eunuchs." On another card, he attempted some Arabic lettering, mentioning an author Abul-Farah Ibn Djur Jauzi (likely the 12th-century Ibn al-Jawzi) alongside the words "Tanvir ul Gabash" and a comment about the Sudan.

He had a lot of index cards.

NOTES TO "CORRESPONDENCE"

[1] Specifically, he would have been interested in Chapters VIII about harems, XI about Ottoman decadence, XX about eunuch nature, and XXII about eunuchs as lovers.
The failed attempt to locate the book: MS Cumming, *Eunuchry*. Letters from Harvard College Library and Boston Public Library, October 1932.
The successful attempt to locate the book: MS Cumming, *Eunuchry*. Letter from Charles F. McCombs at the British Museum in London, Summer 1933.
[2] MS Cumming, *Eunuchry*. Letter from Prof. Philip Hitti of Princeton University, December 28, 1932.
[3] MS Cumming, *Eunuchry*. Letter from the Library of Congress in Washington, September 5, 1933.
[4] The letter was signed: M. W. Stirling, Chief. They referred him to the study by contemporary scholars Dr. Leslie A. White of the University of Michigan at Ann Arbor and Dr. Elsie Clews Parsons of Harrison, New York.
MS Cumming, *Eunuchry*. Letter from M. W. Stirling, Chief, at the Smithsonian Institution, Bureau of American Ethnology, November 23, 1933.

[5] MS Cumming, *Eunuchry.* Letter from Leslie A. White, December 8, 1933.

[6] The term *kokwimu* is from the Keres language spoken by some of the Pueblo people in the southwestern United States. Pueblo people have also used the Spanish *mujerado,* a masculine word literally meaning "made woman." *Berdache,* with an etymology meaning "prostitute" or "slave," is French and was primarily applied by European explorers to native peoples.

For more information, see: "Was We'Wha a Homosexual?: Native American Survivance and the Two-Spirit Tradition." Will Roscoe. *GLQ: A Journal of Lesbian and Gay Studies,* Vol. 2, 1995. pp. 193-235.

http://www.willsworld.org/WasWeWha1995.pdf

Accessed February 21, 2020.

[7] MS Cumming, *Eunuchry.* Letter from Leslie A. White, January 12, 1934

[8] MS Cumming, *Eunuchry.* Letter from A. Kaiming Chiu, the librarian at the Chinese-Japanese Library at Harvard, 1933.

[9] MS Cumming, *Eunuchry.* Letter from Eldon R. James, Harvard Law librarian, 1933.

[10] The library card was dated Nov. 17, 1933 and valid until July 1, 1934.

[11] It identified his home address as 48 Alkamont Avenue, Scarsdale.

[12] MS Cumming, *Eunuchry.* Letters from Barnette Miller at Wellesley College, dated January 31 and February 22, 1934.

[13] MS Cumming, *Eunuchry.* He wrote to them September 7, 1934 and they replied on October 10, 1934. This is in the the 7th folder of a box of correspondence.

[14] MS Cumming, *Eunuchry.* Letters from Lionel Giles to Edward Cumming, August 6 and September 6, 1935. Pasted into the "Text," i.e. the black folder, Vol. 14.

WHERE TO BEGIN? WILL IT EVER END?

I n his manuscript, Ned acknowledged help from librarians at the New York Public Library and the New York Academy of Medicine. He also thanked Mr. H. I. Katibah for Arabic translations and Rev. Donald W. Blackwell for "deciphering and translating the Theodorus manuscript."[1] Since his own manuscript was never published, in these acknowledgments he was talking to himself, but perhaps it's the thought that counts.

#########

E verything in your engineered environment was "architected by another person," Abby Covert explains in *How To Make Sense of Any Mess.*

Information architecture is a term coined by Richard Wurman in the 1970s.[2] It means we begin with a pile of content or data (words, numbers, events) and deliberately structure it to aid others in understanding it, to influence how they interpret it, and thereby to help determine what it ultimately comes to mean—to give birth to it as information.

Now departing from Track 1.
Now arriving on Track 40.

If someone didn't put thought into what the train station is like from the passengers' perspective, we'd have a bad experience. We don't care whether the vehicles are electric and when the engineer goes on lunchbreak. We need to catch our train. The architect's goal is for the system to work so beautifully that we don't even notice that we're in an architected system.

Challenges for an information architect include declaring a mission, drawing connections, and managing other people's interpretations. If done poorly, the result will still be a mess. There may be, as Covert says:

1. Too much information
2. Not enough information
3. Not the right information[3]

The "user"—the reader, the passenger, or anyone who uses the "product" in any way—also plays a role when they pull information from the architected environment. Information, Covert says, is "whatever a user interprets from the arrangement or sequence of things they encounter." It's subjective. So, while information architects "can arrange things with the intent to communicate certain information, we can't actually make information. Our users do that for us." It's a dialogue and a shared responsibility.[4]

✂✂✂✂✂✂✂✂✂

Where to begin? Every book has a first sentence. How would Ned get started with his?

With the castration of the gods? *Horus castrated Typhon. Uranus begat Kronos who begat Zeus, and the sons castrated their fathers. Ba'al Shamin begat El, and you can imagine.*

With legend? *Odysseus against Melanthius. Paris against Peritanus.*

With old histories? *The Greek Emperor Constantinus' envoy Andrea against the Armenian envoy Sergius at the court of Caliph Moahuriyah. Antiochus ordering hit men to poison his son.*

With the Bible? *Joseph. Potiphar.*

With the conventions of political succession? *The Byzantine Empire. The recent past of African kingdoms like Dahomey and Bagirmi.*

With so-called "savages"—the word he used—and their alleged cannibalism? *Peter Martyr wrote of "the wylde and myschevous people called Cannibales or Caribes" in the West Indies who are rumored to geld boys as if they were livestock to fatten them before they eat them.[5] The same was reported of an island chief in Fiji in the South Pacific.*

With Christian martyrs? *Nerus and Achilleus.*

TEN PAST NOON

Calocaerus and Parthenius. Hyacinthus and Protus. Azates, Gouschtazad and Usthazanes.

With passages by ancient would-be scientists? *Aristotle, Galen, and Pliny arguing whether eunuchs go bald and have gout. Archigines and Actius Caelius Aurchimus saying they don't get leprosy. The latter saying epilepsy neither. The several writers who said that eunuch priests were immune to poisonous fumes in Egyptian caves.* (Ned, for the record, was a skeptic on this last point.)

One must begin somewhere. *Relax as if taking a golf swing. Bend the knees, elbows, hips. Twist the shoulders. Lean forward. That's how a eunuch enters the cave. Begin from everywhere all at once.*

An endless march of early Christian moralists like Tertullian, John Chrysostom, and Gregory Nazianzen, and some of their Greek and Roman predecessors like Sextus Empiricus, said eunuchs can't be credited as being "temperate" in sexual matters because they aren't tempted in the first place. A work by Philostratus[6] presented a counterexample of a eunuch who slept with a harem woman, deliberately to refute the idea that eunuchs were uninterested in sex. Epictetus said as much, too. Ausonius said eunuchs engage in sex but are frustrated by their inability to orgasm; Seneca and St. Jerome said they have long-lasting erections; Joannis Cassianus said they wish they could father children.

Theodorus the Pedagogue said that castration effeminizes men. Ned is skeptical because "precisely what these personality qualities were which eunuch[s supposedly] shared with women is never clearly stated" and "the [alleged] female eunuchoidal type was not clearly identified by any ancient writer who were content to call them masculine females."[7]

In Vol. 8, on the first page, Ned announces his intention to examine eunuchs in India within a historical context even though he believes the details are "impossible to trace," while the last page notes a perceived similarity between Indian and Jewish attitudes toward eunuchs even though he believes that such an analysis would be "a hopeless task."[8] He has switched horses midway, abandoning an "impossible" thesis for a "hopeless" thesis.

#########

The information keeps recycling. I have another example of this, outside of Ned's work.

In 1931, Panurge Press, a New York-based mail-order publishing house that sold five-dollar books of prurient interest to subscribers, printed fifteen hundred copies of *Praeputii Incisio* (the title is a Latin expression meaning "circumcision"). Unlike other titles sold by Panurge, no author was given credit. It was, in fact, a plagiarism, mostly of Peter Charles Remondino's *History of Circumcision from the*

TEN PAST NOON

Earliest Times to the Present (1891), plus bits of John Davenport's *Aphrodisiacs and Anti-aphrodisiacs* (1869) and the pseudonymous Jacobus X's *Ethnology of the Sixth Sense* (1899). The plagiarist selected his favorite chapters, cut and shuffled them, slightly modernized the wording, and privately printed a book with no one's name on the cover. That was all there was to it. The Panurge Press director, Esar Levine, apparently signed off on this plagiarism, because, figuratively speaking, he left his calling card within the text. He inserted a plug for his own new release, *Chastity Belts,* within a passage that was otherwise written by Remondino forty years earlier.[9] This is just one example of how information keeps recycling. With or without the author's names, the same words are reprinted, often without a fact-check.

We all recycle information, one way or another.

Ned, however, is trying to give credit to his sources. He is trying to get it right.

#########

The moon landing *"will be believed when it is done."*

#########

This goes on. Ned's handwritten manuscript is, by my estimate, four times the length of the book you are holding right now. He wrote double-spaced on the page, each sheet of paper single-sided, with about six words per line. His script was legible, but hardly a word was typed.

He considered five of his nineteen volumes "supplemental," suggesting uncertainty about whether he wished to include those volumes in the manuscript proper, but those "supplemental" volumes are, I'd argue, the aim of his text. Writers often do this. As I said, it takes a while to arrive at the point of all our prior struggles, and this conclusion is often phrased, unfortunately, as an "oh, by the way."

His writing style was bloated. Here's how he says *generalizations can be useful*:

> The advantage to be gained by taking different aspects of the history of castration out of their appropriate setting in each of the above major departments of human activity and presenting them together in a single volume, lies in the fact that ideas and practices respecting castration frequently have application outside the immediate orbit in which they originate.[10]

Here's how he says *my topic is inherently interesting, but I fear that my writing style may bore people*:

> It is apparent that to the student of any of the various departments of history from which the history of castration derives, the related portion of the present

> monograph can fail [to be] of interest only because of imperfection in the execution of the project not because of indifference to the subjects discussed.[11]

In the following word salad, he assumes that castration was practiced since prehistoric times but that these early humans would have lacked coherent thought. He then puzzles over what to do with competing claims that early humans had complex motives. We shall never, he laments, be able to pin down the origins of castration.

> Primitive man during insanity, disease and strife may accordingly be supposed occasionally to have castrated himself or his fellows. The more nearly man approaches the animal in mentality the closer would castration performed under these circumstances partake of the character of an accident. However the savage peoples who have lived during historic times and of whom records exist have all been so far advanced in intelligence and social organization that the motives for castration as practiced by them have been already extremely diversified and the problem of origins seems both unimportant and insoluble.[12]

Almost by definition, we can't find the historical origins of that which predates history. The dawn of humanity, in his imagination, is a time in which people were—to use his words—simultaneously "savage" and "advanced," a kind of Schrödinger paradox in which both poles are true just because you don't yet know the answer. (But it's not that. It's actually a false binary and not a question that needs to be addressed. Using the adjective "savage" to describe unknown peoples never brings us to a good place, and if "advanced" is meant simply as the opposite term, then that mirror-image is also misinformed and misguided.)

And while noting that there were ten thousand eunuchs in China during the four-hundred-year period "between the Han and T'ang dynasties," he concludes there is "nothing noteworthy" related to them.[13] This conclusion is implausible. Even a naïve reader might think it highly unlikely that thousands of palace officials with their own separate gender role did nothing in a powerful, influential country for four hundred years. The real gap here is that Ned did not read Chinese and was not positioned to learn this history. Nothing noteworthy happened in his New York library carrel, but something surely happened in China.

Despite his ability to produce sentences, he entirely neglected to write proper introductions, analyses, and conclusions. He wrote too many words of the wrong sort. Who knows how long the final draft would have been if he'd added structure and cut filler.

TEN PAST NOON

During my own library research, after handling his manuscript briefly on two separate day-long visits in 2012, I didn't yet understand its limitations, and I indulged the fantasy that I could rehabilitate and vindicate it. I wanted to read it in its entirety, find its boundaries, fill in its gaps, and make it publishable.

Charles Yu tells us *How to Live Safely in a Science Fictional Universe:*

> In any coherent time loop, there are certain objects that are created during and exist within the time loop. One common example of such an item is the hypothetical Book from Nowhere: A man brings a copy of a book with him back in time, giving it to himself, and instructing himself to reproduce the book as faithfully as he can. The book is then published, and after its publication, the man then buys the book, gets in a time machine, and starts the cycle all over again.

* * *

But what if I were to skip forward? Just cut out all of this filler in the middle. After all, as my self told me, I am the author of this. Whatever it is. I am its author and its only reader. I want to know what happens. I want to know if I'll ever get out of here.[14]

In 2013, I paid my third visit, this time

scheduling four days. On my final day, just as the library was closing, I had a sudden epiphany:

Something is wrong. This project isn't organized correctly. He can't do it the way he's trying to do it. Listing eunuchs won't work.

As a complex explanation began to form in my mind of *why* Ned's book project wasn't viable, I had to fold up my laptop and clear out of the reading room. I thought of reestablishing myself in the library cafeteria to recapture my thoughts, but I believed I was late for dinner. I walked quickly through Central Park, passing a stranger who told me to smile.

There are a couple thousand squirrels in Central Park. Scientists do not have time to count them. Hundreds of volunteers once spent a couple weeks taking a census, though.[15]

Arriving at my destination, I discovered that dinner had not yet begun, after all. By the end of dinner, I had already lost my grip on half of the threads of my original idea. I played a mindless game in my smartphone for an hour, hoping the thought would return, and I fell asleep. When I woke up, the epiphany had vanished. All that remained of my insight was: *I know Ned's project is invalid.*

As a writer who juggles my own strange ideas as a hobby, I've accustomed myself to occasionally losing my grip on an insight. Imagination and artistry can't be forced. I've learned to trust that, if a fleeting thought is important and if I'm meant to have it, it will return. It almost always works out.

This insight, however, never returned to me in its original form. Its absence was a deep hole for me and a bit of a wound to my ego, given that my enduring interest in anything having to do with eunuchs was based in my desire to hash out my own identity. I assumed Ned's catalog to be a quintessence of eunuch studies; in my imagination, he was the arbiter of *Eunuchry,* the inventor of the very word. The less I uncovered about him, the more his mystique grew. If I knew that something major was wrong with his *Eunuchry* project but I wasn't ready to grasp and articulate precisely what that was, my ignorance seemed a reflection on my readiness to engage with my own concepts about my identity. It therefore wasn't just an ordinary creative block; it was as if I stood in front of a mirror wearing a nametag: "Hello, I'm Blocked." It was me.

And for reasons having to do with major events in my own personal history, I wasn't able to return to visit the manuscript for another five years. By then, I had convinced myself that Ned's manuscript wasn't fixable, but I still wanted to write *about* it or about my encounter with it. I knew that I had something book-length to say and that whatever I wrote would be in large part a critique. I just didn't yet grasp what my critique would be. For a long time I had known only that *he can't do it the way he's trying to do it,* and I had to reconstruct my reasons why.

Something about how listing people encyclopedia-style treats them like objects. Something about the importance of stating a thesis that gives better meaning to the list. Something else, too, about the strangeness of categorizing and connecting people by something they *don't* have (in this case, a scrotum). Listen to those words: On some level, the connection *isn't there.*

###########

"There are thousands of bulls," says the woman character in *The Sun Also Rises,* touching a bullfighter's hand, pretending to palm-read. She means, in a flirty way, that he will have a long career.

###########

I began by telling Ned's life story. And by telling a little bit of my story at the edges where my work touches his.

"We keep on changing and changing our sculpture till we get it pretty near as we want it, but it's a long and laborious process, and we're never satisfied because we're copying something we can't clearly see," said Robert Irwin, who would go on to murder people.[16]

George Orwell gave writing advice in his 1946 essay "Politics and the English Language": *avoid clichés, prefer short words, delete unnecessary words, use active voice, embrace everyday language.* These rules, he went on to say, are important yet are nothing compared with refraining from saying "anything outright barbarous." There is often "a gap between one's real and one's declared aims," and people weaponize words to confuse and distract, "like a cuttlefish spurting out ink. In our age there is no such thing as 'keeping out of politics'. All issues," he warned, "are political issues."[17]

NOTES TO
"WHERE TO BEGIN? WILL IT EVER END?"

[1] MS Cumming, *Eunuchry*. Vol 1.
[2] "Why IA Matters for UX — A Brief History of Information Architecture." Lucia Z. Wang. UX Collective (Medium). May 15, 2017. https://uxdesign.cc/a-brief-history-of-information-architecture-d26b17205e7b Accessed January 21, 2020.
[3] These items—1, 2, 3—are quoted from Abby Covert. Abby Covert. *How to Make Sense of Any Mess.* Amazon, 2014.
[4] Covert, *ibid.*
[5] MS Cumming, *Eunuchry*. Vol. 1.
[6] A dialogue between Apollonius and Damis.
[7] MS Cumming, *Eunuchry*. Vol. 1.
[8] MS Cumming, *Eunuchry*. Vol. 8, black folder.
[9] *Praeputii Incisio* includes Remondino's chapters 1–10, 12–13, and 17; Jacobus X's chapters 9 and 14; and Davenport's Essays 2 and 3. I discovered this plagiarism and made this determination myself.
[10] MS Cumming, *Eunuchry*. "Text" in black folder, Vol. 1.
[11] MS Cumming, *Eunuchry*. "Text" in black folder, Vol. 1.
[12] MS Cumming, *Eunuchry*. "Text" in black folder, Vol. 1.
[13] MS Cumming, *Eunuchry*. "Text" in black folder, Vol. 8.

[14] Charles Yu. *How to Live Safely in a Science Fictional Universe.* Pantheon, 2010. pp. 113, 116.

[15] "There are 2,373 squirrels in Central Park. I know because I helped count them." Denise Lu. *New York Times.* January 8, 2020. https://www.nytimes.com/interactive/2020/01/08/nyregion/central-park-squirrel-census.html Accessed January 27, 2020.

[16] Harold Schechter. *The Mad Sculptor: The Maniac, The Model, and the Murder that Shook the Nation.* Seattle: Amazon Publishing, 2014. p. 84.

[17] George Orwell. "Politics and the English Language." London: *Horizon,* April 1946. https://www.orwell.ru/library/essays/politics/english/e_polit Accessed October 22, 2019.

WHAT WE CAN STOP TODAY

The train stops *everywhere*.

Eunuchs cannot swallow eggs (Jean Bodin, 16th century); they hemorrhage periodically from their anus as if it were a kind of menstruation (late 18th century); they cannot pronounce the letter 'R' (Barthélémy Cabrol, *Alphabet anatomic,* 1594).

It is unclear if Ned realizes the foolishness.

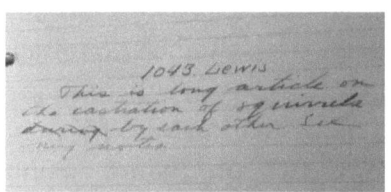

Figure 19 – Source number 1,043 by an author named Lewis. Ned describes it: "This is long article [sic] on the castration of squirrels by each other. See my notes."

He writes down everything he hears about eunuchs.

TEN PAST NOON

Even things that are trivially true. They have to do housework, and they make the best of it? Sure. In China, young castrated boys were called "little eunuchs"? Logical. If someone attempted a significant theft from the emperor, he'd be executed? No kidding.

Even the report that one young man in Abyssinia was taunted by his peers because he never managed to secure a genital trophy from an enemy's body as was socially expected among his group.[1] Well, yes, if someone is socially expected to do something and they miss their target, they'll be taunted.

Even the graphic details of a 14th century execution of an Irish friar who picked an ill-advised battle with the Duke of Lancaster.[2] Yes, if you really upset the Duke, your execution will be exceptionally painful.

Even the note that one late 19th-century English writer "gives [a] long account of man without legs etc who also had no testicles."[3] And?

Even the obvious contradiction, separated by only several pages within Vol. 10, that in Turkey the enslavement of white eunuchs was "completely abandoned more than a hundred years ago, the last white eunuch dying in 1856...Yet white eunuchs still were surreptitiously made or imported and a small remnant lived on into the present century." Only one of those statements can be true.

Even an omen from India said to predict

whether an unborn child will be "boy, girl or eunuch."[4] People imagine they see lots of omens. Some omens are culturally important, but none are objectively real.

Even stereotypes that are meaningless and irrelevant.

> As early as the Middle Ages, Arabian writers noted that devotion to tame song birds was characteristic of all eunuchs. – while the negro eunuchs of Constantinople are said to have been less restricted in their taste in pets among which were included chickens, lambs, cows, monkeys and especially cats.[5]

(The most meaningful thing about this list of preferred pets is that it was reprinted by Penzer, a man I will discuss later.)

++++++++++

Ever since ancient times—as exemplified in the writings of Xenophon, Juvenal, Martial, Claudian—eunuchs were thought to be physically weaker than men.[6] In the late 19th century, men of science began to analyze their bodies, including their skeletons[7] and their body fat distribution, which the scientists deemed feminine.[8] Researchers recorded "body dimensions of a number of Skoptzi," a self-castrating Russian religious sect.[9]

Measurements can be used to diagnose physical disorders and identify trends. My own skeleton was regularly measured from infancy as

TEN PAST NOON

I was found to have a discrepancy in the length of my legs. We know that, after a decade or two of growth, a child will stop growing. (In some ways, for some purposes, that is really the key: we stop.) The different rates of growth of each leg were used to predict my full adult height. This information was used to decide the ideal moment for a childhood surgical intervention, and the intervention was done correctly, insofar as today, having stopped growing, I walk comfortably with barely any tendency to limp.

Unfortunately, body measurements and analyses have often been used in a threatening and harmful way. Height, head size, and the length of appendages like fingers and ears is information that has been used to identify criminals (for *bertillonage*, developed before fingerprinting became standard)[10] and, in aggregate, to draw racial distinctions that are then often used to highlight supposed essential differences between races. Nell Irvin Painter gives several examples of such pseudoscientific miscommunication in her book *The History of White People.* One example is Petrus Camper, a Dutch physician who became a member of the Royal Society in England, who drew a chart that contrasted the "facial angles" of three supposed human races, an idealized work of Greek sculpture, and an orangutan. The chart was published posthumously in 1792 and was embraced by white supremacists.[11] Another is Samuel George Morton, an American anthropologist who, a half-century after Camper's publication, taught anatomy at the University of Pennsylvania and owned nearly a thousand human skulls; he asserted that different races have different brain sizes which in turn determines intelligence. Following Morton's work, "all the prominent anthropologists of the time," Painter said, "assumed that brain size correlated with intelligence." (This manifested in a particular academic controversy in 1861 in which French anthropologists, acknowledging that their entire bodies—including their brains—were smaller than those of their German colleagues, struggled to digest the implications.)[12]

Scientists today don't believe that race is a category with any biological meaning. Grouping people based on head size and then declaring that these groups are "races" with different head sizes is surely question-begging, that is, assuming the very thing that one claims to be demonstrating.

Because of historical missteps like these, it is valuable to be aware of potential consequences of pinning data to marginalized groups of people. Negative consequences may occur regardless of the researchers' intent.

Ned was not a scientist, but he wanted to curate and interpret scientific data about the physical traits of eunuchs. What could he (or the future readers he likely imagined) have possibly done with his presentation of the data, beyond what scientists would already do? Should someone ask eunuchs for physical details and health statuses on a questionnaire modeled after the Deep Springs school application, alongside that application's existing philosophical (and nationalistically motivated) questions like "Why not be a Bolshevist?" In what context would a eunuch submit this information, and what would he benefit from it? Where would his application take him?

#########

Sometimes Ned adds a skeptical remark of his own. Regarding penetrative sex between men, he observes that penetrative partners often desire their receptive partners ("pathics," he calls the latter) to have "a resemblance to the female sex." That, he says, is why men often appreciate eunuch lovers. But why, then, he asks, would the penetrative male not prefer to be with a woman? Why a eunuch? He calls this a "familiar but curious paradox."[13]

We might note that there is nothing paradoxical about an attraction to someone whose gender or body is ambiguous, in flux, unusual, or unique. The attraction is not a problem that needs to be solved. The problem is in the way the question is asked.

#########

Ned was aware of reported beliefs by centuries-old Muslim authors that the left and right testicles had different functions: one to produce children, the other to grow a beard. He was likely aware that this was incorrect information.[14] Trying to describe testosterone, he wrote:

> Although experiments with men have not been entirely conclusive yet experiments with animals have left no doubt that the testicles after puberty do prepare a chemical which is the same for many different species of animals and that this chemical by being absorbed in the blood affects the changes occurring at puberty and that its absence is the cause of the effects resulting from castration.[15]

He was born at an exciting time to reflect this scientific awakening, but scientific sensibility and the body of human knowledge weren't moving fast enough for him. The amount that remained unknown was frustrating.

Some of his material is organized under "sterilization." The Troglodytes (according to Diodorus Siculus) did this to "malformed children"; the Nordic countries, to "vagrants"; and an American physician, Orpheus Everts, said in the late 19th century that criminals should be prevented from creating offspring like themselves.[16] Ned doesn't take the opportunity to ask his own questions, which could have been: *What do these approaches have in common? What assumptions do people make about hereditary traits? What social engineering goals are implicit here? How will we know it when we*

TEN PAST NOON

see it? How should we respond? He doesn't use the proper word: *eugenics.*

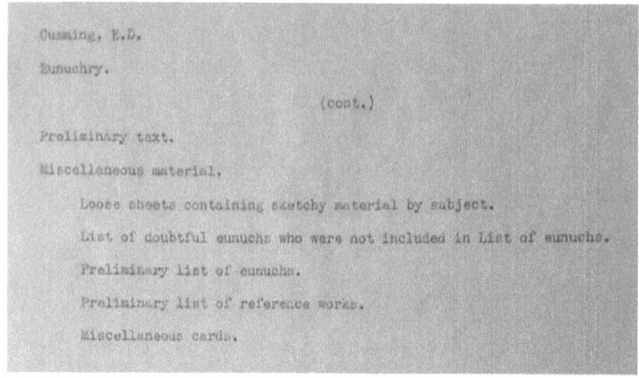

Figure 20 – A rare piece of typed material in Ned's manuscript. He classifies the information he's collected: "preliminary," "miscellaneous," "loose," "sketchy," "doubtful."

The groundbreaking sex research of Alfred Kinsey was still a decade in the future. That human sexual function could be an object of empirical study was a notion in Ned's mind, but he turned to philosophers and theologians for the information. Seneca and St. Jerome had suggested that eunuchs had erections of longer duration (because, of course, eunuchs found it harder to reach orgasm, Ned editorialized); however, these ancient writers said nothing "of the number of orgasms or the period between orgasms" nor did they have credible information about the eunuchs' sexual desire.[17] The idea of interviewing people about their own sexuality hadn't yet taken hold. That would be Kinsey's revolution.

Ned would have had no way to have known this, but, for nearly a year in the early 1930s, a man named Robert Irwin was living five miles northeast of him at the Burke Foundation in White Plains, a rehabilitation center for people with a range of illnesses and disabilities. Irwin, occasionally suicidal, increasingly believed that he needed to cultivate his powers of visualization, and he independently came up with the idea of sublimating his sexual energy by removing his penis. Having left the rehabilitation center and moved in with a Hungarian immigrant family on East 53rd Street in Manhattan, Irwin promptly attempted mutilating himself with a rubber band and a razor blade but gave up and presented himself at Bellevue Hospital, where, for a short time, he continued to pursue the goal, requesting a surgeon's help. He said he did not want to be a woman and eventually suggested he'd be content with a vasectomy. The psychiatrist who met with him daily was not aware of any other attempt at genital self-mutilation in all of psychoanalytic literature.[18]

This was the type of professional knowledge gap that Ned believed his research could bridge.

≠≠≠≠≠≠≠≠≠

Many of his pronouncements, while seemingly intending a humanist bent on the one hand, nevertheless are virulently racist on the other hand. For example, in Vol. 3, he says that anyone who advocates the castration of conquered enemies ought to be be considered "barbarians" who are "not partaking of civilization," and he rather doubts he could find such advocacy "by any group of men pretending to civilization." He then adds that it still happens in "North East Africa...[it] is peculiar to the races of that region and perhaps at certain periods of other races of Africa."[19] Language like this can do nothing to stop violence by chieftains on another continent, but it does increase racist prejudices at home. There were plenty of people "not partaking of civilization" in the United States; they participated in white mobs that lynched thousands of black people during the time that Ned was writing.[20] These extrajudicial murders often included torture and mutilation. If one's real agenda is to tell people to stop hurting each other, it may be best to start by lecturing the people at home.

Noting that old European laws often treated Jews differently, he mentions that a certain Jewish man convicted of illicit sex with a Christian woman in 16th century Prague was executed in one of the most sexually violating, physically painful, and ignominious manners conceivable. But he does not offer an analysis of the effect of such anti-Jewish violence at the time, nor how it might have led to present-day anti-Semitism, and much less does he make a political statement about whether his 1930s contemporaries should be concerned about the fate of the Jews in Europe.[21]

He claims to be aware that, as recently as the 19th century, conquered chiefs were castrated in Dahomey (a West African kingdom lasting until 1894) and Bagirmi (a Central African kingdom lasting until 1897). Invading Europeans could meet the same fate. Following the 1896 Battle of Adwa in Ethiopia where there were thousands of Italian losses, the fallen men were mutilated in their genitals. Many were already dead or presumably died soon after, but dozens survived this treatment. One such Italian crawled to a stream and laid next to dead bodies for a week until he was rescued by a fellow wounded soldier. He had no access to a doctor for a long time. When finally a doctor examined him, he was scarred around "the opening of the severed urethra." The patient was described—though I do not know how the doctor verified this subjective feeling—as "quite resigned to his lot."[22] These details of a battle forty years before Ned was writing may have had special resonance for him, as he had probably heard that Italy, under Mussolini, invaded Ethiopia again in 1935.

Ned racially stereotyped not just the castrators, but the eunuchs themselves. His interests veered toward the psychic life of eunuchs, and he was curious about whether people of different races might have different

TEN PAST NOON

emotional lives. His attempts to catalog racial stereotypes about emotion resulted in contradictory claims. Of "the negro eunuchs in Turkey," he records two judgments: they are vengeful (cited to Omar Haleby)[23] or not vengeful (cited to Gaden)[24]. He doesn't seem to notice the contradiction, and adding more items to the list—which you may be assured that he does—doesn't resolve it. Repeating a rumor does not make it true. It could be a majority opinion or an expert opinion, but that's not the same as being true. It doesn't matter how many times it was said or who said it; if it's untrue, we don't have to accept it.

When he opens his Vol. 13 with the claim that "impotent eunuchs occasionally assault women embracing and fondling them against their will…negro eunuchs being apparently especially given to these displays of uncontrolled passion," it's not a piece of information we can use. It's not information at all. It's made up. Women who were captive in harems were raped, certainly; what's invented is the stereotype that an African eunuch is a rapist by his nature because of his race and gender.

Of Turkish eunuchs, again, he quotes an unnamed Armenian physician: "There is no more personal jealousy in him than there is in a paving stone." Yet he also quotes Amicis saying the opposite: "Sometimes they fall in love and are jealous, and chafe, and become shedders of blood, or seeing that some ardent glance directed towards their lady is returned; they lose their heads altogether and strike..."[25] There's no attempted resolution of the contradiction.

The people referred to as "eunuch dwarfs" of the Turkish Sultan, meanwhile, are supposedly "prized in proportion as they are repulsive and the greater their deformity the more amusing the ladies find them."[26] This rumor had been passed around by European travel writers, and it reflects the way that many visibly disabled people have been treated in many places and times. Phrased in this way with such loaded words, it is hard to know how one might begin to verify the statement, and, even if it was true that many people did assign entertainment value to other people's physical differences, we do not need to let their attitude stand without comment or challenge.

A similar problem comes up with Ned's references to China. Wondering if a recurring claim that eunuchs "lack individuality" might be a prejudiced misperception in the eye of the beholder, he mentions the "common illusion" that "to a European all Chinamen look alike and seem to have fairly uniform facial expressions and manners."[27] He seems to recognize the racist errors in such perceptions, but he has not discovered his own racist error in continuing to reproduce the words without fully and clearly repudiating them and explaining how other "Europeans" (or, more pointedly, white Americans) might change their ways.

TEN PAST NOON

++++++++++

Whiteness itself is a relatively modern invention. Nell Irvin Painter tells us that, until long after the Roman empire was gone, "the various German-speaking tribes east of the Rhine considered themselves distinct one from another, sharing no sense of common identity or common interest."[28]

The Saxons were one of several Germanic peoples who came to England in the 5th century. To the extent that it is coherent to speak of "Anglo-Saxons," they resulted from the intermarriage of "Germanic peoples with Britain's preexisting Celtic inhabitants and subsequent Viking and Danish invaders" between the 5th and 11th centuries, as *Encyclopedia Britannica* says.[29] Those people had called themselves "Anglecynn" or simply "Englisc." Historians called them "Anglo-Saxon" when they wanted to specify something like "not the original, actual Saxons." Beginning in the 16th century, English people adopted this term to buttress their identity, and onward it went into the service of British imperialism.[30]

Sometimes solidarity means broadening one's identity; other times, narrowing it. *English Traits* by Ralph Waldo Emerson was an 1856 thesis on what supposedly made whiteness special. Emerson had been influenced by his English friend, Thomas Carlyle, who identified as a Saxon from the south of Scotland; who considered other groups his inferiors (including the Celts from the north of Scotland, the Irish, and the French); and who believed that the best examples of "Saxons" in England were to be found, conveniently, only within the city limits of London. Both Emerson and Carlyle, through their writings, identified the ideal English and American citizens with the supposed Saxon race.[31]

In 2019, the medieval studies group formerly known as the International Society of Anglo-Saxonists voted to change its name, given that, as the *Washington Post* put it, the term "is co-opted today by white supremacists around the world to advance a false version of white-dominated history."[32]

Being descended from people who lived in Europe—as I am—is a neutral fact. Being "white" is a destructive construct that was built to secure a narrative of European superiority. People of European descent will continue to be white until we collectively do the work to change the reality we share with everyone.

++++++++++

Ned mentions Xenophon's report of several eunuchs who killed themselves because they did not want to outlive their masters,[33] and he suggests that "the murder of a master by his eunuch might well be considered the most perfect example of treachery."[34] Whether we agree with the accusation of treachery depends on how we answer this question: Is a slave's principal moral obligation to obey his master, or is the self-appointed master the one who commits the true treachery against humanity? These sentences are built of moral assumptions. So, too, a sentence discussing whether, at different times, slave traders might have "imported" human beings from Morocco or Egypt depending on which was "the most convenient market for the purchase of this commodity,"[35] and a comment elsewhere that "only eunuchs deprived of all their organs were employed in the harems [in India] and formed an article of trade."[36] It is hard to tell what he thinks about the language of slavery (e.g. "imported," "commodity," "article of trade"), as he reproduces it without explicitly challenging it. He might mentally insert his own "scare-quotes," but he doesn't offer that guidance to his readers.

This happens again when he tries to math out the danger of forced castration. If a eunuch could be sold for triple the price of a man, then, he reasons, "the mortality must have been less than 2 in 3"; otherwise, the slave-traders—in aggregate and over time—would self-inflict a financial loss. He imagines it "likely that the mortality was in fact inconsiderable, which would allow a threefold return to the dealers less incidentals."[37] There is of course a lack of compassion in the idea that deaths are "inconsiderable" as long as they do not impact profit. Moreover, it is unnecessary to rush to assume that slave traders always reasoned according to a factory-scale economic model, when we can easily find examples when they owed favors, took advantage of personal tragedies, believed they were obligated to punish or control someone, or were swayed by their own sadism. What is going wrong in these passages, I think, is an unquestioned assumption that the dominant racial group operates logically—as if we could provisionally set aside the slave-traders' racism and find some logic under it.

It is probably impossible. When we look under racism, we more typically find *illogic.* And I think this is a way in which, by failing to consistently recognize racism as a flag for illogic, a writer can have difficulty forming his own thesis that actually is logical as well as beautiful and ethical. He absorbs and reproduces the racism while refusing to see it, and thus he keeps a major part of his own thought process invisible to himself. He can't agree to grow beyond the dysfunctional parts of himself. As he silences others on the margins, he also silences his own story of living on some of those same margins. He never finishes his book—about others, about himself—because he knows his book is wrong but he can't find the spots where it breaks down. This is a way in which white people hurt themselves with their own racism as well as hurting everybody else.

TEN PAST NOON

"We are compelled to pause," Edgar Allan Poe said, and contemplate "the confines of this Universe of Stars." Should we assume that everything we see is everything that exists? Or is the universe full of sparks whose light, still racing across a distance we do not understand, has not yet reached us?[38]

If we aren't prepared to say which is true, at least we could stop making the doomed effort to forcibly expand or misrepresent the limits of our minds. We may as well stop.

Sunlight takes eight-and-a-half minutes to reach Earth. When we notice the sun directly overhead and we go and tell someone it's noon, it's really ten past noon. It may not work quite the way we believe it does, but we can't speed it up or slow it down.

We may not feel compelled to pause. But it may help to pause. Our feet are stuck to the Earth anyway. If the information is already *en route*, there is nothing to do but wait.

///////////

If you haven't got a meaningful grasp on your available information and you don't have good interpretations, you can't determine what's relevant, and you start to look farther afield for insight in places where it is very unlikely to be found. An example of this is Ned's note on a "long article on the castration of squirrels by each other," shared at the beginning of this chapter. If he needs to know how he can emotionally survive the 1930s, rodents biting each other between the legs in squirrelfights can't help him. His fixation isn't working.

Sometimes the problem is that he reads negativity where there is positivity and thus resists something he could instead embrace. He repeats an anecdote told by an Italian man about an Indian eunuch who was so greedy that he sold his elephant's dung so that he could buy a second elephant.[39] But why, indeed, should we read "greed"? Selling one's resources and expanding one's assets is practical. All the American robber barons did it with their coal and their steel and their railroads. In the elephant keeper's case, it was also environmentally sustainable.

Such comments say more about those who start the rumors and about those who pass them on than about the people presumptively described. Especially without acknowledgment that these sorts of stereotypical comments are racist and factually inaccurate, a catalogue of the comments is not useful. If we spin complicated rationalizations to explain discrepancies between statements that aren't true anyway, our rationalizations will also be wrong.

That is a big part of the reason why Ned's *Eunuchry* project isn't viable. I once lost my grip on my answer to that question while walking through Central Park one evening in 2012, but now I feel that I've found a good and important

TEN PAST NOON

answer again.

Because we live in a racist society, Crystal Fleming explains, we are conditioned to describe race (and racism) superficially, nonsensically, or inaccurately, often while perpetuating racism and simultaneously denying that racism exists. Why were we taught to do this? Because white people benefited from slavery and colonization, continue to benefit from white supremacy, and want everyone else to prop up that system. How do we—whatever race we may be—break the habit? How do we stop complying? *We stop.*[40]

⧣⧣⧣⧣⧣⧣⧣⧣⧣

We stop, and we are no less part of space and time. We must have no fear that those cosmic bonds will dissolve; we are eternally bound to the cosmos.

We stop. The Earth still turns. The Sun still shines.

The moment we stop may be a moment in which we, and others, will feel a little more free.

NOTES TO
"WHAT WE CAN STOP TODAY"

[1] MS Cumming, *Eunuchry.* "Text" in black folder, Vol. 1.
[2] MS Cumming, *Eunuchry.* "Text" in black folder, Vol. 1.
[3] MS Cumming, *Eunuchry.* "Text" in black folder, Vol. 1. This is cited to Davenport.
[4] MS Cumming, *Eunuchry,* "Text" in black folder, Vol. 1.
[5] MS Cumming, *Eunuchry,* Vol. 12.

While Penzer published a similar sentence in 1936, the list predates Penzer. See: George H. Junne. *The Black Eunuchs of the Ottoman Empire.* London: I. B. Tauris, 2016. p. 246. https://books.google.com.co/books?id=YBKMDwAAQBAJ&pg=PA246&lpg=PA246

[6] MS Cumming, *Eunuchry.* "Text" in black folder, Vol. 1.
[7] MS Cumming, *Eunuchry.* He cited: Ecker 1864, Lortet 1896, Becker 1899, Lavinois and Roy 1902.
[8] MS Cumming, *Eunuchry.* He cited: Godard, 1867.
[9] MS Cumming, *Eunuchry.* Vol 2. He cited: Pellikan 1876, Tandler and Grosz early 1900s, Koch 1920, Pernot 1934.
[10] "Bertillon System." Dead Media Archive. New York University, Dept. of Media, Culture, and Communication. http://cultureandcommunication.org/deadmedia/index.php/Bertillon_System Accessed 2 July 2019.
[11] Nell Irvin Painter. *The History of White People.* New York: W. W. Norton, 2010. Chapter 5.
[12] Painter, *ibid.,* Chapter 13.
[13] MS Cumming, *Eunuchry.* Vol. 6.
[14] MS Cumming, *Eunuchry.* "Text" in black folder, Vol. 1. Citing al-Jāḥiẓ and Soyouti.
[15] MS Cumming, *Eunuchry.* Vol. 2.
[16] MS Cumming, *Eunuchry.* All three examples are in the "Text" in black folder, Vol. 1. Diodorus Siculus was cited to Mobius S18. Orpheus Everts was cited to Millant. The quote from Everts was from 1888.
[17] MS Cumming, *Eunuchry,* "Text" in black folder, Vol. 1.
[18] Harold Schechter. *The Mad Sculptor: The Maniac, The Model, and the Murder that Shook the Nation.* Seattle: Amazon Publishing, 2014. pp. 109-121.
[19] MS Cumming, *Eunuchry,* Vol. 3.
[20] "Chilling maps of lynchings in 1930s America." Frank Jacobs. *Big Think.* 16 April 2018. https://bigthink.com/strange-maps/chilling-maps-of-lynchings-in-1930s-america Accessed August 8, 2019.
[21] MS Cumming, *Eunuchry,* third draft of manuscript (the big stack of paper), Chapter 2.
[22] MS Cumming, *Eunuchry,* Vol. 3.

[23] MS Cumming, *Eunuchry,* Vol. 12. Cumming quoted Omar Haleby: "if one of them is aroused to the point of determining to kill someone, either he will accomplish his purpose or in desperation kill himself."

[24] MS Cumming, *Eunuchry,* Vol. 12. Cumming quoted Gaden: "the Negro is by nature a fatalist; in place of preserving useless rancor towards their master, the eunuchs serve him with a fidelity which the sultans are pleased to reward."

[25] MS Cumming, *Eunuchry,* Vol. 12.

[26] MS Cumming, *Eunuchry,* "Text" in black folder, Vol. 8.

[27] MS Cumming, *Eunuchry,* Vol. B-2.

[28] Painter, *op. cit.,* Chapter 2.

[29] "Anglo-Saxon." *Encyclopedia Britannica.* https://www.britannica.com/topic/Anglo-Saxon Accessed February 18, 2020.

[30] "Academics Are At War Over Racist Roots of 'Anglo-Saxon' Studies." Erika Harlitz-Kern. *Daily Beast.* December 1, 2019. https://www.thedailybeast.com/academics-are-at-war-over-racist-roots-of-anglo-saxon-studies Accessed February 18, 2020.

[31] *English Traits* presents "concepts of American whiteness" and was the "earliest full-length statement of the ideology later termed Anglo-Saxonist," as Painter explains. Painter, *op. cit.,* Chapter 10.

[32] "'It's all white people': Allegations of white supremacy are tearing apart a prestigious medieval studies group." Hannah Natanson. Washington Post. September 19, 2019. https://www.washingtonpost.com/education/2019/09/19/its-all-white-people-allegations-white-supremacy-are-tearing-apart-prestigious-medieval-studies-group/ Accessed February 18, 2020.

[33] MS Cumming, *Eunuchry.* Vol. A-3.

[34] MS Cumming, *Eunuchry.* Vol. A-3.

[35] MS Cumming, *Eunuchry.* Third draft of manuscript (the big stack of paper), Chapter 5.

[36] MS Cumming, *Eunuchry.* "Text" (in the black folder),

Vol 10.

[37] MS Cumming, *Eunuchry*. "Text" (in the black folder), Vol 9.

[38] Edgar Allan Poe. "Eureka: A Prose Poem." Gutenberg, 2010. (Originally New York: Putnam, 1848). http://www.gutenberg.org/files/32037/32037-h/32037-h.htm Accessed February 16, 2020.

[39] MS Cumming, *Eunuchry*. Vol. 12. Cited to the 17th-century travel writer Niccolao Manucci.

[40] Crystal M. Fleming. *How To Be Less Stupid About Race.* Boston: Beacon Press, 2018. pp. 4, 14, 54.

NOTHING?
OR ALMOST ANYTHING?

Some eunuchs withdrew socially; some didn't. (If you phrase it like that, at least it's not self-contradictory.) But what do we know directly from eunuchs themselves about how they felt? Not much, Ned says:

> Direct investigation of the psychic life of eunuchs, as already noticed, has never been undertaken. A hint perhaps is given by the old books regarding dreams. It was remarked in the text that the dreams of eunuchs, which the old books pretended to interpret, dealt with the phantasy of recovering their genital organs or of achieving power and prestige. It may be that these passages were based on reports by eunuchs of their actual dreams.[1]

Among eunuchs, "while there is much evidence of realistic thinking, scheming and objectiveness there is absolutely none of artistic thinking, dreaming or introspection." That few eunuchs have displayed "the artistic impulse," he says, may be explained by the fact "that where ever eunuchs have been numerous they have constituted a body closely analogous to the occupational castes of India." (He does not explain what caste grouping might have to do with artistic ability.) "It is true no artistic genius is to be found among them. But if there is any significance in this is [sic] could be discerned only by comparative statistics of a type wholly impossible to formulate."[2]

For any human being, indeed, it's "wholly unanswerable" whether physical or psychological changes determine their "general type of adjustment." And yet, Ned—contradicting himself again—takes a position on that "unanswerable" question, saying that he prefers to think of castration's effects on personality as "hormonal" rather than "psychic" in origin.[3] What he means by that, I suppose, is that if there is a particular eunuch personality, it is not only because the eunuch's pride has been injured or because he has been socialized a certain way, but because he is influenced by the chemical messengers in his own body.

Ned points to Lange (the author of the 1934 German text, one of his favorites as previously mentioned) having found "neurasthenic and vaso-motor disorders" among European war veterans who had suffered castration after puberty. ("Vaso-motor disorders" refers to hot flashes and night sweats.) There were "changes in metabolism and glandular structure which...Lange ascribes to physical disturbances similar in nature to the menopause in women."[4]

Physicians past or present have not suggested that castration causes "insanity," he points out, although it may cause "melancholia" perhaps related to loss of sexual libido.[5] Beyond that, he shrugs, "the effects of castration (in respect to the aspects of personality considered) may be nothing or almost anything."[6]

And what are the results for society? *Positive or negative.* Sometimes "the power of the eunuchs...prolonged the life of the dynasty," except when it "no doubt did contribute to the decline of the dynasties."[7]

He notes that there were relatively few careers open to eunuchs, and maybe, he suggests, that restriction accounts for reduced diversity in their personalities. "It is probably obvious that eunuchs employed as Christian priests must differ greatly from eunuchs employed regularly as pathics [receptive sexual partners]," he says helpfully.[8]

To generalize, then: If eunuchs had more professional and social opportunities, might they also experience more psychological flexibility? That's what he wants to know.

The Skoptzy, a self-castrating Christian sect in Russia, must, he imagines, be less likely to suffer from "psychic causes of dissociation" because of their religious beliefs, their attitude toward body transformation, and their community. He extrapolates: Could "social and occupational therapy" help injured veterans of the World War? (He conjures this proposal based on what he reports as the "fact" that mental disorders don't appear among "oriental eunuchs living in groups or possessing recognized and approved status.") It seems to him that modern eunuchs could "maintain their psychic balance" more easily if

> settled in colonies where they could associate freely with their fellows. Again no attempt at psycho analytic [sic] treatment seems ever to have been attempted in a castration case. There seems to be no necessary reason why a eunuch should not be a reasonably useful and happy citizen.[9]

He realizes that a few crumbling tomes on dream interpretation from the ancient world will be insufficient to provide any substantial comfort or assistance to most people. He also fears that modern psychology may not yet be up to the task, as a psychoanalyst may be unable to help without good biological understanding of a castrated man's hormonal problem.

Introversion and extroversion are typically produced by experience, he says. When eunuchs work with women and children, they "display many of the qualities characteristic of women and children"; this argument, though, is "dismissed by the moderns who maintain that women and children do not constitute true psychological types." Castrated men in modern Europe have introverted personality types, he says. Castration *per se,* however, "does not seem to produce a peculiar personality type nor a tendency to conform to any particular type."[10]

With one exception, that is. Here is where the illusionist who has dedicated so many years to hiding his cards accidentally shows the card that's face-down on the top of the deck.

> Eunuchs never for a moment forget that they are eunuchs—that they are set apart from humanity. It is constant consciousness that they are eunuchs and that decisions must be made by criteria different from those of ordinary men which sometimes makes them introverts. Their sympathy—not pity but 'we feeling'—thus never includes any but eunuchs. Eunuchs as a group work well together. Not so with the uncastrated. Consciousness that he is a eunuch is certainly the type characteristic.
>
> The popular stereotype of the eunuchs seems generally to be accepted by the eunuchs themselves.
>
> Eunuchs thus are probably not in any proper sense psychological types, but they have nearly all always conformed to a few particular social types depending for definition on the state of society and

the accidents of their individual associations.[11]

Although this contradicts what he said at the beginning—that eunuchs can't be classified in reality and that his only reason to classify them is to have an excuse to divide his book into chapters—it seems that he is finally approaching a real thesis: *Eunuchs fall into distinct social categories, and they know what they are.*

How could he possibly know what "eunuchs never for a moment forget" if, as he said earlier, an academic inquiry into "the psychic life of eunuchs...has never been undertaken"?

He could know it if he himself were a eunuch.

And if his own tribal sense "never includes any but eunuchs," he was likely to be lonely indeed.

"A man," said the banker J. P. Morgan, "always has two reasons for what he does—a good one and the real one."[12]

++++++++++

Coming up with a theory can be exhilarating if you're on a roll or if you at least believe that you are. In Lily King's 2014 *Euphoria,* which places white anthropologists in 1930s New Guinea studying a fictional tribe that exists only in her novel, a character gushes:

> We kept at it. The sun came up and went down again. We believed we were in the throes of a big theory. We could see our

grid in chalk on university blackboards. It felt like we were putting a messy disorganized unlabeled world in order. It felt like decoding. It felt like liberation.[13]

But if the theory is rarely rolling, and if there is no collaborative "we" but only a frustrated "I," whence exhilaration? There is no reason to be excited by the process if it isn't yielding wisdom.

The neurologist Robert Burton wrote in 2008 that the "feeling of knowing"—something every human being experiences, something that is probably a "primary brain module"—"cannot be triggered by conscious effort."[14]

And what if the frustrated "I" changes his mind? What if suddenly it seems instead that eunuchs' "characters have not been as sharply differentiated from those of uncastrated men as has been commonly assumed," and it now appears "unjustified" to distinguish them from other men "in the ordinary actions of life"?[15] (Which, indeed, Ned says at one point.) Where's his theory now?

Reading twelve hundred books can be a qualification to write your own book if what you need to know is indeed within those books. If, however, what you need to know is within yourself, your formal source material may be irrelevant.

I am sure that Ned was one of those "introverts" or, as he also put it, someone who often felt "set apart from humanity"—in a word, lonely. I am waiting for him to say this, and I will be waiting forever.

If "no attempt at psycho analytic [sic] treatment seems ever to have been attempted in a castration case," that is partly his fault. First, if a eunuch has not been to the psychoanalyst, a eunuch could go to the psychoanalyst. Second, if being "settled in colonies" with eunuch "fellows" would help him achieve "psychic balance," he could found a Deep Springs ranch school for eunuchs. If he did either of those things, he would probably wind up writing a useful book, too, as a natural consequence—a book about his feelings or about something he built with others. Instead he has a giant stack of constipated papers with no thesis, a list of historical eunuch figures stripped of their contexts because on most days *he* has no "we feeling" for "any but eunuchs," a rolling library cart whose slowly increasing weight is making him feel lonelier.

The tank is made of steel, but it has structural deficiencies, and the molasses is liable to blow.

> "It's mostly the density of the molasses, so how much it weighs, and how tall it is," explained Nicole Sharp, an aerospace engineer and science educator, who has studied the fluid dynamics of molasses. "You basically have a giant stack of something that's really heavy and as soon as you remove whatever's holding that—

in this case, the walls of the tank—all of that is going to rush out, and a lot of that potential energy that you had from stacking this thing up really high is going to turn into kinetic energy. It might as well be a tsunami."[16]

NOTES TO "NOTHING? OR ALMOST ANYTHING?"

[1] MS Cumming, *Eunuchry*. Vol. B-2.
[2] MS Cumming, *Eunuchry*. Vol. B-2.
[3] MS Cumming, *Eunuchry*. Vol. B-2.
[4] MS Cumming, *Eunuchry*. Vol. B-2.
[5] MS Cumming, *Eunuchry*. Text in black folder, Vol. 2.
[6] MS Cumming, *Eunuchry*. Vol. A-3.
[7] MS Cumming, *Eunuchry*. Third draft of manuscript (the big stack of paper), Chapter 9.
[8] MS Cumming, *Eunuchry*. Vol. B-2.
[9] MS Cumming, *Eunuchry*. Vol. B-2.
[10] MS Cumming, *Eunuchry*. Vol. B-2.
[11] MS Cumming, *Eunuchry*. Vol. B-2.
[12] J. P. Morgan, quoted in HuffingtonPost.com. *The Week*. March 8, 2013, p. 19.
[13] Lily King. *Euphoria*. Atlantic Monthly Press, 2014. p. 191.
[14] Robert Burton. *On Being Certain: Believing You Are Right Even When You're Not*. New York: St. Martin's Griffin, 2008. p. 61.
[15] MS Cumming, *Eunuchry,* third draft of manuscript (the big stack of paper), Chapter 9.
[16] "Remembering Boston's Deadly Molasses Flood, 100 Years Later." Julia Press, WNPR. January 15, 2019. https://www.wbur.org/news/2019/01/15/boston-molasses-flood-100-years-later Accessed Nov. 10, 2019.

'LITTLE INFINITE POEM'

Available literature on the history of eunuchs is "vast," two endocrinologists wrote in 1999, mentioning Ned's unpublished manuscript.[1] Their paper does not further suggest that the authors, located in Texas, ever visited the collection in New York to read it; they seem, rather, to have cited Ned's effort only as an illustration of the available material, because Ned quantified his sources.

The more we look for information, the more we find, and thus we become aware of the vastness.

Ned lived in a city that was growing relentlessly. William E. Leuchtenburg wrote:

> European travelers [to New York City] who in 1910 had been awed by 20-story skyscrapers returned in 1930 to find them dwarfed by new giants; some of the old structures had even been demolished to make way for 60-story buildings. The Grand Central section of Manhattan was

almost entirely rebuilt; Fifth Avenue resounded with the staccato of riveters and the sharp clash of steel beams.²

In 1929, Federico García Lorca wrote "Little Infinite Poem" while in New York:

Equivocar el camino
es llegar a la nieve
y llegar a la nieve
es pacer durante veinte siglos las hierbas
    de los cementerios.

To take the wrong road
is to arrive at the snow
and to arrive at the snow
is to get down on all fours for twenty
    centuries and eat the grasses of the
    cemeteries.

"Probably New York," Robert Bly and Marion Woodman speculated of Lorca, "was a kind of underworld to him."³

"Now the value of the *Sefer Yezirah*"—the Jewish esoteric *Book of Creation*—"does not consist in its solution of the riddle of the Universe, but in its attempt to solve it," H. Sperling wrote.⁴ So, too, perhaps, with Ned's *Eunuchry* encyclopedia. Sometimes the value is in the attempt. That is especially true when the content of the response is wrong; in that case, there is more value in having tried to learn something than in the specific wrong response that was called out and fortunately not swallowed. Our education comes from learning to think, not from memorizing a list of things that may not be true anyway.

Kurt Gödel's 1931 incompleteness theorems claim that a formal system can't be both complete and consistent. Or: "There are some things that are true, but they can't be proved using the same mathematical language used to conceive that truth."[5]

In the 1930s, the medical and narrative dimensions of mental health were receiving increasing public interest and confidence. Freud was still alive, still theorizing. Countless thoughts of countless people since then have been influenced by his words. Leuchtenburg again:

> With similar fragmentary evidence, psychoanalytically oriented biographers tried to add a new dimension to their work; some of these ventures were serious, others were little more than vendettas on heroes of the past. Emerson and Thoreau, Ludwig Lewisohn wrote, were "chilled under-sexed valetudinarians." Even when new information or interpretations were established, it was not always clear what use could be made of them. "The superstition persisted," wrote Alfred Kazin, "that to have proved one's subject impotent was to have made a critical statement."[6]

Movie directors were discovering that they could traffic in fear. "It would soon acquire a name of its own: the horror movie."[7] After a decade of archaeological work on King Tut, Matthew Coniam explains, horror movies "were at once a culmination and a permanent afterlife for this inchoate fascination: a receptacle for every stray aspect of weirdness and eeriness and wild speculation…"[8]

No one needs to make a private list of "all the things" (if I may invoke a modern meme).[9] Today we digitize our data because it is obvious that the most thorough lists and catalogs are made collectively and provide online updates in real-time. Data is "born digital" now. These global projects boggle the mind, becoming "hyperobjects" on incomprehensibly large scales. Sometimes we don't know how to refer to any particular data set, which is why the 21st-century meme-phrase "all the things" resonates so well.

Ned was trying to list all the things because he did not have Internet. He didn't even have a typewriter. His list will always be incomplete, and we don't need to pick it up where he left off because we have Wikipedia now. If you want to list some eunuchs, there are editable online articles for that. If you introduce an error or say something confusing or unhelpful, someone else will correct the text. You don't need to kill a tree, put it on a cart, write wrong things on it, and make people travel to see it.

The first Wikipedia article I ever wrote was about the photographs of missing children that used to appear on milk cartons but don't anymore because now we have Internet.

Ned would have been delighted with Wikipedia. It would have solved many of his problems. He would have been able to see all the information that already existed and spend time adding only what didn't yet exist. It would not have cost anything. He could have footnoted easily and cleanly. He could have linked articles. He could have gotten a virtual badge for being a prolific volunteer. It would have fit in his smartphone, meaning the list would never have weighed more than the phone itself, meaning he would not have had to lock himself in his bedroom in Scarsdale to have access to his books and papers and could have worked on his lists while traveling the world. Beyond that, contributing information to a public repository would have taught him to distinguish what is an uncontroversial and properly cited fact that belongs in such a crowdsourced list and what is, by contrast, his unique perspective and hard-won analysis that he might want to keep close to the vest and save for a properly workshopped and professionally edited book.

If, after reading a cursory Wikipedia list, you are still asking, "What does it mean?," then you need to log off and read a book by an expert. An academic history conference called "Neither Woman Nor Man: Eunuchs in antiquity and beyond" was held in 1999 in Wales. Thirteen scholars wrote papers on their areas of expertise and those papers were collected in a book edited by Shaun Tougher. An area of expertise can be defined by a geographical area, an era, or a language—likely all of the above—as well as years of study. No one is an expert in "all the eunuchs." The eunuchs lived in various places and times. Some people are experts in *some* of the eunuchs, and, fortunately, they are writing many excellent books.

Ned's most detailed information was about the Byzantine general Narses and the Italian singer Tenducci. He got off to a good start there. He had pages on them. But if you want to learn about those figures, who deserve entire books, today you can read L. H. Fauber's biography of Narses (published in 1990) or Helen Berry's biography of Tenducci (published in 2012).[10]

If your interest is more closely tied to science, the 21st century is a good time for you to be alive and find material. Millions of scientific articles are published every year. Scientists understand testosterone far better today than they did in the 1930s. For this reason alone, the content of Ned's manuscript does not have much staying power. That part is not his fault. He was alive at a transitional moment.

NOTES TO
"'LITTLE INFINITE POEM'"

[1] "Indeed, the Cumming Manuscript Collection of the New

York Academy of Medicine Library contains more than 1200 references, abstracts, and documents concerning the early history of human castration."
"Long-Term Consequences of Castration in Men: Lessons from the Skoptzy and the Eunuchs of the Chinese and Ottoman Courts." Jean D. Wilson and Claus Roehrborn. Journal of Clinical Endocrinology & Metabolism. 1999. Vol. 84:12. https://issuu.com/rebirthing/docs/test Accessed 28 June 2019.
At the end of the paper, they acknowledge that their studies were aided by "Caroline Duroselle-Melish, Reference Librarian in the Historical Collections of the New York Academy of Medicine Library, [whose help] made it possible for us to broaden their scope."
[2] William E. Leuchtenburg. *The Perils of Prosperity: 1914-32.* Chicago and London: University of Chicago Press, 1958. p. 182.
[3] Robert Bly and Marion Woodman. *The Maiden King: The Reunion of Masculine and Feminine.* New York: Henry Holt and Company, 1998. p. 38.
The original poem: Federico García Lorca. "Pequeño Poema Infinito." *Poeta en Nueva York.* Originally published in Ciudad de México: Séneca, 1940. NoBooks Editorial, 1972.
https://books.google.com.co/books?id=amX2DQAAQBAJ&pg=PT77&lpg=PT77 Accessed February 22, 2020.
Translation by Robert Bly: "Little Infinite Poem."
Published in Robert Bly. *Leaping Poetry: An Idea with Poems and Translations.* University of Pittsburgh, 2008.
https://books.google.com.co/books?id=CSfMDwAAQBAJ&pg=PT20&lpg=PT20 Accessed February 22, 2020.
[4] "Jewish Mysticism." H. Sperling. *Aspects of the Hebrew Genius.* Edited by Leon Simon. London: George Routledge & Sons, Limited. New York: Block Publishing Co. 1910. p. 156.
[5] "The Best Answer to Life's Questions." Zat Rana. June 9, 2019.
https://designluck.com/the-best-answer-to-lifes-questions/

[6] Leuchtenburg. *op. cit.,* p. 167.
[7] Matthew Coniam. *Egyptomania Goes to the Movies: From Archaeology to Popular Craze to Hollywood Fantasy.* McFarland, 2017. p. 55.
[8] Coniam, *ibid.,* p. 3.
[9] "Know Your Meme: All The Things."
https://knowyourmeme.com/memes/all-the-things
Accessed August 5, 2019.
[10] L. H. Fauber. *Narses: Hammer of the Goths.* New York: St. Martin's, 1990.
Helen Berry. *The Castrato and His Wife.* Oxford University Press, 2012.

TELL ME, HOW'S IT GOING?

I n 1933, Ned was inquiring after a work that he identified as "Chamberlain, H. R. M. *The Eunuch in Society*, London 1927." He probably learned about it through a citation in N. M. Penzer's *Ocean of Story*. He provided this title to the Library of Congress in Washington, but they responded that they could not find any information for it.[1] He apparently never found it because his enormous bibliography does not include it.

This was an unfortunate missed connection. Herbert Roy Maslen Chamberlain was a few years older than Ned and alive in England, and he was someone who actually *did* finish a book on eunuchs, albeit a self-published one. I made an effort to find it, digging into primary sources to learn who its author had been.

"Roy," as Chamberlain was called, grew up in a poor neighborhood in London as the son of an artist who made signs for shop windows. In late 1915, as a six-foot-tall, 21-year-old man, he presented himself to military examiners and joined the service the next day as a private with the London Regiment. He eventually attained the rank of Acting Captain and was demobilized after the war. He was permitted to wear the uniform for one month beyond that and was still wearing it when he appeared on the campus of the London School of Economics in the Fall of 1919. He was knowledgeable about secondhand bookstores and knew the niece of the *Manchester Guardian* editor.[2] He graduated with honors in Modern Economic History and stayed on to complete a masters thesis on the West African slave trade.

In 1927, however, he told the school he was having difficulty. His faculty advisor, Prof. Lilian Knowles, had died the previous year; he realized belatedly that he needed to narrow the scope of his research; his mother fell ill and moved to the country; he had to move out of the family house in Clapton and sell it; and he didn't have money.

He reported to the school in July 1927 that he had finally completed his thesis and wished to be examined that October. However, he never earned the M.Sc. degree. The final distraction may have been his 1928 marriage.

Prof. R. H. Tawney—son of the Sanskrit scholar C. H. Tawney and a prolific socialist writer just then assuming the presidency of the Worker's Educational Association[3]—had briefly served as Chamberlain's faculty advisor, pinch-hitting for the role of the late Prof. Knowles. It is likely that this was how Chamberlain learned of the recent serial issue of the late elder Tawney's English translation of Indian fables called *The Ocean of Story*. This beautiful edition, with its black buckram binding and gilt edges, was annotated by Norman Mosley Penzer, a scholar, London resident, and fellow veteran two years older than Chamberlain who had studied at the University of Cambridge. Penzer spearheaded the project with the financial sponsorship of Charles J. Sawyer booksellers. (The elder Tawney had consented to the reprint of his work, but his advanced age did not permit him to assist further with the project.)

In 1927, Chamberlain completed his own book-length work called *The Eunuch in Society*. Perhaps it was part of his thesis on the slave trade. Penzer noted it in a bibliographical addendum to the *Ocean of Story's* ninth volume (1928), saying that Chamberlain's book was "privately printed" (implying that a few copies were distributed to friends as a vanity project). When Penzer published *The Harem* (1936), he wrote that "there appear to be only three or four works entirely devoted" to eunuchs. *The Eunuch in Society* must have been the half-counted fourth title, given his comment: "I believe, [it] still awaits a publisher."

TEN PAST NOON

This book cannot be found. Chamberlain, a stamp collector, became president of the British Society of Russian Philately, which barely even keeps a photograph of him. One of their newsletters has a 1952 group photo captioned with his name among others, but it is not obvious which names correspond to which faces, and in any case the reproduction was so grainy as to leave all the faces featureless.[4]

In 2013, I inquired with Charles J. Sawyer booksellers, the sponsor of Penzer's *Ocean of Story*. I knew that, forty years previously, Richard Sawyer had sold the collection of Penzer correspondence to a private collector (who subsequently donated it to a library, where I read it). I thought perhaps he might know what had happened to the books that Penzer owned and used as sources for the *Ocean of Story*. I was informed that Richard Sawyer had recently died.[5]

I felt certain that *The Eunuch in Society* existed for me to find, even as I kept turning up emptiness.

"She had awakened in this mood," Christine Weston wrote in her 1946 novel *The Dark Wood,* "sure that there would be a message for her, today, from Mark. Once or twice in her life she had experienced this kind of certainty germinating in the very center of doubt, emerging at last as undeniable as the sun itself."[6]

Chamberlain, after divorcing, had a second wife, the widow of Leonard Harry Vardon.

(Leonard, the nephew of the famous golfer Harry Vardon, had also been a golfer. He had mysteriously disappeared around age forty.) Knowing that Chamberlain had a second wife did not help me find his papers. He left everything to her in his will. She died without a will. They had no children.

In 2018, I flew to Texas to read the papers of John Rodker, a London publisher who I thought might have been the likely printer of *The Eunuch in Society*. It was a shot in the dark. Negative.[7]

The golf ball was hit out of our line of sight. It may be near, it may be far. We have no idea where to look. All we see is grass.

Ned had inquired with librarians after the whereabouts of *The Eunuch in Society* in 1933. When communicating with Penzer two years later, he may have forgotten to ask Penzer the same question. Penzer would have had it.

The Eunuch in Society is, therefore, lost. There are living eunuchs who make their way in their societies, but a book called *The Eunuch in Society* will not turn up for me.

There may still be a Carolina parakeet flying over Cypress Gardens and hiding in the trees. But after so much searching for something we've lost, at a certain point, we stop.

TEN PAST NOON

Penzer sent a short handwritten letter from London dated July 30, 1935, asking Ned, "How is the eunuch book going along?"

It is a casual question that, minus the specificity of its fourth word, strikes dread into the pit of the stomach of every writer. Penzer requested

> to be allowed to see a copy of what you have done, and possibly quote in advance from your MS [manuscript]. The point is that I have to do a chapter on eunuchs in my new book on the Harem, and I really have very little new information to give. I am interested in the extent of the operation in different countries at different times, the origin and spread of the use of eunuchs to grand women, the exact nature of their duties etc. etc. Any help you might give would be very greatly appreciated, and, of course, fully acknowledged.[8]

Indeed, Penzer subsequently credited Ned in *The Harem* (1936) for pointing him toward Millant's famous 1908 work *Les Eunuques à Travers les Ages*, referring to him as "Dr. E. D. Cumming," an accidental and honorary title for a man who had never finished any academic program, and optimistically mentioning his manuscript-in-progress.[9]

Dr. Archibald Malloch, the librarian at the New York Academy of Medicine, mailed Ned an advertisement for *The Harem* on March 19,

TUCKER LIEBERMAN

1937. Ned saved it.

Penzer's chapter called "The Black Eunuchs" is unavoidably sticky in the imagination, and, at least from that perspective, he wrote it effectively. He begins with his strength—the map of the palace—and speaks as if he's a tour guide, narrating us architecturally through the harem doors. He describes the formal roles and costumes of the various positions for eunuchs. He backs up to describe Turkish history related to these customs, incorporating European travel writers, then backs up further to quote ancient historians. He graphically describes the painful mutilation that carried risk of death and introduces Greek words that categorize people based on what was done to their bodies. Before moving on to discuss the reported erotic activity of eunuchs (including details like "anal massage"), he regales us with this astonishingly bizarre litany of stereotypes and slurs:

> The physical effects of castration are well known—complete lack of bodily hair, the feminine 'cracked' voice (deeper, however, in the black races), the gradual flabbiness of the body, often accompanied by obesity and ugly wrinkling of the skin in later life. Among other effects of castration may be mentioned a weak bladder, loss of memory, insomnia, and bad eyesight. Eunuchs have no liking for alcohol, of which the smallest amount is sufficient to

> make them incapable. They prefer cakes and sweetmeats to meat. Their favourite colour is red. They like music, especially the rhythmic beat of the drum or tambourine and all Central African instruments. They are neat in their habits, but are miserly and fond of accumulating wealth. They unite the small brain of the negro with the childish imagination of the ignorant Oriental. Consequently they believe the wildest stories, and once an idea has entered their minds nothing can change it. A terrible story about a Chinese eunuch, related later, goes to illustrate this point. They adore what we call 'fairy stories,' and can listen to recitations of the *Thousand Nights and a Night* and similar collections for an indefinite period. They love children and animals, including chickens, sheep, cows, and monkeys—but most of all cats, which they keep as pets and treat with the utmost care and attention.[10]

Despite (or perhaps because of?) this paragraph, the book was reprinted posthumously and remains well known.

It is a reminder of how the most brazen lies can appear plausible or are at least easily swallowed. Indeed—to project the shadow of this paragraph back at ourselves—we humans, all of us, tend to "believe the wildest stories" and, once an idea enters our minds, "nothing can change it."

Nothing changes, that is, unless we really try.

#########

Here's Alexander Chee in his essay "100 Things About Writing a Novel": "If I do not answer the question What is the novel about? or How is the writing going? it is because my sense of a novel changes in the same way my knowledge of someone changes."[11]

#########

A half-century after the publication of *The Harem*, the artist Barbara Chase-Riboud published her novel *Valide* (1986), which was soon discovered to contain passages quoted nearly verbatim from Penzer without attribution. Chase-Riboud's defense given to the *New York Times* reporter was that she treated nonfiction books of a certain age as "reference materials" within the "public domain" and that it was fair for her to incorporate those words into her fiction.[12]

Penzer's book will legally enter U.S. public domain in 2031.

So many people do it. Sometimes people get caught. The history of eunuchs has been written as an endless web of anecdotes and rumors. *How is it coming along?* It is hard to say.

#########

TEN PAST NOON

Ned, in the mid-'30s, was deep in his scribblings.

Eighty years later, in the present day, Dan Barker explains how free will and determinism are related, drawing from his knowledge as a jazz pianist:

> Musicians usually think of melody as horizontal and harmony as vertical. In common notation, melodies run from left to right while chords are vertical stacks of notes. Reading music is like looking at a graph. On the axis of time, melodies run from earlier to later while harmony is a time-irrelevant backdrop that gives melody its context. Chords usually change less frequently than notes of a melody.[13]

Our lives are a time-bound series of determined actions, this determinism being like our melody, Barker says, while our free will is more like the harmony.[14]

⟊⟊⟊⟊⟊⟊⟊⟊⟊

Underground, Ned was nevertheless starting to see the light.

This should be unsurprising: after all, there is infinite light, and the light has taken long enough already to arrive. Yet it always feels like a surprise.

The enlightenment is coming slowly, one small starpoint at a time—and what a chronotope we are in!

TUCKER LIEBERMAN

NOTES TO
"TELL ME, HOW'S IT GOING?"

[1] MS Cumming, *Eunuchry*. Letter from the Library of Congress, July 14, 1933.

[2] The *Manchester Guardian* editor was John Atkinson Hobson.
My brief biography of H. R. M. Chamberlain is based on my original research in 2013. I received assistance from Kate Elms at the Brighton History Centre and from Sue McMahon at the Worthing Reference Library. I also purchased copies of civil documents from the U.K. National Archives.

[3] "R. H. Tawney." *LeftWord.*
https://lefttest.tulikabooks.in/author/post/r-h-tawney
Accessed January 21, 2020.

[4] The BSRP organization still exists but does not store anything Chamberlain wrote about eunuchs. Chamberlain had no descendants (nor does his sister Doris appear ever to have married); in his will, he left everything to his second wife Mabel; Mabel in turn left no will; and the London School of Economics keeps no copy of his eunuch manuscript nor of his thesis on the slave trade. Chamberlain's name may appear on the back of the BSRP's president's badge. A 1963 newsletter said that Mabel had given the organization "a President's badge worked in solid gold in the form of the monogram 'B.S.R.P.' as shown on the cover of the Journal. The letters are picked out in dark blue lacquer, and the badge is hung by ribbon from the shoulders. The reverse is suitably inscribed in Roy Chamberlain's memory."
"A Collector's Calendar." P. T. Ashford. *British Journal of Russian Philately,* No. 33, October 1963. p. 32.
https://www.bsrp.org/wp-content/uploads/2019/11/bjrp_33_1963.pdf

TEN PAST NOON

Accessed January 24, 2020.

[5] Richard Sawyer had been working in the bookstore with his father in 1972 when the Penzer collection was sold, but he died several months before my inquiry in 2013.

[6] Christine Weston. *The Dark Wood.* New York: Charles Scribner's Sons, 1946. p. 300.

[7] The John Rodker papers are at the Harry Ransom Center at the University of Texas—Austin.

[8] MS Cumming, *Eunuchry.* Letter from N. M. Penzer, July 30, 1935.

[9] N. M. Penzer. *The Harem.* (1936) New York: Dorset Press, 1993. p. 151.

[10] Penzer, *ibid.,* pp. 144-145.

[11] "100 Things About Writing a Novel." Alexander Chee. *The Yale Review.* Undated. https://yalereview.yale.edu/100-things-about-writing-novel Accessed February 22, 2020.

The essay originated as several blog posts, apparently in 2011, on Chee's former blog "Koreanish."

[12] "Writer Who Cried Plagiarism Used Passages She Didn't Write." Margarett Loke. *New York Times.* Dec. 19, 1997. https://www.nytimes.com/1997/12/19/movies/writer-who-cried-plagiarism-used-passages-she-didn-t-write.html Accessed August 31, 2019.

[13] Dan Barker. *Free Will Explained: How Science and Philosophy Converge to Create a Beautiful Illusion.* New York: Sterling, 2018. p. 33.

[14] Barker, *ibid.,* p. 39.

EVERY EFFECT
IS ITSELF A CAUSE

In Tonkin, a region of north Vietnam, near China, where eunuchs were "household servants and government officers" until the French took control in the 19th century, people seemed to perceive castration as "a misfortune not without compensating factors," as Ned put it. While a eunuch may have been "hated" or "envied" as an individual, Ned is aware of no general prejudice.[1]

He leans toward a certain prejudice, though, at least in the way he expresses himself. After all, he urges doctors not to castrate, and to do so he takes the stance that there is something bad about castration. "All must concede that the eunuch is in many respects both individually and socially inferior to the uncastrated," he says (as mentioned earlier), and he charges the pro-castration advocates with the "burden of proof" for articulating benefits over costs "entailed to the individual and to society."[2] In this passage, he is not speaking of inviolable human rights, but of utilitarianism, and he is recusing himself from providing his utilitarian calculation.

Elsewhere, though, mentioning lands where there was a cultural habit of employing eunuchs, he does object as a matter of principle: "All participated in the benefits and none protested loudly the wrong."[3] That is a serviceable indictment of white supremacy and other kinds of oppression.

If you sleep with your book under your pillow—be patient, wait a few years—the thesis fairy comes and leaves you a present. It might be a blessing. It might be a curse.

On the penultimate page of his Vol. 9, Ned defends eunuchs as "men" whose characters, as a class, are not "sharply differentiated" from those of other men, and who are, to the contrary, "in many respects more manly" than other men. Thus, he concludes, discrimination against eunuchs is "unjustified."

Yet, on the final page of Vol. 9, he backtracks and says that the character of eunuchs is not properly or fully understood:

> It is said that a eunuch, a certain Labys, attached to the temple of Apollo at Delphos, was the first to pronounce the words of the familiar precept "Know thyself"; but there is no evidence that any eunuch ever followed this instruction; nor, for many years to come, is anyone

likely to attain a right understanding of the eunuch character.

He had used the same sentence, with only minor differences, to conclude Vol. 2 where he had ended with the phrase "a complete understanding of the effects of castration on the human organism." That he had deliberately replaced this language with "a right understanding of the eunuch character" in Vol. 9 reflects how he was moving away from biology and toward psychology, an effort I will now explain.

In the late 1930s, perhaps because he had exhausted his sources, he moved away from hand-indexing the history and science of eunuchs and began gravitating toward his "supplemental effort." He discovered a new interest: *Psychology. Emotions. Personality types. Disorders.* Putting aside his original fourteen loose-leaf binders, he now filled five more binders with information from modern psychologists. He mostly repeated schema and theories, in many cases doing little more than copying the tables of contents, or an introductory sentence or two, from dozens of books. He did not seem to have deep knowledge of the field.

Though he labeled his amateur foray into psychology as "supplemental" to his eunuch manuscript, it was actually foundational to what he'd always wanted to know. If he could understand how human minds worked, he had a hope of understanding what made eunuchs different. The specific is a divergence from the general. He wanted to back up and explore the general.

#########

On January 16, 1937, thirty-six-year-old Felix Kittredge finally married. "My chicken" was his pet name for his bride, Carola de Peyster Kip, who wore "a draped gown of white romaine crêpe and a veil of point d'esprit lace that has been in her family for five generations."[4] The ceremony was held at St. Bartholomew's, an Episcopal church in midtown Manhattan.

Ned was likely invited to dance at his cousin's wedding. They might have played the hit songs from the past couple years: Ethel Merman's "I Get a Kick Out of You," Eddie Duchin's "I Won't Dance," Fats Waller's "I'm Gonna Sit Right Down and Write Myself a Letter," the Dorsey Brothers' "Lullaby of Broadway," Fred Astaire's "I'm Putting All My Eggs in One Basket," Guy Lombardo's "When Did You Leave Heaven?," Jimmy Dorsey's "Is It True What They Say About Dixie?" and Marian Anderson's "He's Got the Whole World in His Hands."

#########

TUCKER LIEBERMAN

The day before Felix's wedding, a boy in Atlanta celebrated his eighth birthday. Like Felix, he was also a "Junior." This boy had originally been called Michael after his father, but now he was called Martin, his father having changed both of their names.

#########

In one of his "supplemental" volumes, under the heading "Motor traits," Ned listed:

> Total output of energy
> Maximum muscular effort
> Organic speed of resprase-galvanometer
> etc.
> Dancing
> Taciturn vs. voluble
> Hyperkinetic vs. Hypo
> Feeling of fatigue[5]

He wrote: "There does seem to be some correlation between motor traits and emotion. The hypokinetic seem to be usually of low affectivity."[6]

He didn't dance or express emotion. His younger cousin published a novel and got married. Ned could do neither.

#########

Still ringing in his ears was the echo of the singing, that of the eunuch musicians.

> On his first appearance in Rome, the eunuch singer Farinelli then only seventeen years old, matched his art

against that of a famous trumpeter and was able to outlast him, the trumpeter stopping for breath while Farinelli burst into an additional cascade of trills and runs.[7]

Petronius' *Satyricon* has a eunuch singing in a brothel. Brison, a eunuch of the 4th-century Empress Eudoxia, teaches the Arians how to sing hymns. Manuel, a eunuch in Russia in the 12th century, trained choirs and was made a bishop. A travel writer says that eunuchs in the entourage of the King of Dahomey sing his praises.

> Of the Italians an English traveller remarked in 1648 that "They are so addicted to Musick, especially that of the Voyce, that great persons keep their Castrati; whose throats and complexions scandalize their breeches."[8]

Wolcot's poem "Lord Brundell and the Eunuch" features a singer named "Signor Squaline" who's called a "squeal eunuch." Meanwhile, Whitehead: "What piping, fidling, squeaking, quav'ring, bawling, What sing-song Riot, and what Eunuch-squawling."[9] And some of these singers had attitude:

> ...when Katharine II of Russia refused to agree to pay the eunuch Gabrielli 500 ducats for two months services on the ground that such a sum was more than she paid a field-marshall, the eunuch retorted that then she might let her field-marshall sing.[10]

Despite all this beautiful noise, in the 16th century, Juan Huarte de San Juan said that castration results in the loss of

> wit and ability... even as if he had received in the Brain some considerable Hurt.... even in Music, which is their ordinary profession, we see plainly how blockish they are, and the reason of it is, that Music is a work of the imagination, which power requires much heat, whereas they are cold and moist.[11]

In general, Ned uncritically accepted pronouncements that eunuchs were incapable of artistic ability, even though this is irreconcilable with the attention he paid to the Italian opera singers.

He briefly mentions a ceremonial chant in 19th-century Korea. The relative confidence and lyricism of the English in this paragraph, compared to the rest of his text, drew my attention. The words turn out not to be Ned's. They belong to the American diplomat William Woodville Rockhill, who reported in 1891 that several hundred Korean palace eunuchs perform an annual ceremony "to insure bountiful crops in the ensuing year. They chant in chorus prayers, swinging burning torches around them the while. This is said to be symbolical of burning the dead grass, so as to destroy the field mice and other vermin."[12] I'm sure the plagiarism was accidental; Ned wouldn't have annotated twelve hundred sources and risked stealing one paragraph. But I point it out because this is the song. This is the art. Every note matters.

Translation, says Lindsay Lerman, "has allowed me to spend hours wondering if *puissance* should be rendered as *power* or *force*," but "it's all a kind of gamble. Will this word or the other one be better? Is one of them 'right'? Does it matter?" She wrote her first novel "letting each word matter" but also decided she "could not let any one word, or any one collection or cluster of words, matter more than the whole and how it hangs together to *feel* inside the mind/body of the reader."[13] Every note matters, but we rarely listen to notes in isolation. Together they form a song.

♯♯♯♯♯♯♯♯♯

Sometimes, when someone is depressed, he feels as if he is moving through molasses.

The tar pits museum at La Brea offers a demonstration of the stickiness and density of asphalt. Never mind molasses; asphalt is a next-level problem. At the museum, you can plunge a foot-sized plug into the goo and try to pull it out. It's likely at the edge of your ability if you are, in this respect, an average man of about forty, as I was when I visited and tried it. Whether you can free yourself depends on how your foot landed. Luck of the draw. You might not be able to do it. Not even if you're a mastodon. Not even if another mastodon has stretched out its trunk and is offering to help pull. The asphalt, it has you.

Ned tried to solve it with combinatorics.

> The loss of sex desire is less common than impotence.
>
> Desire may: Persist Weaken Increase
>
> Erections may Persist Weaken Increase
>
> There are nine possible combinations / six of which represent discrepancies.[14]

At the bottom of one headache-inducing diagram, with lines drawn between different possible factors influencing personality, he complained that "psychical and physical factors are interrelated all the way down the line—all that can be done is to attempt to segregate *controlling* factors." But "the great difficulty," he wrote, "arises from the fact that every effect may itself be a cause."[15] An *ourobouros*; a self-consuming snake.

One page has the centered heading "Previously Normal." Below this, a numbered list:

1. Erections
2. Ejaculations
3. Other organic phases of orgasm
4. Sensory experience in erections ejaculations and other aspects of orgasm
5. Desire
6. Direction[16]

Each of these topics was assigned its own

page. For the first five, he elaborated. The sixth page for "direction"—by which he meant the object of sexual affections, what we would today call sexual orientation or perhaps fetishism—was left blank.

NOTES TO
"EVERY EFFECT IS ITSELF A CAUSE"

[1] MS Cumming, *Eunuchry,* Vol. 8.
[2] MS Cumming, *Eunuchry,* Vol. 14.
[3] MS Cumming, *Eunuchry,* Vol. 14.
[4] "Carola de P. Kip Becomes a Bride." *New York Times.* January 17, 1937.
https://timesmachine.nytimes.com/timesmachine/1937/01/17/98858466.pdf Accessed October 23, 2019.
The DePeyster name on her mother's side had arrived in the Dutch settlement of New Amsterdam (the original name of New York City) in the 1600s. Her father's surname, "Kip," means "chicken" in Dutch, which would explain the term of endearment.
[5] MS Cumming, *Eunuchry,* Vol. A-1.
[6] MS Cumming, *Eunuchry,* Vol. A-3.
[7] MS Cumming, *Eunuchry,* Vol. 2.
[8] MS Cumming, *Eunuchry,* Vol. 8.
[9] MS Cumming, *Eunuchry,* Vol. 13. (Wolcot and Whitehead references.)
[10] MS Cumming, *Eunuchry,* Vol. 13 (and repeated elsewhere).
[11] Probably from *Examen de ingenios para las ciencias* (The Examination of Men's Wits, 1575-1594). Quoted in MS Cumming, *Eunuchry,* Vol. 2.
[12] MS Cumming, *Eunuchry.* He plagiarizes the paragraph in his Vol. 8. The original is: "Notes on Some of the Laws, Customs, and Superstitions of Korea." W. Woodville

Rockhill. *American Anthropologist.* Vol. 4, No. 2 (Apr., 1891), pp. 177-188 (12 pages) p. 185. https://www.jstor.org/stable/658250?seq=9#metadata_info_tab_contents Accessed August 5, 2019.

[13] "Finding the clarity and sobriety that grief forces us to feel: An interview with Lindsay Lerman, author of *I'm From Nowhere.*" Chuck Augello. *Cease Cows.* October 21, 2019. http://ceasecows.com/2019/10/21/finding-the-clarity-and-sobriety-that-grief-forces-us-to-feel-an-interview-with-lindsay-lerman-author-of-im-from-nowhere/ Accessed October 22, 2019.

[14] MS Cumming, *Eunuchry.* Vol. A-1.

[15] MS Cumming, *Eunuchry.* Vol. A-1.

[16] MS Cumming, *Eunuchry.* Vol. A-1.

TESTOSTERONE

Beginning with raw, natural material, Ernst Laqueur isolated testosterone in the early 1930s. He used a quantity of bull testicles that weighed as much as a large man, and he reduced them to a ten-millionth of their mass so that all that was left was the crystalline hormone, roughly the amount a man produces in one day,[1] roughly the weight of a grain of sand or a dust particle cast by Halley's Comet.[2]

In 1935, researchers synthesized the hormone. What makes bulls bulls? They found a definitive answer. Now we know. It's the chemical structure of testosterone. Look at the constellation.

TEN PAST NOON

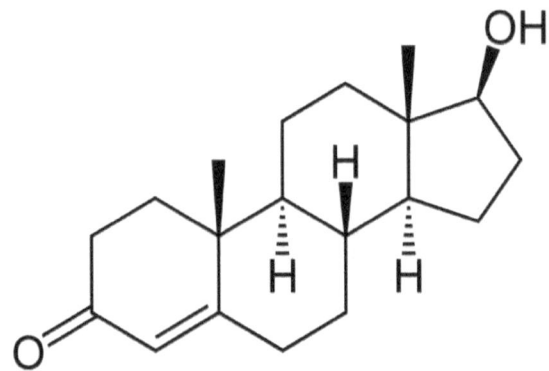

Figure 21 – The chemical structure of testosterone.[3]

The National Committee on Maternal Health wrote to Ned in 1937 asking if he'd like to meet Dr. Errol T. Engle, a part-time director of the board who was researching castration. Ned was invited to Engle's office on West 168th Street.

Engle's career included research into hormonal processes of menstruation and the pituitary gland's regulation of reproductive organs.[4] Originally from the Midwest, he earned his Ph.D. in 1925 at the California university named for Gov. Leland Stanford who had made a fortune on the building of the transcontinental railroad. Robert T. Frank congratulated Engle in 1928, writing that his recent publication "is the first time, to my knowledge, in which a proof has been submitted, that while both sex hormones are circulating in the blood, the male organs are not interfered with." (In other words, that men naturally produce some estrogen, too.) In 1929, an OB/GYN colleague in Detroit corresponded with him about commercially available estrogen injections. The following year, he was invited to present at the Second International Congress for Sex Research in London.[5]

Engle's preserved papers have some colorful documentation of his own scientific collecting habits:

> "The big chunky tooth which you thought might be Titanotherium I believe belongs rather to one of the Oligocene rhinocerae."
>
> —Letter from Freeman Ward, state geologist of South Dakota, University of South Dakota (Vermillion, S.D.), Oct. 19, 1922

> "If, however, you wish to make a preliminary investigation in order to determine the most favorable stage for your study of the inner ear, I can send you a few heads of [opossum] embryos fixed in Bouin's fluid."
>
> —Letter from Carl Hartman, U Texas Austin, dept of Zoology, Nov. 21, 1923

> "I am also in need of some large cryptobranchus [giant salamanders] which must

also be fresh from their natural habitat [and alive]."

—Letter to Mr. George M. Gray, Dept. of Supplies, Marine Bio Lab, Woods Hole, Mass, on March 22, 1929[6]

At the time Engle reached out to Ned, Engle was a new transplant to New York. He would begin teaching at Columbia University the following year, where he would build his reputation by showing that anterior pituitary hormones control the descent of human and animal testes. Perhaps someday these hormones could be used to treat "cryptorchism" (undescended testes).[7]

Engle, sponsored by Columbia and the American Museum of Natural History in Manhattan, traveled to French Cameroon with three other professors.[8] In a brief handwritten memoir of that trip, he uses humor, mentioning "John Haig" (Scotch whiskey) along with quinine hydrochloride to prevent malaria. It is hard to tell whether he is trying to be funny when he says that "I first learned that my colleague was organizing an expedition to go to Africa to accumulate a few gorillas, and maybe a native or two, for purely scientific study." The story is only a few pages long, within which he comments that memoir-writing engenders his fear of criticism and is "discouraging."[9]

Although Ned's own interests had begun to veer toward psychology, I assume he was nevertheless thrilled by the chance to speak to a medical specialist like Engle and to be implicitly flattered as an as-yet-unpublished author. After all, he saved Engle's invitation letter. On the other hand, he saved a lot of information.

He was still researching in 1937.

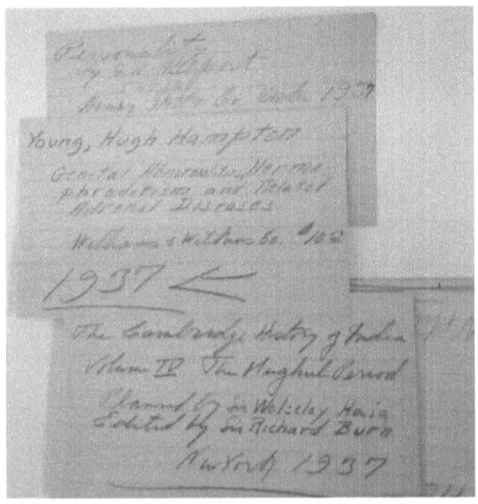

Figure 22 – His handwriting lists publications dated 1937: G. W. Allport's Personality, *Hugh Hampton Young's* Genital Abnormalities, Hermaphroditism and Related Adrenal Diseases *(ten dollars), and Sir Richard Burn's* Cambridge History of India, *Vol. 4.*

Here is his undated statement of intent to finish his book. It is a note to self. It's another indication that he indeed wanted, at least at one point, for these papers to be a published book.

This goal, unfortunately, is not broken into achievable steps.

TEN PAST NOON

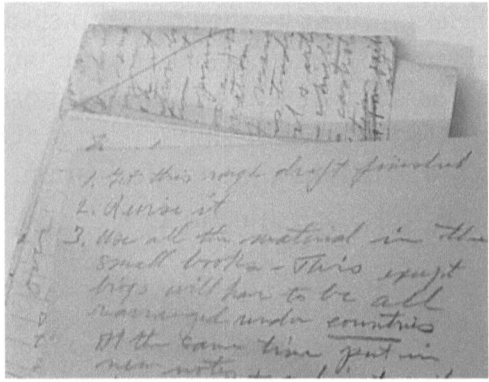

Figure 23 – Handwritten goals.

1. Get this rough draft finished
2. Revise it
3. Use all the material in the small books—This except biog[raphie]s will have to be all rearranged under *countries* — At the same time, put in new notes...

There is no further record of what happened.

NOTES TO "TESTOSTERONE"

[1] "...in the early 1930s, Dutch pharmacologist Ernst Laqueur managed to isolate 10 milligrams of crystalline testosterone from 100 kilograms of bull testicles, and that changed everything. Suddenly, researchers could pick apart testosterone's chemical structure; suddenly, they could experiment. Synthetic versions soon followed..."
Steven Kotler. *Tomorrowland: Our Journey From Science Fiction to Science Fact.* New York: Amazon Publishing, 2015. p. 193.

[2] "...the tiny meteoroids from Halley are so light. A typical

debris particle is about the same size as a grain of sand, but it is much less dense, weighing only 0.01 gram."
"Halley's comet returns in bits and pieces." Tony Phillips. NASA Science. October 20, 1998. https://science.nasa.gov/science-news/science-at-nasa/1998/ast20oct98_1 Accessed Nov. 12, 2019.

[3] Public domain image of the chemical structure of testosterone. Author: "NEUROtiker." Wikimedia Commons. June 29, 2007. https://commons.wikimedia.org/wiki/File:Testosteron.svg Accessed Nov. 10, 2019.

[4] 1958 obituary by The Endocrine Society. http://jcem.endojournals.org/content/18/6/670.extract

[5] The Second International Congress for Sex Research (London, August 3–9, 1930) sent him a letter on February 1, 1930.

[6] Correspondence. Errol [Earl] T. Engle papers, 1896-1970 (bulk 1922-1930). Health Sciences Library Archives and Special Collections, Columbia University Medical Center, New York, New York.

[7] From his eulogy by Dr. John K. Lattimer at the meeting of the New York Society of the American Urological Association.

[8] "Further Adventures of Meshie: A Chimpanzee That Has Lived Most of Her Life in a New York Suburban Home." H. C. Raven. *Natural History,* Nov–Dec 1933. http://www.naturalhistorymag.com/htmlsite/editors_pick/1933_11-12b_pick.html Accessed Sept. 24, 2019.

[9] Unpublished memoir of his trip to Africa. Errol [Earl] T. Engle papers, 1896-1970 (bulk 1922-1930). Health Sciences Library Archives and Special Collections, Columbia University Medical Center, New York, New York.

TRACKS 37-39
NO BOOK

UNANSWERED QUESTIONS

In the early 2000s, I wanted to read everything about eunuchs I could find. As I mentioned in my introduction, I wanted stories and language that could interpret who I was. The language about transsexuality in the *Diagnostic and Statistical Manual of Mental Disorders* was designed for health providers to feel better about their own decisions to help me, and I had to become fluent in that language for their purposes, but the language was never designed to tell me anything profound about myself. So I looked elsewhere.

Due to the physical and social similarities I perceived between ancient eunuchs and modern transgender men like myself, I thought the language used for eunuchs might be instructive. I thought it might reveal archetypes: ones that came purely from the people they described, not ones written by medical gatekeepers for their self-assurance and satisfaction. I wanted archetypes because, I figured, if we have a shared set of symbols that is sufficiently complex, we can use it for tarot readings to explore our feelings.

I am not, however, a eunuch, and it is funny that I sought authenticity outside myself, namely in the way that male writers described eunuchs. What I really needed to know was how transgender men could begin describing ourselves. But the influence of the *Diagnostic and Statistical Manual of Mental Disorders* was overwhelming, transgender men didn't have book deals, and the Internet was still new. So, tales of eunuchs it was, then.

I found N. M. Penzer's *The Harem* in which he mentions that "Dr." E. D. Cumming had a book in progress. I could not find any publication by a man by that name, however. And when I learned that this unfinished, handwritten manuscript was in a library, I wanted to read it. It took me about seven years to finally make the trip. Once I saw it, I had to keep returning, and then it took me another seven years to understand it. This endeavor was never going to give me the answer as to how to express my own authenticity, but I didn't know that at the time. The value for me was in trying to answer the question, even though my answer was wrong.

#########

One of my first published essays contains an esoteric joke. I had told the story of using a men's ritual bath in Israel and having a traveling companion look at my naked body and laugh at what he thought must be my penis "shrinkage" in the frigid water. (I had not had genital surgery, and my genitals were roughly the size they had always been, so being naked around other men was a bit transgressive, which is what made my memoir a specifically transgender travel story.)

The editor—who overall made quite helpful comments that improved the piece—also suggested that I bring in the kabbalistic idea of *tzimtzum* (צמצום): God choosing to pull back and not take up all the space so that there would be room for Creation. I had not been aware of this concept. *What would God do to get out of Creation's way?* I wondered. *Crawl into a black hole?* The editor said I could tell him if I disliked the idea.

Indeed, I felt uneasy about the proposal. My memoir, in repeating a joke that someone else had made about my invisible penis, attributed the comment to that person. The editor was taking the opportunity to extend the penis joke and to ask me to include it, too, this time in my own voice.

It wasn't even my joke. It was not the sort of thing I would have come up with. It seemed to me that, if this *tzimtzum* theology were true, then comparing God's creative methodology to the size of my penis was certainly in bad taste, and, if this theology were not true, the joke made little sense. That was really the problem—that the comment felt performative rather than authentic.

Probably all writers feel they are being performative when a publisher asks them to add something to their memoir. Being transgender made it more fraught insofar as I was twenty-four years old before anyone ever made a penis joke in reference to my body, and now my version of this anecdote was going to be printed in a magazine.

I agreed to the editor's addition, though, because I wanted my essay to be published. Indeed, my essay appeared in the magazine in 2007 and then in an anthology in 2010 which won a literary award.[1] Once, in Boston, someone on the street to whom I'd just introduced myself asked me if I was the author of that "iconic" essay. I am happy that the essay reached some readers who understood it. I don't contemplate the inclusion of the embarrassing *tzimtzum* joke; if I did, my mind would be sucked into a black hole.

✂✂✂✂✂✂✂✂✂

Negotiating a role change at my office in 2014, I had to suggest a title for myself. I was going to do less proofreading of others' organizing principles, designs, and finished products. Instead, I would finally be the designer. As this was a new role at the office, it didn't come with an off-the-shelf name.

My boss suggested the title of Product Manager.

This did not strike my fancy. It sounded as if I *owned a thing*. I preferred the implication that I *organized the concepts*.

I briefly argued that I should be called an Information Architect.

The boss looked thoughtful. "No," he said, "I think Product Manager is good for you."

≠≠≠≠≠≠≠≠≠

Similarly, in the *Eunuchry* project, the late Ned Cumming remained its Information Architect. I started off as Product Manager. Ned had already organized his research according to his own principles. My role was only to find a way to bring the book to press.

Dante complains at the beginning of *Inferno:*

> *Nel mezzo del cammin di nostra vita*
> *mi ritrovai per una selva oscura,*
> *ché la diritta via era smarrita.*

> [Midway in the journey of our life
> I came to myself in a dark wood,
> for the straight way was lost.][2]

And Virgil counsels:

> *Ond' io per lo tuo me' penso e discerno*
> *che tu mi segui, e io sarò tua guida...*

> [Therefore, for your sake, I think it wise
> you follow me: I will be your guide...][3]

That *was* my role, anyway, until I realized it just couldn't be. I wasn't going to own a product that, upon inspection, I did not find useful or beautiful and did not even agree with. I would have to be Information Architect as well as Product Manager. I would have to rearchitect the book.

When I did that fully and correctly, it would no longer be his book. It would be mine.

#########

I don't mind that I had this particular relationship with a dead author and this fascination with his work. It gave me the chance to raise some questions:

Why didn't he finish his book? Why isn't it the kind of thing you can borrow from a local library or buy in a store?

Why, for that matter, was it handwritten? Had he never learned to type? Was his typewriter broken, or did he not like changing the ribbon? Did his creative process require a pencil? Was he a Luddite artist, objecting to machines on principle? Did he want his manuscript to look old-timey? Was he so particular about consistency that, once he began to handwrite, he did not want to switch? Was he holding out typewriting as a future reward to himself—*I'll hire a girl*, maybe he thought—to incentivize himself to finish? Was he self-sabotaging by reducing the likelihood that an editor would ever accept his book proposal? Was this a way of entrenching his social isolation?

If I can pick only one answer, I will imagine a

different one: His housemates complained about the clacking of the keys. *"Ickira, trecketre, stedenthal."* He wrote in pencil so he could work at night while they slept.

For anyone who believes that their mission is to write and yet is not actually finishing their book, that impasse is a matter of personal importance. If Ned could not justify his writing process and his failure to conclude his project, it may have been a source of anxiety.

NOTES TO "UNANSWERED QUESTIONS"

[1] "Hearing beneath the Surface: Crossing Gender Boundaries at the Ari Mikveh." Tucker Lieberman. First published in *Zeek*, March 2007, and then in *Balancing on the Mechitza: Transgender in Jewish Community*. ed. Noach Dzmura. North Atlantic Books, 2010. The anthology won a 2011 Lambda Literary Award in the "Transgender Nonfiction" category.

[2] Dante, *Divine Comedy* (first printed in 1472). Translated by Robert Hollander and Jean Hollander. Doubleday/Anchor, 2000. Canto 1, lines 1-3.
http://etcweb.princeton.edu/dante/pdp/
Accessed February 21, 2020.

[3] Dante, *ibid.,* Canto 1, lines 112-113.

IMPULSE, OBSESSION, DOUBT

"Every second of our life has its own premise, whether or not we are conscious of it at the time," the dramatist Lajos Egri wrote in 1942. He was a Jewish Hungarian immigrant who taught dramatic writing in Manhattan in the '30s. We hold beliefs that motivate us, and, even if we can't prove any such belief, "there was one we meant to prove...The premise of each second contributes to the premise of the minute of which it is part, just as each minute gives its bit of life to the hour, and the hour to the day. And so, at the end, there is a premise for every life."[1]

"Ill-temper leads to isolation," "Materialism conquers mysticism," or "Prudishness leads to frustration" are among the dramatic premises that Egri gave as examples. A brief premise like one of these implies "character, conflict, and conclusion" and serves "a thumbnail synopsis of your play."[2]

TEN PAST NOON

#########

In his supplementary volumes to *Eunuchry*, Ned listed the various kinds of mental distress. The type of "Insanity" called "Volitional Insanity" was further broken down into "Impulse," "Obsession," and "Doubt."[3]

#########

It has to be organized. You can't keep your content and forgo architecture.

"If you rip out the content from your favorite book and throw the words on the floor," says Abby Covert, "the resulting pile is not your favorite book."

Meticulous architecture that changes the meaning of the content isn't right, either.

> If you define each word from your favorite book and organize the definitions alphabetically, you would have a dictionary, not your favorite book.

> If you arrange each word from your favorite book by gathering similarly defined words, you have a thesaurus, not your favorite book.[4]

#########

You may expand your dramatic premise to include subpremises, Egri advised, but if the original premise comes to look "untenable," you must "formulate a new premise and discard the old." You cannot "start out with one premise and switch to another...No one can build a play on two premises, or a house on two foundations."[5]

In *Eunuchry,* for Ned, there was no habit of discarding. There was only expansion. "Psychosis," supposedly, according to Ned's notes for his supplement, can encompass manic-depressive and epileptic psychoses and all their subtypes. He found nine kinds of "alcoholic psychosis."[6] I want to warn him: *At this point, if you change your thesis to alcoholism, you will never finish writing your book.*

I learned that you cannot write your book by listing everything you have ever heard. That will become a hypno-saga at best.

Here is a list of reasons why.

NOTES TO
"IMPULSE, OBSESSION, DOUBT"

[1] Lajos Egri. *The Art of Dramatic Writing: Its Basis in the Creative Interpretation of Human Motives.* (1942) New York: Touchstone, 1972. p. 1.
[2] Egri, *ibid.,* p. 8.
[3] MS Cumming, *Eunuchry,* "Text," black folders, Vol. 15.
[4] Abby Covert. How to Make Sense of Any Mess. Amazon, 2014.
[5] Egri, *op. cit.,* p. 22.
[6] MS Cumming, *Eunuchry,* "Text," black folders, Vol. 15.

MONSTER MANUSCRIPTS

A dragon within the human imagination, wrote Jorge Luis Borges and Margarita Guerrero, is "a *necessary* monster" as evidenced by the recurrence of dragon tales "in many latitudes and ages."[1] The dragon resides in the collective unconscious of all humanity.

So, too, is the Oedipal complex, according to 1930s psychologists. Probably in the later part of the decade, Ned transcribed a passage from Geza Roheim, who had claimed that tribal rituals for male puberty (Roheim used the word "savage" to refer to such people) are designed to mitigate the unconscious aggression of sons toward fathers. The son's fear of being castrated by the father is further "socialized" into fear of being magically slain by "the sorcerer who can kill people," and the evil magician eventually is interpreted as a "divine king" who reveals "the whole ontogenetic and phylogenetic infancy of mankind."[2]

TEN PAST NOON

That's some tarot reading, indeed.

"An illusion is rooted in reality but does not become a reality in the mind," Dan Barker said. "A delusion is not rooted in reality but becomes a reality in the mind."[3]

I don't know how old Ned was when he became acquainted with the frustrating obtuseness of medical castrators, nor do I know who in his family might have brought him to see the surgeon. But the late 1930s, more generally, may have been one of those times when much of humanity began to feel its own helplessness in the face of its aggression toward itself.

Though a mythical creature does not exist, the idea of it may be instructive. In his 2001 *Hermaphrodeities*, Raven Kaldera explains that he

> does not attempt to separate ancient and therefore "legitimate" myths from "illegitimate" ones borne of personal revelation, since I believe that any myth and symbol that is associated with a transgendered deity or archetype has something to tell us, if only about the society we transgendered people have to survive in, or the value in which we are held in varying cultures.[4]

Some investigations of a beast are scientific and historical in nature; in those, the question of whether the beast ever existed is exactly the point at issue. Other investigations are about how stories of a beast anchor to the real world in some other way, regardless of whether the beast existed and of what value the stories have for us.

With imagination, we can sketch a monster we've never seen. The "palaeontologist," Sabine Baring-Gould wrote in 1865, "has constructed the labyrinthodon," an early amphibian, "out of its foot-prints in marl, and one splinter of bone." She hoped to similarly describe werewolves "although I have no chained were-wolf before me which I may sketch and describe from life."[5] The language we use creates what exists. "The methodology of science creates a wolf," wrote Barry Holstun Lopez, "just as surely as does the metaphysical vision of a native American, or the enmity of a cattle baron of the nineteenth century."[6] The animal is physical, but the role the animal plays for us is partly made of our own thoughts and feelings.

"This will always be a story about the limits of what's known, or maybe of what can be known," Gemma Files wrote. The story is "open to interpretation, not so much because it has missing pieces, but because missing pieces are all it was ever made from."[7]

Some people seriously maintain "that the ten elementary numbers and the twenty-two letters of the alphabet," as according to the *Sefer Yezirah*, "were the instruments by which the Almighty created the world."[8]

In *The Magic Mountain*, the residents make

their own Ouija board by placing their hands on a wine glass that glides across a table toward letters of the alphabet. *Will the spirit answer questions? Will the spirit reveal the face of a deceased friend? Yes, yes.* But what to ask? Whom to conjure? No one wants to request any specific friend. They all feel it "unthinkable," the author explained, as, "at bottom, and boldly confessed, the desire does not exist…What we call mourning for our dead is perhaps not so much grief at not being able to call them back as it is grief at not being able to want to do so."[9]

The writer begins with someone else's archive carts and his own blank page. He could write "nothing or almost anything."

Heavy cart. Where to start?

Maybe Ned was on hiatus for a while. Working a job, traveling, doing anything other than being stuck in a room with a metastasizing manuscript, almightily creating a world of endless classification and loneliness. Pulling back a bit to allow for a better creation.

Had he ever finished anything, really? He raced through prep school and didn't finish college or graduate school, nor his Deep Springs or St. George's teaching assignments, and his engineering career was short-lived. He probably did not go to the Canadian flying corps after announcing that he would.

Had he ever ejaculated? Had he ever discussed it with anyone?

TUCKER LIEBERMAN

People are allowed to go on hiatus. And they will go on hiatus even if they are not given permission.

Bess Rahner, the widow of Harry Houdini, had always kept a candle burning for him. She finished her tenth annual séance attempting to communicate with his spirit. He had never responded. She snuffed out the candle.

NOTES TO "MONSTER MANUSCRIPTS"

[1] Jorge Luis Borges and Margarita Guerrero, *The Book of Imaginary Beings [El libro de los seres imaginarios]* (1967), translated by Andrew Hurley. The quotation is from the foreword by the authors (1954). New York: Viking, 2005. p. xii.

[2] "Psycho-Analysis and Anthropology" by Geza Roheim. Printed in Stindor Lorand. *Psycho-Analysis Today: Its Scope and Function.* London: George Allen & Unwin, 1932. This may be a reprinted excerpt from Geza Roheim's *Animism, Magic and the Divine King* (1930).
https://archive.org/stream/psychoanalysisto032422mbp/psychoanalysisto032422mbp_djvu.txt
Accessed August 31, 2019.
Quoted in: MS Cumming, *Eunuchry,* "Text," black folders, Vol. 15.

[3] Dan Barker. *Free Will Explained: How Science and Philosophy Converge to Create a Beautiful Illusion.* New York: Sterling, 2018. p. 61.

[4] Raven Kaldera. *Hermaphrodeities: The Transgender Spirituality Workbook.* USA: Xlibris, 2001. p. 123.

[5] Sabine Baring-Gould. *The Book of Were-Wolves.* London: Smith, Elder & Co, 1865. Chapter I.

[6] Barry Holstun Lopez. *Of Wolves and Men.* (Originally, New York: Simon and Schuster, 1978.) Touchstone, 1995. p 203.

[7] Gemma Files. *Experimental Film.* Toronto, Canada: ChiZine, 2015. p. 238.

[8] "Jewish Mysticism." H. Sperling. *Aspects of the Hebrew Genius.* ed. Leon Simon. London: George Routledge & Sons, Ltd. New York: Block Publishing Co. 1910. p. 156.

[9] Thomas Mann. *The Magic Mountain* (originally S. Fischer Verlagberlin, 1924). Translated from the German by H. T. Lowe-Porter. England: A. Wehaten and Co., Exeter, 1971. pp. 660, 664, 674-5.

MOLOSSUS

Each of us has a worldview whether we are aware of it or not; to deny that it exists is just to be unwilling to question it.[1] And we must question it. Why be afraid to judge our methods and our motivations for our perceptions? Our awareness of our mental shortcomings may at least help us escape the room.

Directing our attention is a way of managing our identity and sense of place in the world. No matter how "tightly attentive" we are to what we fixate on, said Ram Dass and Paul Gorman, it's not the case that "everything else disappear[s] from awareness"; we just don't "get totally lost in identifying with it."[2]

When we direct our attention, we are beginning to choose our worldview.

TEN PAST NOON

Usually, we don't know exactly what others want. We only know that they "live in a state of want," Ben Kafka writes, and that "they seek explanations for why they can't get what they want. When we can't get our wants met, we at least want an explanation."[3]

Sometimes the problem is that we cannot see or grasp the problem. The problem casts an unruly demonic shadow. Henry Adams, the history professor at Harvard, third-personed himself in his autobiography: "Did he himself quite know what he meant? Certainly not! If he had known enough to state his problem, his education would have been complete at once."[4] If we do not have questions, then, no matter how much information we gather, we will never find answers. Our search will yield only "ignorance… accumulate[d] in the form of inert facts."[5]

Other times, we identify the problem on which we wish to labor, but we do not understand why it should be of interest. "It is sad but common for a graduate student to work her dissertation problem through to completion while never knowing," Jeff Schmidt demurred, "its social origin."[6] In other words, the student might not realize what outside forces cause her to ask the question and shape the way she asks it. If this is so, then she will likely also fail to realize how that bit of ancestral wisdom would have made it easier to ask her question and thus to complete her dissertation.

TUCKER LIEBERMAN

#########

In one of L. L. Nunn's final addresses to the boys at Deep Springs, he said:

> His [an individual's] active, conscious effort plays but a small part. His environment and, above all, the quiet listening to God speaking to his soul,— the being led without effort, but with thoughtful reasoning, step by step,— create his character, his real being.
>
> Those of you who have read Hawthorne's "Great Stone Face" will understand my meaning when I say that the passive creates more than the active. This is because man is created in the image of God, is in touch with his Creator, and is separated from Him by too much activity.[7]

That last bit is a manifesto taking a side in an old spiritual debate: contemplation over action. Indeed, while the act of writing makes someone a writer, we often need to take a step back and contemplate our underlying motivations, fascinations, and problems.

If I am providing advice, which I am, Ned should not have been writing to librarians and scholars asking for yet another photostat of a tangentially relevant article in languages he didn't read, especially not if those collaborators didn't care and were charging him ten dollars he didn't have. That was useless activity. He should have been getting in touch with himself—that form of "passive creation," to coin a phrase off Nunn—and then actively telling people: "This is why I care." He should have found other people who also cared. The closest he got, perhaps, were Barnette Miller and N. M. Penzer. They cared because they were interested in the Turkish seraglio, architecturally and historically. They may have cared less about genders and bodies. Miller didn't need help writing her book (she was merely waiting for her publisher to resolve its financial problems), and Penzer only wrote a chapter on eunuchs because he felt it was obligatory. Ned needed to find people who were more like him and shared his motivation. Dr. Engle cared about bodies, but he wasn't a psychologist.

First person: The importance of talking about who you are. It may seem simple—selfish and self-centered, even, with shifting standards that don't require any particular field of expertise—and yet when you finally allow yourself to do it, it may be difficult. You are never conscious of all the parts of yourself. When you start to become conscious of them, other people will object, and systems will toss up barriers.

###########

The idea of authenticity is immediately problematic because, the moment you start to think about it, your behavior becomes more performative and thus less authentic. Your family's authentic cuisine, to take an example, is whatever your parents and grandparents ate. It's a conservative fiction, the idea that nothing has changed and that you are performing the past as it always was. You can't reproduce your own history perfectly because the ingredients may not be available, the food may not be healthy for you anymore, and the people with whom you're having dinner want something else, so you adapt. Authenticity is in the past and you're in the present. Or, rather, authenticity invokes past and present simultaneously and makes a virtue of nostalgia. But what's here now is never exactly what was; everything is always modernizing. The backward-looking glance yields details and generates feelings that can never be recreated.

Something like that happens with gender and sexuality, although, in that case, authenticity is said to reside in some invisible homunculus, a little man behind the curtain, seated in your center of true being, while part of you already knows that you are a hall of mirrors. There's no homunculus. Your real authentic self is however you're living right now. There is nothing to search for. Yet you keep reaching into your own emptiness looking for that homunculus so you can mimic it and become "more truly yourself." It's an act. The more you worry about authenticity, the more you're performing an imagined version of yourself. Authentic is how you are when you stop worrying whether you are existing correctly.

That's a problem of self-awareness. You have to be aware enough to recognize and label your past behavior and to judge whether your present behavior matches it. But you can't do this too self-consciously or you will have moved from simply *being* who you are to *performing* who you are. Your authentic nature is supposed to be your givenness. If you have to seek it out, evaluate it, and choose it, what makes it different from anything else that wasn't yours to begin with? Authenticity is self-contradictory for this reason: the moment you identify a part of yourself and label it "authentic," you make a conscious choice to own it, and then it's no longer given but chosen.

This contributes to the excitement around the idea of "gender performativity," a phrase that Judith Butler made popular thirty years ago.[8] To the extent that gender is a social role to which we must conform, we perform at least parts of our gender, and most of us are already aware that we do so. We do it to please our family and our bosses, and we inculcate it to the next generation of children and employees. Confusion arises when we remain attached to the idea that our gender identity is a "true self," for how could we "perform" that?

I suspect the desire for authenticity is the desire to return to a childlike, innocent state of "just being" in the years before personal identity becomes crowded with questions and problems, or to escape to an idealized era where there never was and never will be any demand to conform.

Yet somehow we go on living authentically. We do it when we trust ourselves. For transgender people, the way we exist often leverages "knowledge systems unrecognized by colonial authority," C. Riley Snorton said. What we already know about our own lives may challenge "transsexuality as a development narrative" that requires "certain medical surgeries and legal recognition."[9] Even if we do happen to want surgery and legal recognition, we can still challenge an external narrative that says we are *supposed* to want it.

Other people's narratives about us don't have to define our fate. Prejudices and demands often affect us, but they are not a logically inevitable part of the cosmos. There is a possible world in which these hurdles, which other humans have imagined into being, don't exist or aren't controlling us.

Chase Strangio, a lawyer who argued for transgender rights at the Supreme Court in 2019, explained in an interview that the 20th-century gay rights movement's focus on the immutability of gay sexuality was part of a strategy to pursue legal protections. There's a compromise involved in negotiating one's own survival with a constitutional court: the U.S. legal system was "foundationally about preserving chattel slavery," Strangio admitted, and "every intervention within this system is always going to be harmful in some way."[10] Legal rights are "this notion that the legal system sets forth for you," and because of that, in his analysis, part of queer people's collective attempt to become "a coherent legal subject" that can be granted rights has been the making of blanket generalizations that *gay people were born that way*.[11] A group defined by an immutable feature with which they were born is a group whose legal rights can be coherently discussed. The "born this way" narrative may be politically necessary for gay people, but it may simultaneously be psychologically false. The story spun for the sake of winning public dignity may then have to be unspun to regain the private dignity of understanding the truth about oneself.

Bisexual and transgender people's narratives were often bluntly cut from these political arguments because the idea of immutability doesn't apply as neatly to our lives. But why should that call our experiences into question? What about human experience is ever cleanly defined?

For example, "we actually organize society based on a self-determination of gender," not a biological determination of it, as Strangio pointed out. "We don't show an ID, and we certainly don't show our genitals, when we walk in the bathroom." The social rule has always operated this way. It wasn't created by transgender people. Those who suddenly claim to want to enforce their own notions of biologically-based gender in an attempt to control transgender people may assume "that their rule is neat and our rule is messy. But the reality is that it's all messy."[12] Political arguments that center biological sex are sometimes phrased like attempts to return to a past when everything was obvious, nothing was ambiguous, and commonsense interpretations reigned. This past never existed; the rhetoric is a reactionary attack on transgender people.

The thicker the air grows with political attacks, the more distant authentic self-understanding begins to feel. Transgender people are often asked to justify our gender identity, and then, having provided a justification, we are often criticized for having described our gender in a stereotypical way and thereby allegedly having reinforced the same boring sexism that has always affected everyone else. ("It's as if it's somehow trans people's fault that gender exists," Strangio said.)[13] But how should the transgender person have responded to the original question? The very demand to *Explain what your label means* seems to prompt the person to give a stereotype in the answer, since a new concept is always "contingent on the ones that were there before," especially if the speaker wants to be publicly comprehensible.[14]

An alternative response is for the transgender person just to let go of the existing concepts and refuse to answer the question on those terms. In that case, one might say that one's own gender doesn't need to be justified because everyone already has the knowledge of their gender inside themselves and should be trusted on that matter without being prompted to reassert existing stereotypes and social agreements. There may not be a pure, inner, "true self" of gender identity to which we can each be unfailingly authentic; nevertheless, we do know something about our own genders. Strangio said:

> 'How do you know what your gender is?' If you ask anyone that, they'll say, 'Well, I just know'…I know that about myself [as a trans person] too; it's just that no one believes me when I say it…the more you're challenged [about your gender], the harder it is to explain. And I think this is how we end up reifying these [gender binary] categories as well: through the doubt of the listener…We have to repeat a norm that is familiar [if we want] to be believed [when we assert our gender].[15]

The dilemma can occur with all sorts of choices and identities. We may have to choose something minor, like whether to wear yellow or purple, or more significant, like whether to argue cases for the prosecution or defense. Does our color preference reflect something essential and unchanging about us, or is it something we picked up from social cues and acculturation? Does our argumentation style reflect our true personality, or is the idea of a plaintiff and a defendant itself a social construct? Yellow and purple may be on opposite ends of a color wheel, and plaintiff and defendant may be on opposite ends of a courtroom, but do we always have to consider them as a binary? More to the point, I am thinking about what happens when someone interrogates us about why we picked a certain color or accepted a certain client. In our response, either we invoke a bunch of common assumptions about The Meaning of Things, or else we ditch the assumptions and just say, *Because I wanted to, so I did.*

Adding details can make the problem thornier. "What color shall I wear?" might sound as though it can be a gender-neutral aesthetic question, but, in the actual world, there is no color-in-the-abstract or clothing-in-the-abstract. That's a trick of language. In the actual world, there are physical articles of clothing, and they are often gendered, and that is probably how the question presents itself on any particular morning: "What *necktie* shall I wear?"

Backing up and asking bigger questions can also be dizzying. When the question is broadened— *Why do lawyers wear neckties, and why only those who are men? Why be a lawyer at all?*—the discussion becomes more diffuse. The question of identity and choice is now being asked not just of any one individual but of all individuals within a cultural context.

TEN PAST NOON

The difficulty in answering remains the same, however, whether we're talking about individuals in their private interiority or in community: It is hard to explain why we are who we are.

The questions aren't really answerable because they are meta-questions, lightly disguised, about whether rationalization itself is valid. We are really asking if the "question-and-answer" language game makes sense, if philosophy is possible, and if personal and cultural worldviews are likely to change in response to new information.

Argument itself is a construct. The notion that we have to justify our corner of reality (or to explain how we perceive and inhabit that reality) is also a construct. The argument, undergirded by the belief that we must participate in the argument, is a construct that co-creates the reality about which we are arguing.

We spend much of our time on earth rationalizing our decisions, and we often forget that most of this analysis is done in retrospect. Even when we haven't taken an action yet, the decision may already have been made—we just aren't aware that we've decided. Rationalization is an important human activity, but it probably doesn't mean what we think it means, and we are never going to argue it into becoming something else.

#########

TUCKER LIEBERMAN

The popular debate over whether queerness is inborn is sometimes a proxy for a debate over determinism and free will. Many (perhaps most) people argue that determinism and free will are compatible, or that, as Dan Barker argues, that these concepts apply to such different areas that there's nothing that could be incompatible between them anyway. Our judgments and our behavior are actually determined; free will is the subjective, conscious impression we feel when we judge our behavior. Free will is a happy illusion. It's closely tied to our ability to argue. "Any action that you *decide* to take only requires free will if you need to justify your decision. Otherwise, you just do it," Barker says. "Free will is irrelevant—it doesn't even exist—until you judge behavior. It is a retroactive product of judgment."[16]

I have never personally advanced the argument that my queerness is caused by queer genes or a queer brain. As far as I know, geneticists and neurologists have not yet conclusively identified that queerness is to be found in genes and brains. I am not a scientist and am unqualified to weigh in on the subject. Still less could I assert that, whatever this biological queerness is, that I am an example of it, i.e. that it is definitely to be found in *my* genes and brain. It is possible that other people have certain biological markers of queerness and that I do not share them. I am unable to see into my own brain. My eyes don't roll back that far. If I were to say, "I married a man because I have the gay gene," or "I changed my sex because I have a male brain," I'd be making a statement I'm unable to support or defend.

It is a claim I do not wish to make for five reasons:

Because whether I am respected (in human rights needs and in ordinary social contexts) should not be dependent on whether queerness exists as an objectively verifiable feature in biology and on whether I have that biology. Queerness doesn't need to be "proven" to be "excused."

Because queer biology might turn out to be a liability rather than a boon. People who are demonstrably queer in their biology (regardless of whether they behave queerly or admit to feeling queer) might be penalized. Someone might even attempt to erase queerness through eugenics. This concern does not seem far-fetched to me.

Because whether I consider myself queer wouldn't change based on my receipt of those biological test results, and hopefully other queer people would be similarly indifferent to the outcome of my test and we wouldn't use science to gatekeep each other's identities or cross each other off invitation lists for Pride March afterparties.

Because my experiences wouldn't change either: I *did* marry a man and I *did* change my sex regardless of whether I can explain why I did so.

Because the social understandings of queernesses change all the time, and sometimes a specific queerness emerges in mid-life due to a situation, decision, or insight. I wouldn't send anyone on a wild goose chase for biological markers for identities that are (at least for those individuals) cultural and conceptual, since to do so is to misunderstand the person's identity and to devalue their own explanations of it.

Because because because because because is a song lyric from Oz honoring manifest wizardry.

Why would I need my brain to have a sex? Who's ever going to see inside my brain? God? Do I *really* believe in God, or do I merely have an instrumental need for God to exist as a witness to bolster my claims about my sex?

I don't need to invent God for this. I already know my own gender. I won't reroute that inquiry to God. If people aren't listening to me about my own gender, they can start. *I just know.* This is an elementary fact on the ground. It is not a problem for upper management.

Nor do I find it productive to make statements about God in general. Is God man, woman, or genderless? How would we know, if we can't even agree on whether God exists? Who has the technology to find God and pinpoint God's gender? Why do we believe it's important to find out whether there is a God? Theology hasn't asserted (to my satisfaction, anyway) exactly what we're looking for and why we'd be looking for it, so I prefer to say that God probably doesn't exist and that our self-conceptions and our human rights certainly shouldn't depend on our beliefs about whether God exists. When people cite God's existence to win arguments that should properly be about something else and should be handled on other grounds, it always sounds like a dominance game to me. *"I just know, because God, whom I also just know."*

It is possible for two people to say "I just know" regarding their own identities and experiences and for them to listen and accept each other. That is not a dominance game. It is an attempt to dominate when one person adds, "Because God," if that is an attempt to shut down what the other person is saying by invoking God as a partisan referee.

It is as if some people say, "Everyone is born heterosexual, because God," and others counter, "Well, no, some are born homosexual, because God." Never mind the God part: I don't want to make this counterargument that some people are born gay because I don't actually know this. I don't believe—despite my body being made of genes—that I know much about them. Scientists have this knowledge; I don't. But I don't need to understand genetics to believe in the importance of human dignity. I can find other grounds for human dignity. This also frees me from committing myself to categories like "heterosexual" and "homosexual" that don't even stay fixed in culture for more than a decade at a time.

"On résiste à l'invasion des armées; on ne résiste pas à l'invasion des idées," Victor Hugo wrote in 1852.[17] We can resist an invading army, but we have less choice when the culture introduces a new concept.

I am neither a theologian nor a scientist, and I have no confidence that I could ever find divinity or queerness in anyone's genes or brains. I understand divinity and queerness as concepts that may not have any footprints in nature. We don't need those footprints to be who we are and to know what we know. Some concepts, even without tangible footprints as evidence, are useful.

Divinity is a concept I can't find a use for. The world has value in itself, and that's that. There's no need to refer to any other type of value that is unpinpointable and somewhere-else by definition.

Queerness, though, is a useful concept to me, because it is something we can see play out in countless interactions. Queerness arises as a byproduct when we assert what we "just know" about ourselves and when we lose the dominance game that our conversation partner is playing with us.

TEN PAST NOON

Authenticity is not just about our idea of our "true selves." It is also about how we navigate bumps in the road, how we deal with people who are in our way, and how we talk about this. Sometimes people want to hurt us for talking about it. Facing this work is an existential dread in itself, because, if we fail, we dishonor the importance of our own perspectives.

For Ned, speaking about himself would have been hard because—despite his overall social privilege—his project on physical sex and gender roles (with its inevitable references to sexuality) presented particular risks. During his lifetime, sexual activity between men was a felony in every U.S. state.[18] Although this charge was infrequently prosecuted, it nevertheless enabled blackmail and weaponized shame. The social threat was so powerful that it constrained people's behavior often without having to show itself in court. Obscenity laws were enforced against publishers in New York, as the state had its own New York Society for the Suppression of Vice, and some of the booksellers Ned would likely have had to contact directly were being arrested.[19] There is no way he remained unaware of these laws while obtaining twelve hundred printed sources about eunuchs. It is possible that he was threatened. Maybe that's why he didn't publish. And if he faced this sort of oppressive challenge, it would be inescapable for us to consider it as a possible factor in his death.

Which leads me to wonder why he did not write directly about the challenges of his time.

If I could visit him in that moment, I'd bring an MP3 player with a downloaded file of Chase Strangio's interview. Bringing more written material to Ned would feel to me as though I were bringing beer and cake to someone who already drinks and eats more than enough, but maybe listening to an oral argument would help him move forward in a different way.

I don't know how MP3 players work. Maybe they have little Victrola motors inside.

I'd let him listen to it over and over until the battery ran out and the light turned off.

#########

The rhythm of the words *"I just know."* In Greek and Latin poetry, this metrical foot—three long syllables—was called a "molossus." That's the name of an ancient Greek ethnic group that disappeared after its defeat by the Romans twenty-two centuries ago. Why is the metrical foot called that? Because a molossus *just is* a molossus. Listen to it.

In English, we perceive syllables more by their "stress" than by their "length," but the idea is similar and the label transfers well enough for my purposes. When we have occasion to say *"I just know,"* we are drawing out and stressing those syllables. In such a situation, we have decided to stop categorizing and arguing. *I—just—know!*

TEN PAST NOON

We point to the thing itself or to the one who perceives it; we point to the phenomenon of knowing, clear as day.

This is our molossus. We can hear it in our voices.

We don't usually "just know" the interiority of other people, or at least, we don't excel at it (unless we are empaths of the highest order), but we are very good at "just knowing" things about ourselves. We know that we have a sexual orientation, a gender identity, a body, a lived experience. We know if these things have stayed the same or if they have changed. We know where we came from. We know what we want. This might be simple for us, but if it's complicated, so much the better for "just knowing": we definitely know that "it's complicated." We also "just know" a few things about the social and political structures and the natural and artificial environments of which we are part.

There are known things that don't benefit from argument. *I just know* that I am transgender. *I just know* that I live as a man in society—that this is possible and achievable and actually works for me. *I just know* that this doesn't hurt anyone else. What is argument going to do here? Would it serve any purpose other than to challenge my feelings and experiences and to posit false grievances against me? What if I were allowed to start with what *I just know* and conserved my energy to debate something else?

I wish to coin this new application of the word "molossus" to mean our personal starting gate for what we think we know about the world as we relate to it. It is a bit of academic fun. "Ontology" is the term for a theory of being; "epistemology" is the term for a theory of knowledge. Occasionally someone uses "onto-epistemology" to refer to thinking-about-being-and-knowing. These words are not much fun. "Molossus" is shorter while still sounding pretentious. It sounds like "molasses," which contributes to tasty desserts but can be unpleasantly strong when tasted directly. And, like molasses, thinking-about-being-and-knowing is a fluid that moves so very slowly that it might be mistaken for a solid.

≠≠≠≠≠≠≠≠≠

Here's how I would use "molossus" in a story. The story is about a certain argumentation game.

Alpha Bear says, "Really? You think you know something?" and Beta Wolf says, "Yes." Alpha Bear says, "I'm not so sure you do. Here's my molossus of *'I just know.'* Go figure it out and come back and explain it to me." Alpha Bear throws their molossus across the East River, and Beta Wolf has to dogpaddle all the way to Rikers Island, fetch and bite down on the molossus, and carry it back in their teeth. This can take years. If their tail is not wagging when they return, they

TEN PAST NOON

will be yelled at for having a bad attitude. Meanwhile, Alpha Bear has given themselves the uninterrupted opportunity to do things like build railroads and make money. Beta Wolf has instead had quality time to reflect on why their own molossus doesn't taste like Alpha Bear's molossus, and they are soaking wet.

"Are you still on that?" Alpha Bear asks with surprise when Beta Wolf crawls out of the East River. Alpha Bear had forgotten that Beta Wolf even existed.

"Yes. Here is something," says Beta Wolf, "that I've learned from this exercise: What you know and what I know were never in binary opposition."

"I was never really interested in your ideas anyway," says Alpha Bear. "I just threw something across the river to get you out of my hair so I could focus on my actual work. I am still right, and you are still wrong."

Beta Wolf has some opinions about that. "What we each know about ourselves is, I maintain, not contradictory. You are right about yourself, and I am right about myself. Rather, it was your request for me to 'go fetch,' and my perception that I was compelled to engage with your request, that put us in opposition and that created a binary of the dominant and the oppressed. You are acting as if you assume me to be wrong, and your behavior reinforces your perception of my wrongness. Despite your attitude, *I still know* what I always knew."

"Why do you people talk about your molossus all the time?" Alpha Bear sneers.

The question is infuriating. Alpha Bear was the one who, long ago, had asked Beta Wolf to explain their differences. Beta Wolf takes a deep breath and points out the obvious: "You, too, have a molossus. You were just asserting that your knowledge is correct, and, in doing so, you showed me that molossus."

"No, I live without a molossus," Alpha Bear insists. "I threw it into the river years ago."

≠≠≠≠≠≠≠≠≠

It is a problem to alternately insist-on-and-then-deny what one already knows, and this behavior can mean different things. But once you admit that you already have your own answer, that yours counts as much as anyone else's, and that your truth is not diminished just because they are not listening to you, what do you do with your answer? How does it get you where you need to go?

Zakiyyah Jackson asks what "non-self-identical onto-epistemology" would look like: how we would understand the "relation of being to knowing" if not by the cruelty and constraint of "our antiblack present" and instead by "the conditions of possibility for representation itself."[20] To phrase it more simply and according to my own understanding: When we say we *just know* something, we are often talking about ourselves and our immediate plight. We are invoking ourselves, and the subject matter we claim to know is basically identical with whatever we're worried about. We might, however, consider pointing our being-and-knowing toward a vision of a better future in which we will not be defined by our suffering. We might consider imagining how, and what, we would *just know* in that future.

A future in which people could have conversations that aren't constructed as cruel games in which a person in a socially constructed beta role needs to beg for equal treatment while an alpha assumes that even listening to the request constitutes a threat to their own status.

A future in which this is not endless work.

※※※※※※※※※

Argumentation is important and valuable. There is a role for it. I believe this. This belief is part of my identity as a person who studied philosophy and journalism. I might have what is called *motivated reasoning* to believe this. I want arguments to matter. I want good arguments to count more than bad ones.

However, as I previously mentioned, what we think of as "reasoning" is often just rationalization cast by the shadow of a decision or action that has already been made. Furthermore, as also previously mentioned, our sense of "free will" may be yet another downstream result. Our rationalizations and the illusion that we ever had free choice are "retroactive products," to use Dan Barker's phrase.

It feels harder to distinguish good and bad arguments if I begin with the assumption that even my opinions about logic and rhetoric are predetermined. Admitting the loss of a free will I once believed in—my own, and that of others—leaves me a little less motivated to argue about arguing. Even as a philosopher and journalist, I am ready to stop arguing-about-arguing.

A determined universe still leaves room for this form of human dignity, importance, and confidence: *I just know* some things. *You just know* some things. We may not have to fight over this. We may not have to dispute who knows their stuff more intensely. The knowledge we feel serves as a ground for our sense of dignity, importance, and confidence. It is our home base. We have different home bases. It is OK to "just know" what we know. It is OK for other people to "just know" something different. We can listen patiently. We can trust and believe. We can have a conversation that doesn't turn into a game to reassert who is in charge.

From this place of dignity, importance, and confidence, we can begin to make good arguments and judgments. These arguments and judgments are about something more than the thought processes that create arguments and judgments; instead, they move us forward. We are led to the beautiful illusion that we have free will. This is one way to be free.

⧣⧣⧣⧣⧣⧣⧣⧣⧣⧣

The path is not always straight. Sometimes it doubles back.

Sometimes the ground is shiny, reflective, a black mirror of sorts, except where the leaves have papered it over. Little bubbles of methane pop through slowly. It's a tar pit. It will suck you in. I know it because I have pulled on an asphalt sample in a museum and found it difficult. I have a muscle memory of this. The tar pit is a chronotope that is the very opposite of an escaping hot air balloon. If your feet are stuck in the tar pit, you cannot tap your heels and go back to Kansas ever. You had better walk all the way around the far edge of this trap.

⧣⧣⧣⧣⧣⧣⧣⧣⧣⧣

"Molossus" is also the name of a rare dog breed. These are massive guard dogs. They stand up to wolves and probably to bears. They have opinionated barks.

⧣⧣⧣⧣⧣⧣⧣⧣⧣⧣

You have to work to honor the importance of your perspective and if you fail then you dishonor it and then you have to talk about the dishonor to honor it. You fall off the horse and you get back on again and then sometimes you fall off again.

The train goes from New York to Boston and back again.

We are on a loop here.

NOTES TO "MOLOSSUS"

[1] "The Twee Revolution." James Parker. *The Atlantic.* July/August 2014. p. 36–38.

[2] Ram Dass and Paul Gorman. *How Can I Help?: Stories and Reflection on Service.* (1985) New York: Alfred A. Knopf, 2004. pp. 108–109.

[3] Ben Kafka. *The Demon of Writing: Powers and Failures of Paperwork.* New York: Zone Books, 2012. pp. 78-79.

[4] Henry Adams. *The Education of Henry Adams.* The Massachusetts Historical Society, 1918. "Chapter XXII: Chicago (1893)."

[5] Adams, *ibid.,* "Chapter XXV: The Dynamo and the Virgin (1900)."

[6] Jeff Schmidt. *Disciplined Minds: A Critical Look at Salaried Professionals and the Soul-Battering System that Shapes Their Lives.* Rowman & Littlefield, 2000.

[7] Stephen Bailey. *L. L. Nunn: A Memoir.* Ithaca, N.Y.: Printed for Telluride Association, 1933. p. 12. Boxes 1 and 2.

[8] Judith Butler. *Gender Trouble.* Routledge, 1990.

[9] C. Riley Snorton. *Black on Both Sides: A Racial History of Trans Identity.* Minneapolis: University of Minnesota Press, 2017.

[10] "Trans Rights with Chase Strangio." September 3, 2019 podcast episode of "Why Is This Happening? with Chris Hayes." 23:30-25:00 https://feeds.megaphone.fm/with

[11] "Trans Rights with Chase Strangio." *ibid.,* 17:30-19:00

[12] "Trans Rights." *ibid.,* 1:01:30-1:02:45

TEN PAST NOON

[13] "Trans Rights." *ibid.,* 34:15-35:00
[14] "Trans Rights." *ibid.,* 35:00-35:15
[15] "Trans Rights." *ibid.,* 33:15-34:15, 34:45-35:15
[16] Dan Barker. *Free Will Explained: How Science and Philosophy Converge to Create a Beautiful Illusion.* New York: Sterling, 2018. p. 29.
[17] Victor Hugo. *Histoire d'un Crime [The History of a Crime].* (Written 1852, published 1877.) Translated by T.H. Joyce and Arthur Locker. Conclusion, chapter X.
[18] "…homosexual acts remained felonious in every state of the United States until well past mid-century under nineteenth-century sodomy laws…The legal tide began to turn in 1961…"
David F. Greenberg. *The Construction of Homosexuality.* University of Chicago, 1988. Chapter 11, "Gay Liberation," p. 455.
https://books.google.com.co/books?id=RKhFRgR-1awC&pg=PA455&lpg=PA455
Accessed February 22, 2020.
[19] See: Jay A. Gertzman. *Bookleggers and Smuthounds: The Trade in Erotica, 1920-1940.* University of Pennsylvania, 1999.
[20] Jackson, Z.I. (2016). Sense of things. *Catalyst: Feminism, Theory, Technoscience,* 2 (2),1-48. Pages quoted: pp. 9-10.
https://www.academia.edu/33860733/Sense_of_Things
Accessed November 11, 2019.

END OF A DECADE

The Constitutional amendment prohibiting the sale of alcohol had been repealed in 1933.

By the Scarsdale train station, in Ned's neighborhood where he spent the 1930s writing, a large new apartment building was planned to accommodate the suburb's expanding population.[1]

A short story set in this era said, "A las doce había empezado el calor. El tren se detuvo diez minutos en una estación sin pueblo para abastecerse de agua." *By twelve the heat had begun. The train stopped for ten minutes to take on water at a station where there was no town.*[2] Gabriel García Márquez would publish the story, "La siesta del martes," in 1962. It imagines a fictional town in Colombia in which the midday heat is so severe that the townspeople require a five-hour siesta. They cannot function normally under those conditions.

The philosopher Mikhail Bakhtin had

previously—just when Stalin was taking leadership of the Communist Party—been the victim of an anti-intellectual purge, but he had avoided a labor camp due to a bone disease that caused severe pain in his leg. He was now freshly out of Kazakhstan exile and taught briefly at a university in the Mordovian Autonomous Soviet Socialist Republic. Fearing he would be caught in another purge, he resigned the university position and moved to a town near Moscow in the fall of 1937.[3] He began writing his essay, "Forms of Time and of the Chronotope in the Novel: Notes Toward a Historical Poetics."

On Easter Sunday 1937, Robert Irwin entered the East 50th Street Manhattan home of the family with whom he'd once lodged, the Gedeons, and murdered the mother, a daughter, and their current lodger. Irwin went on the run for three months. "HE MAY BE MASQUERADING IN FEMALE ATTIRE!" the magazine *Inside Detective* warned. (He wasn't. The magazine was clearly attempting to code his villainy as queer, marking him specifically as a eunuch[4] or as a transgender person before the word "transgender" even existed.) Irwin surrendered in June. Would his defense lawyer pursue an insanity defense? *"Res ipsa loquitur,"* the lawyer answered with calculated restraint; "the thing speaks for itself." Before the trial began, a *Daily News* editorial remonstrated that Irwin should be executed or sterilized.[5]

On May 6, 1937, a hundred miles to the

south, the hydrogen-filled Hindenburg airship exploded. It was ignited by static electricity as it landed. The ship had belonged to the Nazis.[6]

On July 24, 1937, Rudolph Johnson, the owner of the Scarsdale house where the Cummings lodged, was involved in a fight with his neighbor who lived around the corner. The neighbor called police for help, saying that Johnson had physically attacked him in his home. Later the same day, there was a fierce retaliation; Johnson reported that "four or five men had come to his home and attacked him, blackening his eyes and causing other injuries." Both assault victims were briefly treated at the hospital and reportedly agreed to settle.[7]

The year that Ned's landlord was assaulted in their home was the year that Ned stopped working on his manuscript. It was also around this time that Ned, his mother, and his sister moved out of the Johnsons' Scarsdale house where they had lived for a decade and returned to the city.[8]

David Gelernter writes:

> The brilliance of New York at the decade's close was a temporary thing and people knew it, as if the whole city had bustled momentarily into a shaft of sunlight on the floor of Penn Station's monumental waiting room and knew implicitly that it would be bustling right back out again soon. Ephemerality may

have intensified the era's beauty, as it does autumn's.[9]

Two private companies that ran the subways, the Interborough and the Brooklyn-Manhattan Transit, had financial difficulties in part because the city would not allow them to raise fares above a nickel. The city opened its own line, the Independent, and prepared to take over the other two lines.[10]

Forty-two-year-old Bakhtin's right leg was amputated on February 13, 1938. He would walk on crutches for the rest of his life. He finished writing his essay, "Forms of Time and of the Chronotope in the Novel: Notes Toward a Historical Poetics."[11]

The Peruvian poet César Vallejo died in Paris after predicting:

> Me moriré en París con aguacero,
> un día del cual tengo ya el recuerdo.
>
> *I will die in Paris, on a rainy day,*
> *on some day I can already remember.*

He felt disjointed:

> ...los húmeros me he puesto
> a la mala y, jamás como hoy, me he vuelto,
> con todo mi camino, a verme solo.
>
> *...I have put my upper arm bones on*
> *wrong, and never so much as today have*
> *I found myself*

with all the road ahead of me, alone.[12]

The War of the Worlds, the science fiction novel first published four decades earlier, became the basis for a radio broadcast the night before Halloween 1938. The performance was delivered in a "breaking news" style, as the reader claimed that Martians were attacking New York City with poison gas. The next day, newspapers took the opportunity to discredit radio as a form of mass communication, claiming—though perhaps without sufficient evidence—that the broadcast had caused panic in the streets.[13]

The multiple-murderer Robert Irwin was found sane enough to stand trial, pled guilty, and was put on a train to spend the rest of his life in Sing Sing prison.[14]

#########

The Cumming family—Ned, his sister Emily, and their mother Lucy—had two apartments: West 116th Street and East 43rd Street. All three of them were associated with both addresses.

The usual rent in the West 116th building was forty dollars per month.[15] It was a convenient location for Emily, who attended a secretarial program at Columbia's extension school in the Spring of 1939. It seems she did not enroll again in the fall, and she never graduated from the program, but she had clerical employment.[16]

The East 43rd Street neighborhood—a mile

TEN PAST NOON

from Times Square, less than a mile from St. Bartholomew's Church where Felix had married, on the East River, where the thirty-nine-story United Nations building had not yet risen—"was once one of the worst neighborhoods in the city," Jeffrey Deaver writes. At the end of the 19th century, in addition to coal yards and power plants, it featured cattle pens to support an unregulated industry of slaughterhouses, meatpacking, leather, and glue,[17] giving the neighborhood one of its nicknames, "Blood Alley." It was a dangerous place to live and work. The lovely brownstone homes built earlier in the 19th century, Harold Schechter explains, were used as "cheap boardinghouses for the foreign-born workers eking out a living at the waterside factories and abattoirs," although these began to gentrify again in the 1920s under the Vanderbilts and Rockefellers.[18] A real estate developer put up a dozen Tudor-style apartment buildings that faced away from the river. The Cummings, upon moving there in the late '30s, paid ninety dollars a month for a unit in a building called "The Hermitage."[19]

From their apartment, it was a five-minute walk to the river, and from there they could see the smallpox hospital on what was then called Welfare Island. There was an empty penitentiary there, too. A decade earlier, after performing a show called "Sex," the actress Mae West had spent a week at the penitentiary on a charge of corrupting the youth. It had just closed and reopened on another island farther north: Rikers.

Three neighborhood murderers had helped kick off a sudden public interest in sex crimes. Vera Stretz shot her lover Fritz Gebhardt in November 1935 (and was freed); John Fiorenza killed a randomly selected older woman, the novelist Nancy Titterton, in April 1936 (and went to the electric chair in less than a year); and then there was Robert Irwin's triple murder in April 1937. From this neighborhood epicenter, a morbid fascination spread across the nation. "Beginning in 1937, the boogeyman that haunted the American psyche was the 'sex fiend,'" Harold Schechter wrote, as "popular newsstand magazines...ran panic-inducing articles about the purported plague of psychopathic sex-murders."[20] In the summer of 1937, the mayor of New York City ordered the creation of a clinic on Rikers Island for sex offenders.[21]

Dorothy L. Sayers, a prolific English detective novelist of the '20s and '30s, offered up the literary criticism that murder mysteries should offer psychological depth as well as a technically adept storyline.[22] If people bother to read a book about anything, they should be stirred by it, she thought. She began to worry, too, that it may have a coarsening effect to treat dead bodies as mere props in stories. As her literary interest shifted to religious themes, she warned that Jesus would have been crucified by "not only the Nazis" but even by the liberal "internationalists" because every human ideal contains the mechanism for its own corruption. "Anyone would" have killed Jesus, she warned, "because it is our nature to do so."[23] Perhaps we all are in the murder mystery.

W. H. Auden, while in New York in 1939, wrote:

> I sit in one of the dives
> On Fifty-second Street
> Uncertain and afraid
> As the clever hopes expire
> Of a low dishonest decade...[24]

"When a man dies," Antoine de Saint-Exupéry wrote in *Wind, Sand and Stars* (1939), "an unknown world passes away."[25]

#########

German scientists had demonstrated nuclear fission with uranium. Hitler ordered Heisenberg to build the atom bomb.[26] Jewish towns in occupied Poland with populations under five hundred were disbanded and their residents were moved to urban ghettos that could be more efficiently exited, when the appointed time came, by mass transport.[27] The Jews would be asked to lift their feet and board the train.

#########

The Wizard of Oz came to theaters in the United States. At the beginning of the film, set in rural Kansas, a woman has obtained written legal permission to confiscate and destroy a little terrier. She rides away on her bicycle with her neighbor's dog in the rear basket, but the dog jumps out and runs back to its farm. Dorothy, the teenage owner of the dog, seizes her chance to leave with her pet to save its life.

Dorothy happens upon a wagon, painted with the advertisement: "Professor Marvel: Acclaimed by the Crowned Heads of Europe. Let him read your past, present and future in his crystal." The man begins to tell her future:

> "You're traveling in disguise? No, that's not right...You're going on a visit? No, I'm wrong...You're running away."
>
> "How did you guess?"
>
> "Professor Marvel never guesses, he knows. Now, *why* are you running away? No, no, now, don't tell me. They— they don't understand you at home. They don't appreciate you. You want to see other lands, big cities, big mountains, big oceans."
>
> "Why, it's just like you could read what was inside of me!"

She asks to travel with the professor to "see all the Crowned Heads of Europe." He reacts with surprise: "Do you know any? Oh, you mean—" he says, gesturing to his own advertisement. He says he'll ask his crystal for advice.

> "This is the same genuine magic authentic crystal used by the priests of Isis and

TEN PAST NOON

Osiris in the days of the pharaohs of Egypt, in which Cleopatra first saw the approach of Julius Caesar and Mark Anthony, and so on and so on. Now, you'd better close your eyes, my child, for a moment, in order to be better in tune with The Infinite. We can't do these things without reaching out into The Infinite."

While Dorothy's eyes are closed, he sneaks a peek at a photograph in her travel basket, which shows her standing outside her house with her aunt. He gazes into the crystal and begins to narrate her fortune. The aunt's existence is the boundary from which he supposes Dorothy's fate.

"What's this I see? A house with a picket fence, and a barn with a weathervane of a running horse."

"That's our farm!"

"There's a woman. She's wearing a polka-dot dress. Her face is careworn."

"That's Aunt Em."

"Yes, her name is *Emily*."

"That's right! What's she doing?"

"Well, I can't quite see—Why, she's crying. Someone has hurt her. Someone has just about broken her heart."

Worried about Aunt Em, Dorothy runs home under the darkening stormclouds, where the tornado catches up with her and her bedroom window frame is blown into her room, hitting her in the head. She begins to dream, stepping out of her black-and-white hometown into a parallel dream universe in Technicolor.

She journeys with dream friends, including the Tin Man, who seems like a pleasant fellow, but he says he has no heart.

When they find the long-sought, so-called "Wizard," he appears as an enormous green hologram like a Great Stone Face amidst fire and smoke.

"Do not arouse the wrath of the Great and Powerful Oz!" its voice booms through a speaker. "I said: Come back tomorrow!"

"If you were really great and powerful, you'd keep your promises!" Dorothy objects.

This is the dream version of Professor Marvel, who turns out to be only a little man hiding behind a curtain, puppeteering this hologram.

They reconcile with the Wizard in his human form. He gives the Tin Man a gift of a heart-shaped pocketwatch. The time is ten past noon.

The Wizard then climbs into a hot-air balloon to escort Dorothy back to Kansas. "I, your Wizard," he says with puffery to the adoring crowd, "*per ardua ad alta,*" a riff on the motto of the Royal Air Forces of Britain and Canada, "I am about to embark upon a hazardous and technically unexplainable journey into the outer stratosphere!" The balloon is secured by a rope

TEN PAST NOON

to a docking station. Dorothy's friends stand by to release the ropes at the appropriate moment, but a sudden distraction causes them to abandon their posts. The Tin Man, whose honorary heart is pinned to his breast (the time is *still* ten past noon—after all, this is a dream), actively and inexplicably unravels the knot as if mindlessly following some original order. He looks surprised at the result: The Wizard's balloon rises. Dorothy and her little dog were supposed to be in the basket for the journey home, but they are not. This is not the way for Dorothy to leave this story.

The Wizard, like Icarus flying toward the sun, waves and yells, "I can't come back! I don't know how it works! Goodbye, folks!"

"Goodbye!" the folks reply cheerfully.

Dorothy remains in No Time and No Place. Her magical guide invites her to tap her heels together three times, like a clock, and to say "there's No Place like home."

Our authenticity, our sense of self and home, is a continual pointing into thin air. But we do have selves and homes, even though they are made of concepts and don't pin well to time and space. For Dorothy, the incantation works. She's home.

TUCKER LIEBERMAN

Writing from Amsterdam in the summer of 1939, Felix Kittredge recommended to a family member the novel *Black Narcissus* by Rumer Godden.[28] It was about a fictional palace in the Himalayas that converts from a harem to an Anglican convent. One of the newly arrived nuns, an Irish woman, asks a dashing gentleman if he personally shot the birds whose feathers adorn his hat. The palace convent is a confusing, ethereal place, where, just walking, she feels as if she were "standing still and the air flowed past her and the ground spread away in rings under her feet." As she sounds the bell for Angelus at sunrise, another nun trips and falls to her death. She dreams of people who "had mirrors in the palms of their hands and they were talking to themselves."[29]

Freud died.

A couple months later, Samuel Dana Kittredge died, having named two of his nephews (Felix and the oldest Canfield boy, but not Ned), as executors of his will.[30]

> Failure is easy to measure. Failure is an event. Harder to measure is insignificance. A nonevent. Insignificance creeps, it dawns, it gives you hope, then delusion, then one day, when you're not looking, it's there, at your front door, on your desk, in the mirror, or not, not any of that, it's the lack of all that. One day, when you are looking, it's not looking, no

TEN PAST NOON

> one is. You lie in your bed and realize that if you don't get out of bed and into the world today, it is very likely no one will even notice.
>
> —Charles Yu, *How to Live Safely in a Science Fictional Universe*[31]

I don't know what was happening to Ned in 1940. Did he have a job change, a relationship change, a medication change? Did he have a paycheck at all, or was he deliberately blowing the last of his money on a greater sense of independence by helping his family maintain a second apartment? Was he living alone? Was he talking to his family? Was he spending a great deal of time buried in his manuscript—after all, he did have a few sources dated in the mid-to-late '30s—with great expectations of finishing and publishing it and earning money off it? Or did he leave it in a corner of his room, where the hulk of it sat, staring at him, threatening to mold?

H. I. Katibah, Ned's Arabic translator, self-published his book *The New Spirit in Arab Lands*.

Vichy France passed its Statut des Juifs, the laws depriving Jews of citizenship and the right to hold office.

"Some people sitting there ever since morning, / Other people missing their train by a minute," wrote Rabindranath Tagore, nearing the end of his life, about a train platform in India. "Who are those coming from one direction? / Who are those floating the other way?"[32]

Having been released from a concentration camp in the Pyrenees, Arthur Koestler remained in France and spent early 1940 completing a novel that imagined a trial of one of the Stalinist regime's own revolutionaries. In May, his girlfriend, Daphne Hardy, quickly translated it into English and sent it to London. The pair immediately fled France, making their separate ways to London. Koestler attempted suicide when he believed that Hardy's boat had been torpedoed.

In the summer, France surrendered to Germany.

How did it feel to Ned, having his grand "meaning of life" *oeuvre* pieced together from French and German sources, an investigation that none of his fellow Americans needed to read (in case they needed an excuse beyond not *wanting* to read it) at an hour in which they were realizing more practically grounded existential fears? On top of which, no one else had ever wanted to read about castration? And his favorite castration study, Dr. Johannes Lange's *Die Folgen der Entmannung Erwachsener*, turned out to belong, culturally, to the Nazis? How did that feel?

✂✂✂✂✂✂✂✂✂

Halley's Comet is used as a frame for Lindsey Drager's novel *The Archive of Alternate Endings*. She wrote:

TEN PAST NOON

Under Wilhelm's pen, the stories have morphed, moved further from their origins to become more palatable and refined. But something unsettles Wilhelm about the way he's shaping them. He worries that in honing them, the stories are growing toward his desires and wants and not those of the folk. He looks over to his brother, then looks up at the sky. He thinks: Illness, glass enclosures, spider webs. He thinks: Preservation, collaboration, loss. He thinks: Ashes, mazes, mouths. He thinks: Once upon a time. The comet is coming, he thinks. He steps outside to look up at the stars and what he thinks is: The infinite expanse.[33]

++++++++++

Did Ned approach a traveling doctor in a painted wagon: "Hey, Professor Marvel, I heard testosterone was synthesized five years ago in Göttingen and that it was just approved for medical use in the United States. When might I be prescribed some?" And was the doctor played by Frank Morgan and did he have a little crystal ball and did he reply: "I'm sorry. The Nazis are using it to experiment on unwilling human subjects. The Nazis have just opened Auschwitz. A million people will die there. It will not be liberated for another five years. 'Professor Marvel never guesses; he knows!' You have to wait for your testosterone."[34]

TUCKER LIEBERMAN

The Blitz had begun in London, and the subway system was seen as a refuge. Tens of thousands of people spent the night of September 21, 1940 underground.[35] Sixty-eight people died when a tunnel in the Balham suburbs was bombed on October 14.[36] An empty station known as "St. Mary's (Whitechapel Road)" was repurposed as an air-raid shelter but was destroyed on October 22.[37]

Maybe Ned wondered if the librarians to whom he'd once written had died in the war.

Maybe he wondered if he should use his language skills to assist in the war. Or his engineering skills. Or his Columbia and Harvard connections.

Maybe he offered and they didn't want him.

Maybe someone he knew was killed.

Maybe he had very low hopes that anything would be left.

He couldn't self-interpret or self-soothe. He stayed home and made handwritten lists of things. His lists transitioned from types of eunuchs to types of mental illness. They were lists nonetheless. The music didn't resolve. Colonel Barog had been tunneling from both sides of the mountain and the tunnels didn't connect in the middle.

TEN PAST NOON

At times, a person may suffer a "feeling of cosmic panic," as Peter Wessel Zapffe described in 1933.

> All things chain together in causes and effects, and everything he wants to grasp dissolves before the testing thought... Eventually, the features of things are features only of himself. Nothing exists without himself, every line points back at him, the world is but a ghostly echo of his voice—he leaps up loudly screaming...he feels the looming of madness and wants to find death before losing even such ability.

Four major mechanisms, maybe more, are used to repress and remedy this panic, he says. One may attempt to ignore and isolate oneself from the destructive thoughts. One may reassure oneself and anchor to something that feels more reliable. One may self-distract and avoid one's own interiority through entertainment or busy-work. One may transform and sublimate the panic into art, "fastening onto its pictorial, dramatic, heroic, lyric or even comic aspects."

If the human's "critical surplus of cognition" can be kept busy, they may feel that the problem is being well managed for the moment. Their mental circuits can be occupied in any number of ways. A method of "violence" is Communism. A method of "guile" is psychoanalysis.

None of this, however, says Zapffe, stops the panic.[38]

Nunn challenged the Deep Springs Student Body in 1920: "If the prevalent question of the West has been: How much knowledge have you? the prevalent question of the East was: How are you using your knowledge, for good or evil?"[39]

Arthur Koestler's character in *Darkness at Noon* has a different slant on this. "Practicing politics," Rubashov says obliquely during his interrogation, is like using an unknown x in an algebra problem "without worrying about its properties. Making history," by contrast, "means recognizing what the x stands for in the equation."[40]

A character in Markus Sakey's 2013 novel *Brilliance* observed:

> "The man on the radio was right, Nick. About a war. That's our future." A strange resolve came over her, and she slipped her hands into her pockets. "You can't stop the future. All you can do is pick a side."[41]

You also need a premise. Among the dramatic premises suggested by Lajos Egri in 1942:

"Ill-temper leads to isolation."

"Materialism conquers mysticism."

"Prudishness leads to frustration."

You need both: the dramatic premise and the moral position you take on it. The premise does

TEN PAST NOON

not in itself suffice to write a play, Egri said, because, still, "the author's conviction is missing. Until he takes sides, there is no play."[42]

Especially when it is directionless and ethically constipated: Fastidious technical perfectionism leads to despair.

+++++++++

Ella Sterling and George de Brey meet on a train platform in Felix's 1930 novel, *Crowded Solitude.*

"Now, where's Shaltikoff?" he asked when her luggage had been collected.

"Ivan? Why, he's in Paris," she said, amazed.

"Are you sure? He wired today that he was coming by this train. You did not see him?"

He was looking beyond her, down the length of the train from which people were still descending.

"I think I see him," de Brey said, and waved. "Yes, that's he. Funny you did not meet."

She could not look around and in the panic that now swept her she found herself saying, inanely,

"But I saw him yesterday. He did not tell me he was coming."[43]

+++++++++

TUCKER LIEBERMAN

On Saturday, October 26, 1940, Ned Cumming met his cousin Felix Kittredge in Manhattan. I am not sure if he knew that was going to happen. ("It is often, perhaps most often, the case that individuals meet their 'fate' because it is contingent on some crucial event or inheres in a larger pattern," Jules Brody wrote with Homer's *Iliad* and *Odyssey* in mind.[44]) A third person would be present and would ask Felix, "Do you recognize this man?" and Felix would say, "Yes."

The weekly *New Yorker* magazine featured a cover with a six-panel cartoon by William Steig in which boys played football and street hockey, flew kites, ate candied apples, laughed at a dress-up mask with a handlebar mustache, and roasted marshmallows over a fire in the street next to a hydrant.[45]

The headlines of the front page of the late edition of the *New York Times* were all war. "Lewis declares for Willkie; says Roosevelt means war and dictatorship in nation." "U.S. asks France to state her aims; hopes she won't join war on Britain; R.A.F. pounds Berlin; London hard hit." Wedged between them in a tight column: "Wallace charges Nazis are ordered to assist Willkie." Wendell Willkie was challenging Franklin D. Roosevelt's bid for a third term as president. The election was ten days away.

TEN PAST NOON

Around lunchtime, I imagine, Ned left the apartment on West 116th Street, ran six blocks down Amsterdam, passed his old graduate school in engineering at Columbia University and the Episcopal Cathedral of St. John the Divine, turned right, and ran one long block to Broadway to the train station at 110th Street. The fare would be a nickel. If he only had a dime, it was not a problem; at that intersection there was a Horn and Hardart's Automat restaurant where the machine slots took one nickel per food item, and he could ask a nickel thrower to change his large coin for two small ones.[46] The employees were always brewing coffee and refreshed the dispenser every twenty minutes. Ned might want the coffee to taste like the Newmark's at Deep Springs, but those days wouldn't come back. He could drink a coffee or not; he would still have a leftover nickel for the train.

The subway line had been run by Interborough Rapid Transit until the city had finally bought out that company several months previously. Now all the lines belonged to the Independent. It was an underground train. Time: "P.M.," but the sun still high. Sunset would be at five o'clock.

As Heinrich Wilhelm Olbers posed the paradox in 1823: "How fortunate that the Earth does not receive starlight from every point of the celestial vault!" For then we would only ever see a sky full of light. White text on a black background, photostats overprinting photostats, until there are only words and no more context.

Or maybe the headlights had always been with him. "A photon," as the sci-fi novelist Charles Yu describes a physics theory of Richard Feynman's,

> takes every possible path through space-time to get from point A to point B. In a sense, every photon in the universe is everywhere in the universe at every time in the universe. Or, put yet another way: there is only one photon in the entire universe, and that photon, spread across all of creation in a vast probabilistic smear, that one photon is responsible for all the light we see.[47]

The train was past and future. It barreled into the inescapable present. *"Ickira, trecketre, stedenthal."*[48] On the tracks, he stopped. These headlights, created at the beginning of time, had crossed the entire universe to find him and had finally reached him.

This was unlike the incident when Dean Thornhill's private vehicle had an argument with the Oregon Short Line in 1919. This was not one car with another car. This was two fast, modern cars rolling over Ned's unarmored body. The future travels faster than anything you can imagine and yet there is still darkness ahead of it.

TEN PAST NOON

"You've forgiven me for running away as I did?" Ella asks in *Crowded Solitude.* Her romantic interest responds affirmatively:

> "Of course. But why on earth did you? What happened? I thought I would never come to my senses—I just stood there in the hotel insisting you must have left some message until they all thought I was mad."
>
> "I'm sorry," she said gently. "I was afraid it would hurt you, but there seemed nothing more to say—I could not have said good-by."[49]

#########

It had to have been early enough in the afternoon that someone was able to remove his body from the tracks; that the medical examiner was able to take charge of it at the 24th Precinct; that someone called Felix (who, close to his own fortieth birthday, was living with his wife and baby daughter an hour north of the city in Carmel); that Felix arrived in Manhattan and identified the body; and that the clerk typed up the death certificate, all on the same day. Let's imagine it was a few minutes past noon when his balloon was set free.

Several pieces of information on the death certificate are questionable (if I may echo the saddened skepticism that Ned himself frequently expressed about historical sources). First, the home address provided was West 116th Street while the newspaper the next day said he lived at East 43rd Street. Since he and his sister were still maintaining these two apartments and their mother was in her late seventies and not working, he might have needed income, but the death certificate lists his occupation as "none." His "approximate age" was listed as "37"; he was 39. A funeral director was named, Hillside Cemetery was indicated, and a permit number was given, but Hillside has no record of Ned's remains ever arriving and no gravestone. The cause of death, aside from the physical observation of "mangling of the body," was that he was "said tohave [sic] jumped in front of subway train.. [sic] Suicidal." It does not specify who said this. The paper the next day said that he "jumped or fell." The death certificate's typist hit the period key exactly twice after "subway train," leaving it, as framed by its ambiguous punctuation, halfway between a declarative statement and an ellipsis—neither finished nor unfinished, an ambiguity of an ambiguity, a teasing cantillation mark in bureaucratic silence.

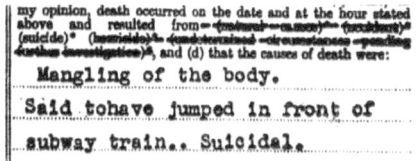

Figure 24 – Ned Cumming's death certificate.

TEN PAST NOON

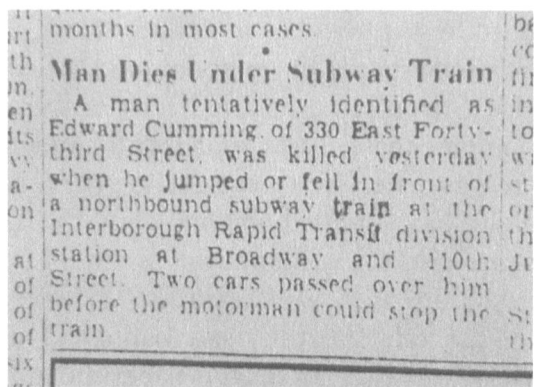

Figure 25 – *"Man Dies Under Subway Train,"* New York Herald-Tribune, *October 27, 1940.*

The typist didn't need to perfect the death certificate. The office was in possession of a human body crushed by two train cars and a piece of paper was needed to transfer those remains to the funeral director. The paper served its purpose.

The death certificate has informational holes, and my main takeaway from it is that Felix didn't know his cousin very well. He knew the address of his 76-year-old aunt, but he may have been unsure where her son lived or worked. He mistakenly remembered Ned (who had started at Harvard two years earlier than he) as being three years younger than he. Someone had reported that Ned felt "suicidal," but perhaps that came from Ned's mother or a witness of his suicide.

And yet Felix was the person Ned's mother called for help, which makes me realize that I do not know if Ned ever had a friend.

Or a cat.

If, until the end of history, he will simultaneously have and not have that unobserved cat.

If he had gained or lost weight.

If he owed or was owed money.

If he liked to walk in nature.

I do not know if he ever took out a personal ad. What would he have written: *Lonely heart, heavy cart?*

I do not know if he wore ugly sweaters or drank tea.

Or alcohol.

If he was autistic.

I have only four photographs of him, and none after the age of eighteen.

And yet I have so much of him, when I look at it from this perspective:

From all the Chinese men who worked on the railroads in the American West, as Chang, Fishkin, and Obenzinger explain, "there is no extant letter, diary, memoir, or even oral history that tells us something about their lived experience from their point of view. To this day, not one piece of textual evidence from them offering even a glimpse into their experiences has been located. With few exceptions, received histories carry not a single name of a Chinese railroad worker."[50] Those workers were, by the accounts of others, literate in Chinese. Yet, probably in large part due to the violence directed at them and the instability in which they lived, everything they wrote is gone. Twenty thousand men and not a single piece of paper. Not so much as their own explanation as to why everything is gone. They left behind broken dinner plates and shirt buttons, but the only remaining paper is their paystubs: the result of their labor, the part the bosses didn't take.

Nor do we have, for that matter, as Saidiya Hartman points out, "one extant autobiographical narrative of a female captive who survived the Middle Passage" of the slave trade across the Atlantic Ocean.[51]

We have stories from concentration camps, but usually from people who possessed some relative privilege within the camps, a privilege that at least kept them, above all other things, alive.[52]

I might well be astonished that there is an entire cart left of Ned, a small tree's worth of Hammermill Bond paper with his pencil looped all over it, if I consider this artifact in the context of all the other people whose stories I might have tried to pursue.

On October 27, a *New York Times Book Review* headline declared that H. G. Wells, the English futurist author of *The Time Machine* and *War of the Worlds* who was then touring in the United States, considered himself "a Journalist,

Not a 'Literary' Writer."[53] When he wrote about time travel and hostile space aliens, he believed himself to be, in some sense, telling the truth.

The "date of burial or cremation" handwritten at the bottom of Ned's death certificate was October 28.

His age, 39, was the same as that of the mathematician and theologian Blaise Pascal when he succumbed to stomach cancer; as the civil rights activist Dr. Martin Luther King, Jr. when he was assassinated; and as the fictional Winston Smith when he perpetrated thoughtcrime in George Orwell's *1984*.

> "Does the past exist concretely, in space? Is there somewhere or other a place, a world of solid objects, where the past is still happening?"
>
> "No."
>
> "Then where does the past exist, if at all?"
>
> "In records. It is written down."
>
> "In records. And—?"
>
> "In the mind. In human memories."[54]
>
> —George Orwell, *1984*

Train suicides are memorable for the drivers,[55] for whom these events come as unpleasant surprises and who live to remember them. I don't know who was driving the train that day. The *Herald-Tribune* reporter wrote, "Two cars

TEN PAST NOON

passed over him before the motorman could stop the train." The train probably was braking as it entered the station anyway. The reporter's phrasing assumes that the driver, when he saw a man on the tracks, would have liked to stop the train early but was unable to prevent the death.

≠≠≠≠≠≠≠≠≠

The "trolley problem" is a philosophical quandary told from the perspective of the one who has to choose to direct the course of the train. (It is also a quandary for the victims, but in a different way.) It's a question of moral agency when our options are constrained.

This type of thought exercise, in which someone must decide whether to divert a train on a fatal path, is usually posed as a question of whether it is better to choose one victim to spare multiple random victims. Would you decline to be involved in the situation and allow the train to plow into a crowd, or would you get involved and send it down a different track where it kills a different person—someone who would have otherwise been unhurt? Many of us have conflicting moral intuitions, or no moral intuition at all, about this. The trolley problem is not a molossus. It's used by philosophy professors to point out to students that not every moral choice can be best resolved by saying *"I just know."* We'd like to know, but sometimes we don't. Sometimes we make it up. Sometimes we get it wrong.

Fortunately, almost no one ever has to make this decision, and, "even if they did," Will Oremus writes in 2019, "studies suggest their reaction in the moment would have little to do with their views on utilitarianism or moral agency." This was my own complaint about the trolley problem when I encountered it in college around the turn of the millennium: By the time we articulate the features of the problem, the accident has already happened. I am someone who likes to collect and ruminate upon details. A good ethical problem for me is one that takes seven years to figure out. I have no idea what I'd do if I were present at a train crash. It seems not to be a situation in which *ideas* are very helpful; muscle reflex, probably, would be more useful. I don't even like driving cars for this very reason. We have to react in emergencies, but emergencies don't accommodate the slow-motion contemplation that most of us mean when we talk about "ethics."

On the other hand, if a disaster happens *too* slowly, everyone is responsible, which means, in practice, that no one will take the necessary action to stop it.

A 21st-century real-world application of the trolley problem is the programmed behavior of self-driving vehicles. If the moral question is difficult for humans to answer even in theory, however, how can humans give robots the correct response? Private companies have simply gone ahead, Oremus notes, and launched the first autonomous vehicles on the roads.

Corporations are motivated by engineering accomplishments and the capitalist rewards of being the first to bring a product to market. Consequently, in 2018, when a self-driving test vehicle caused a fatal accident, it was found that the car "didn't take into account the possibility of pedestrians jaywalking. So even though the car's sensors detected the woman walking into the road long before the crash, it struggled to identify her as human and failed to predict that she would keep walking." The system realized the problem with one second to spare. At that point, according to its programming, it used the remaining time for "calculating various options and alerting the human driver to take over."[56] The human driver, who was present in the test vehicle as backup, did not respond to the one-second warning to take action because she was watching a popular singing competition on her smartphone.[57]

The first fatality caused by a self-driving car had occurred two years earlier. That one was not the outcome of a "trolley problem" calculation, either. It was, rather, the result of a robot's visual processing error. The sky was bright; the truck was white; the car's system guided it into the side of the truck it never saw properly.[58] Everyone agrees that robots ought to have vision that is adequate for whatever they are trying to do. Exactly what they should try to do is a harder question.

TUCKER LIEBERMAN

#########

Police officers stop Boston traffic to protect a procession of eight ducklings behind their mother in *Make Way for Ducklings,* a 1941 children's book by Robert McCloskey. The ducks waddle happily, not sensing how their pathway is carefully architected by others. They live happily ever after.

#########

After the self-driving car's first human fatality, as a public relations maneuver, the responsible company did nonetheless try to guide the public's focus back to the trolley problem, an argument it felt it was still winning.

(The robot hadn't used the trolley problem to choose to inflict this fatality; humans were using the trolley problem to justify having a robot.)

The company's systems had driven many millions of miles before incurring a fatality, which meant that, per mile, robot drivers might still be judged a bit safer than human drivers. The argument is a little hard to swallow. Yes, these self-driving cars were safer *on average.* But they were not safer for the *particular* human passenger of the *particular* car that drove itself into a truck. We want to say that one fatality is preferable to two. We are resistant to making that our "final answer" when the latter fatalities are merely statistical probabilities—or, as Sir Henry Maine might have described it, "what might have happened but didn't"—and when the former has a name, a face, and a corpse, as well as a responsible party.

This is the trolley problem: one molossus doing battle with another. Or a molossus doing battle with something that is not a molossus but is some other kind of argument. Ethics is both computational and visceral.

We tell the robots how to write books and then we wait for them to write them.

#########

Ned doesn't have a tombstone at his family plot, and it seems unnecessary for there to be one. His bones may not even be there. Maybe he did not want his bones to be anywhere. His bones were broken. He asked the future to obliterate him. He wanted to be paper, if anything. We could photostat a few pages of his *Eunuchry* manuscript, white text on black background. Maybe copies are memorials. Shadows in the striations, trying to resemble a body in their size and permanence, trying to take up space in the world as the body once took up space—

And the only way out is a train. And the Europeans in Nazi-occupied countries boarded the train and didn't come back. And the train is what his father wanted him to engineer.

#########

TUCKER LIEBERMAN

The three-ring binder pops open. The papers are unfettered.

"I'm free!" says Oedipus, flexing his ankles.

"No, you're not," says the Sphinx.

≠≠≠≠≠≠≠≠≠

The novelist Anthony Doerr in *All the Light We Cannot See* has a character who "imagines the electromagnetic waves" in a machine:

> Torrents of text conversations, tides of cell conversations, of television programs, of e-mail, vast networks of fiber and wire interlaced above and beneath the city, passing through buildings, arcing between transmitters in Metro tunnels, between antennas atop buildings, from lampposts with cellular transmitters in them...flying visibly over the warrens of Paris, over the battlefields and tombs, over the Ardennes, over the Rhine, over Belgium and Denmark, over the scarred and ever-shifting landscapes we call nations.

Why not sounds, too, the character asks? Can we sense the flight of departed souls,

> faded but audible if you listen closely enough? They flow above the chimneys, ride the sidewalks, slip through your jacket and shirt and breastbone and lungs, and pass out through the other

side, the air a library and the record of every life lived, every sentence spoken, every word transmitted still reverberating in it.[59]

#########

Of sunlight, space, and time in California, L. Jackson Newell shares this observation in *The Electric Edge of Academe:*

The sun seems to rise in the west at Deep Springs, not because time runs backward here but as a function of the unique morphology of the valley. The modern ranch and college sit tight against the mountains on the eastern edge of the valley, keeping it in the morning shadows until...the sun bursts brilliantly against the snow-capped 14,000-foot Sierra Nevada Peaks...Now, as in the distant past, all eyes are drawn to the west in the morning and return there in the evening...[60]

#########

The paradox is not: *If gay men desire men who resemble women, why don't they desire women?* That's not a paradox. That's just a recognition that each person has their own molossus. People take the lovers they wish.

The paradox is: *If there is infinite light, where is it all?* If the universe goes on forever and there's no limit to the stars, why is there still any dark spot anywhere? A moment in which to witness a solar eclipse? A tunnel in which the train needs a headlight?

Language is an interplay of light and darkness: what we see and what we don't see. There are reasons to balance the polarity.

Sometimes we do not want to see because we have already seen too much. If there were infinite light, it would be useless, because our world would be so bright that we couldn't see anything at all. The shadows, as much as the illuminated surfaces, tell us where we stand. The part we don't see is part of what it means to see.

And then again: Sometimes we do not need to see because we have different ways of knowing.

‡‡‡‡‡‡‡‡‡

Language lives and often serves as a memorial.

The Wikipedia entry for Ota Benga said he "had free run" of the grounds at the Bronx Zoo. All three words are wrong. He "had" permission, not incidentally or because it was the natural order of things, but because someone made that decision. He wasn't "free." No one should decide for him that he wants to "run" in circles like a horse. Words imply values and assumptions. An encyclopedia entry is important because it is the way someone is remembered. Ota Benga has a grave in Virginia, which can be a place to remember him, though it was deliberately left unmarked for years to frustrate possible attempts by the Congolese to retrieve his bones. Today there is a sign at his grave with the legend: *"I am a man. I am a man."*[61] That particular sign is not mine to control, but a Wikipedia entry is everyone's responsibility. There are six million English-language articles to guard on Wikipedia, one word at a time. The Wikipedia entry does not use that three-word phrase anymore because I changed it. White people wrote the encyclopedia wrong, and white people should spend their mornings fixing it. This is the tiniest imaginable form of reparations. It is a start.

Abby Covert advised in *How To Make Sense of Any Mess:*

> Sometimes, we have to move forward knowing that other people tried to make sense of this mess and failed. We may need to shine the light brighter or longer than they did. Perhaps now is a better time. We may know the outcomes of their fate, but we don't know our own yet. We can't until we try.[62]

I am not positioned to change the architecture of Wikipedia, but I can change a piece of the content.

If someone doesn't like what I wrote, they, too, can edit.

In this collaboration, we are the guardians of each other's words, though it is probably still important to begin by guarding our own.

※※※※※※※※※

"*Why not be a Bolshevist?*"

The question was not asked by someone in close proximity to actual Bolshevism. If our vague idea of "Bolshevist" values and tactics stands for whatever political activism happens to give us the xenophobic heebie-jeebies, the question will be hard to answer. We may, instead, need to work harder on deciding what ideologies to oppose. We can do that.

"*Explain briefly.*"

Because we have to try.

NOTES TO "END OF A DECADE"

[1] "Village of Scarsdale, New York: Reconnaissance Level Cultural Resource Survey Report." Li-Saltzman Architects, P.C. and Andrew S. Dolkart. July 12, 2012.
https://s3.amazonaws.com/scarsdale/120712+Scarsdale+Cult+Resc+Survey+Rpt.pdf
Accessed Sept. 27, 2019.

[2] Gabriel García Márquez, "La siesta del martes," 1962. Translated by Gregory Rabassa.

[3] R. Bracht Branham. *Inventing the Novel: Bakhtin and Petronius Face to Face.* New York: Oxford University Press, 2019. p. 5.
https://books.google.com.co/books?id=xsS4DwAAQBAJ&pg=PA5&lpg=PA5 Accessed January 16, 2020.

[4] Irwin, as previously mentioned, had spent time in a psychiatric institution for his attempted self-mutilation of his genitals. For information on the "villain-coding" of eunuch characters in fiction, see my 2018 book *Painting Dragons: What Storytellers Need to Know About Writing Eunuch Villains.*

[5] Harold Schechter. *The Mad Sculptor: The Maniac, The Model, and the Murder that Shook the Nation.* Seattle: Amazon Publishing, 2014. p. 249, 258, 266.

[6] "How The Hindenburg Disaster Changed Aviation History." Adam Taylor and Alex Davies. *Business Insider.* May 6, 2013. https://www.businessinsider.com/how-the-hindenburg-changed-aviation-history-photos-2013-5 Accessed November 10, 2019.

[7] The neighbor's name was Noah Quinn. "Summer Calm Is Disturbed By Several Fires, Accidents." Scarsdale Inquirer, Volume XIX, Number 26, 30 July 1937. https://news.hrvh.org/veridian/?a=d&d=scarsdaleinquire19370730.2.10 Accessed Sept. 26, 2019.

[8] In a Columbia student directory for the 1938–1939 academic year, the first address given for Emily—she enrolled in the Spring of 1939—was provided as 420 West 116th St, followed by the old Scarsdale address. She probably had the city apartment by 1938, if not earlier. Columbia University in the City of New York. *Catalogue Number for the Sessions of 1938-1939.* Morningside Heights, New York. http://www.ebooksread.com/authors-eng/columbia-university/catalogue-volume-19381939-ulo/page-112-catalogue-volume-19381939-ulo.shtml Accessed February 4, 2020.

[9] David Gelernter. *1939: The Lost World of the Fair.* Quoted by Michael N. McGregor. *Pure Act: The Uncommon Life of Robert Lax.* Fordham University Press, 2015.

[10] "…unification could be achieved only by the City of New York's acquiring the assets of the two private companies and converting their operations into public-sector

responsibilities. This would happen during the month of June in the year 1940..."
Brian J. Cudahy. *A Century of Subways: Celebrating 100 Years of New York's Underground Railways.* New York: Fordham University Press, 2003. p. 51.

[11] "The Grotesque of the Body Electric." Peter Hitchcock. Printed in *Bakhtin and the Human Sciences: No Last Words.* ed. Michael Mayerfeld Bell and Michael Gardiner. London: SAGE, 1998. p. 80.
https://books.google.com.co/books?id=_8zyAwAAQBAJ&pg=PA80&lpg=PA80 Accessed January 16, 2020.

[12] "César Vallejo's 'Piedra negra sobre una piedra blanca.'" John Alba Cutler. May 2, 2014.
https://sites.northwestern.edu/jac808/2014/05/02/cesar-vallejos-piedra-negra-sobre-una-piedra-blanca/ Accessed February 5, 2020.
"Black Stone Lying On A White Stone." César Vallejo (1892-1938). Translated and edited by Robert Bly. *Neruda & Vallejo: Selected Poems.* Beacon Press, 1971. https://poets.org/poem/black-stone-lying-white-stone Accessed February 5, 2020.

[13] "75 years ago, 'War of the Worlds' started a panic. Or did it?" Mark Memmott. NPR. October 30, 2013.
https://www.npr.org/sections/thetwo-way/2013/10/30/241797346/75-years-ago-war-of-the-worlds-started-a-panic-or-did-it
Accessed January 14, 2020.
"The War of the Worlds panic was a myth." Martin Chilton. *The Telegraph.* 6 May 2016. https://www.telegraph.co.uk/radio/what-to-listen-to/the-war-of-the-worlds-panic-was-a-myth/ Accessed January 14, 2020.

[14] He went to prison in late 1938.

[15] None of the Cummings are reflected at 420 West 116th Street when the census was taken on April 19, 1940. However, Emily had provided this as her address when she enrolled at Columbia in the Spring of 1939, and the address was provided again for Ned and Lucy on Ned's

death 1940 certificate.
1940 U.S. Federal Census. New York, New York. Enumeration District 31-920. Images 19-20 of 51.
https://www.ancestry.com/interactive/2442/
m-t0627-02645-00932?backurl=&ssrc=&backlabel=
Return#?imageId=m-t0627-02645-00949

[16] She is listed as a student in Spring 1939 supplement to the student catalog of Columbia University. She had registered for classes, not in any particular school, but under the designation of "University Classes." According to my own correspondence with the registrar's office, she never graduated.
Columbia University in the City of New York. *Catalogue Number for the Sessions of 1938-1939.* Morningside Heights, New York.
http://www.ebooksread.com/authors-eng/columbia-university/catalogue-volume-19381939-ulo/page-112-catalogue-volume-19381939-ulo.shtml

[17] "Turtle Bay, that portion of east Manhattan near the United Nations, was once one of the worst neighborhoods in the city. In the late 1800s the area was littered with unregulated businesses — tanneries, slaughterhouses, breweries, power plants and coal yards — where the rate of injuries and death among workers was horrific. Dark, overcrowded tenements were squalid and stank and were nearly as disease-ridden and dangerous as the blue-ribbon winner of depraved decay in the New York City of that era: Five Points, near where City Hall is now."
Jeffery Deaver. *The October List.* New York: Grand Central Publishing, 2013. p. 181.

[18] Harold Schechter. *The Mad Sculptor: The Maniac, The Model, and the Murder that Shook the Nation.* Seattle: Amazon Publishing, 2014. p. 4.

[19] "Everything You Need to Know About Tudor City in 1,032 Words." *Tudor City Confidential.* May 4, 2016.
http://www.tudorcityconfidential.com/2016/05/everything-you-need-to-know-about-tudor_4.html Accessed October 14, 2019.

Emily and Lucy lived together on East 43rd Street when the census was taken on April 1, 1940.
1940 U.S. Federal Census. New York, New York. Enumeration District 31-1027A. Roll T627_2648. Page 2B.
[20] Harold Schechter. *The Mad Sculptor: The Maniac, The Model, and the Murder that Shook the Nation.* Seattle: Amazon Publishing, 2014. pp. 47-48.
Schechter describes the two murders:
    The Stretz-Gebhardt murder, pp. 8-22.
    The Fiorenza-Titterton murder, pp. 31-46.
[21] "Pollens, Bertram. *The Sex Criminal.*" ed. Julius J. Marke. *A Catalogue of the Law Collection at New York University.* (Originally published: Law Center of New York University, 1953.) Union, N.J.: The Lawbook Exchange, 1999. p. 476.
https://books.google.com.co/books?id=wLgoiBn75P8C&pg=PA476&lpg=PA476
Accessed October 14, 2019.
[22] Mo Moulton. *The Mutual Admiration Society: How Dorothy L. Sayers and Her Oxford Circle Remade the World for Women.* New York: Basic Books, 2019. p. 105.
[23] Moulton, *ibid.,* pp. 77-78, 81.
[24] W. H. Auden. "September 1, 1939."
https://m.poets.org/poetsorg/poem/september-1-1939
[25] Antoine de Saint-Exupéry. *Wind, Sand and Stars [Terre des hommes].* (1939) Translated from the French by Lewis Galantiere. London: The Folio Society, 1990. p. 105.
[26] Michio Kaku. *Parallel Worlds: A Journey Through Creation, Higher Dimensions, and the Future of the Cosmos.* (2004) Anchor eBooks, 2006.
[27] *Holocaust and Human Behavior.* "Chapter 8: The War on Jews in Poland." Brookline, Mass.: Facing History and Ourselves, 2016. https://www.facinghistory.org/holocaust-and-human-behavior/chapter-8/war-jews-poland Accessed August 1, 2019.
[28] Letter from Benjamin Kittredge, Jr. July 31, 1939, from Nieuw, Amsterdam. Kittredge family papers, South

TEN PAST NOON

Carolina Historical Society.
[29] Rumer Godden. *Black Narcissus.* (1939) New York: Open Road, 2016.
    Feathered hat: Chapter 33.
    "…the ground spread away in rings…" Chapter 14.
    A nun falls to her death: Chapter 31.
    "…mirrors in the palms of their hands…" Chapter 9.
[30] The estate was managed at the Chemical Bank & Trust Company, 165 Broadway, Manhattan. George Dana Canfield and Benjamin R. Kittredge, Jr, the executors of S. D. Kittredge's will, put a notice in the *Dobbs Ferry Register* paper on January 10, 1940 requesting all creditors of his estate to step forward.
[31] Charles Yu. *How to Live Safely in a Science Fictional Universe.* Pantheon, 2010. pp. 180.
[32] Rabindranath Tagore. "Railway Station." *Selected Poems.* Translated from the Bengali by William Radice. London: Penguin, 2005. p. 225.
[33] Lindsey Drager. *The Archive of Alternate Endings.* Ann Arbor, Mich.: Dzanc, 2019.
[34] Testosterone is generally not "orally bioavailable" because it is destroyed by the liver. Thus it's usually taken as injection and sometimes as topical gels. An oral version has been developed that destroys, rather than is destroyed by, the liver—i.e. it is "hepatotoxic."
"Anabolic androgenic steroid-induced hepatotoxicity." Bond P., Llewellyn W., Van Mol P. *Med Hypotheses.* 2016 Aug; 93:150-3. doi: 10.1016/j.mehy.2016.06.004. Epub 2016 Jun 5.
https://www.ncbi.nlm.nih.gov/pubmed/27372877
As an example of the types of experiments that took place: Carl Vaernet, a member of the Nazi party in Denmark, claimed around 1940 to have "a hormone therapy which could convert the sexual orientation of homosexual persons," namely an implant that would release testosterone slowly. He was promoted to the rank of major and in 1943 he began working for "an SS medical company in Prague, Deutsche Heilmittel GmbH." He placed the

implant in several dozen prisoners. Upon the liberation of Denmark in 1945, Vaernet was imprisoned but "succeeded in awakening the interest of the British and Danish authorities in his hormone treatment ideas. He was allowed to keep contact with the outside world from his cell for the purpose of promoting his hormone therapies. Værnet seems to have gained promising contacts with the British-American pharmaceutical company 'Parke, Davis & Comp. Ltd., London & Detroit' and maybe also with the American chemical giant Du Pont." Falsely claiming a terminal heart condition, he was released and sent to a family home to die, then escaped to Buenos Aires where he opened a medical clinic. He lived another twenty years.
"Dr. Carl Peter Værnet (1893–1965)," by Matt & Andrej Koymasky, 1997–2004. *The Gay Holocaust—Nazi Criminals.* Oct. 29, 2011. https://www.fold3.com/page/285875837-nazi-persecution-of-homosexuals/stories Accessed Sept. 25, 2019.

[35] Christian Wolmar. *The Subterranean Railway: How the London Underground Was Built and How It Changed the City Forever.* London: Atlantic, 2004. p. 281.

[36] Wolmar, *ibid.,* p. 289.

[37] Wolmar, *ibid.,* pp. 84-85.

[38] "The Last Messiah." Peter Wessel Zapffe. *Janus,* Vol. 9, 1933. Translated from the Norwegian by Gisle R. Tangenes. English version first published in *Philosophy Now,* Issue 45, March/April 2004. https://philosophynow.org/issues/45/The_Last_Messiah Accessed January 20, 2020.

[39] "To the Trustees," in "Jurisdiction," 12.
"Jurisdiction," L. L. Nunn. Letter to Student Body, October 18, 1920, 14 pp. Subgroup 15, Box 1, fd. 7, 6, DSA; LJN Papers.
Quoted in L. Jackson Newell. *The Electric Edge of Academe: The Saga of Lucien L. Nunn and Deep Springs College.* Salt Lake City: The University of Utah Press, 2015. p. 152.

TEN PAST NOON

[40] Arthur Koestler. *Darkness at Noon.* Translated from the German by Philip Boehm. New York: Scribner, 2019. p. 92.

[41] Markus Sakey. *Brilliance.* Las Vegas: Thomas and Mercer, 2013.

[42] Lajos Egri. *The Art of Dramatic Writing: Its Basis in the Creative Interpretation of Human Motives.* (1942) New York: Touchstone, 1972. p. 9.

[43] Benjamin Kittredge. *Crowded Solitude.* New York: Coward-McCann, 1930. p. 210.

[44] Jules Brody. *'Fate' in* Oedipus Tyrannus: *A Textual Approach.* (Arethusa Monographs, XI.) Buffalo, N.Y.: SUNY Buffalo, 1985. p. 15.

[45] Art by William Steig. Cover of *The New Yorker,* October 26, 1940.
http://archives.newyorker.com/?i=1940-10-26#folio=CV1

[46] In 1938, Horn and Hardart had a location at Broadway and 110th St.

Source: *Investigation of Alleged Wire Tapping: Hearings Before a Subcommittee of the Committee on Interstate Commerce.* United States Senate, 76th Congress, 3rd Session, Pursuant to S. Res. 224 (76th Congress), a resolution authorizing and directing an investigation of alleged wire tapping and installation of listening or recording devices. Part 1, May/June 1940. Washington: U.S. Government Printing Office, 1940. p. 887.

Google Books, accessed January 14, 2020.

See also:

"Automatic for the People: Remembering the Automat Restaurants." Bill Demain. *Mental Floss.* April 21, 2015.
https://www.mentalfloss.com/article/29508/automatic-people-remembering-automat-restaurants
Accessed January 14, 2020.

"After Automats Died in New York, They Flourished in the Netherlands." Quinn Hargitai. *Atlas Obscura.* July 15, 2019.
https://www.atlasobscura.com/articles/automat-history
Accessed January 14, 2020.

[47] Yu, *op. cit.,* p. 27.
[48] Again, this is a line from Katharine Kilalea's poem, "Hennecker's Ditch," mimicking the rhythm of a train. *PN Review* 195, Volume 37 Number 1, September–October 2010. https://www.pnreview.co.uk/cgi-bin/scribe?item_id=8078 Accessed February 16, 2020.
[49] Benjamin Kittredge. *Crowded Solitude.* New York: Coward-McCann, 1930. p. 96.
[50] Introduction by Gordon H. Chang, Shelley Fisher Fishkin, and Hilton Obenzinger. *The Chinese and the Iron Road: Building the Transcontinental Railroad.* ed. Gordon H. Chang and Shelley Fisher Fishkin, with Hilton Obenzinger and Roland Hsu. Stanford, Calif.: Stanford University Press, 2019. p. 3.
[51] "Venus in Two Acts." Saidiya Hartman. Small Axe (2008) 12 (2): 1–14. p. 3. https://read.dukeupress.edu/small-axe/article/12/2/1/32332/Venus-in-Two-Acts Accessed February 13, 2020.
[52] Andrea Pitzer. *One Long Night: A Global History of Concentration Camps.* Introduction: "Sailing to Guantánamo." New York: Hachette, 2017. "A Note on Sources," p. ix.
[53] "H.G. Wells Discusses Himself and His Work; He Insists On Being Thought Of as a Journalist, Not a 'Literary' Writer." Robert Van Gelder. *New York Times Book Review.* October 27, 1940.
[54] George Orwell. *1984.* (Originally published 1949.) New York: The New American Library, 1961. p. 205.
[55] As an example, see Dave Goodwin, a train driver interviewed about his experiences. "Train driver opens up about the traumatic impact of rail suicides." *Daily Mail.* October 10, 2018. https://www.youtube.com/watch?v=phT375xVRQc Accessed October 16, 2019.
[56] "The Real Moral Dilemma of Self-Driving Cars." Will Oremus. *OneZero* (Medium). Nov. 7, 2019. https://onezero.medium.com/the-real-moral-dilemma-of-

self-driving-cars-ab6bb5f216b Accessed Nov. 11, 2019.

[57] "Uber Operator Was Watching 'The Voice' Before Self-Driving Crash." Mehr Nadeem and Emily McCormick. *Bloomberg.* June 22, 2018.
https://www.bloomberg.com/news/articles/2018-06-22/uber-operator-was-watching-the-voice-before-self-driving-crash Accessed Nov. 11, 2019.

[58] "Tesla driver dies in first fatal crash while using autopilot mode." Danny Yadron and Dan Tynan. *The Guardian.* July 1, 2016.
https://www.theguardian.com/technology/2016/jun/30/tesla-autopilot-death-self-driving-car-elon-musk
Accessed Nov. 11, 2019.

[59] Anthony Doerr. *All the Light We Cannot See.* New York: Scribner, 2014.

[60] Newell, *op. cit.,* p. 72.

[61] Ota Benga, 1883-1916. Photograph of the gravesite by Art Wells, 2011.
https://www.findagrave.com/memorial/20167712

[62] Abby Covert. *How to Make Sense of Any Mess.* Amazon, 2014.

SUICIDE NOTE

"What is it about the number forty," the novelist Ace Boggess asks regarding birthday parties, "that sends people into fits of absurdity? Is it the religious significance as in forty days and forty nights? The roundness of the number? Or of any number that ends with an oblique spheroid and signifies crossing from one decade to the next?"[1]

Is it something about the predictability of the human lifespan? Henry Adams, struggling to describe gravitational orbit, mentioned the Great Comet of 1843, visible from Earth when he was five years old. A comet "drops…directly into the sun" and "turns back unharmed…by the path on which it came."[2] He said this seems contrary to law. But of course it is the law; it is the rule by which we are pulled.

#########

TEN PAST NOON

If I were to attempt an autobiographical story of mental illness, right here, right now, it would be a hard story to tell, largely because it would require additional hundreds of pages that are only distantly related to the way I was haunted by Ned's ghost. So, I am not going to tell that story. Instead, I will talk around it.

In 2015, when I was thirty-five, I was working as a Product Manager. I was busy in the office managing the product. One day, around lunchtime, I told my boss I had to leave to handle a personal emergency. A thing was happening or about to happen. I drove home. I dealt with the thing. You already know what hour and minute it was.

The pin slid out of the grenade. "There was silence in heaven for about half an hour," as the Christians say in their Book of Revelation. Then my brain exploded.

The story of my life cleaved in two. There was everything before that moment, and then everything that has come since then. I just know.

I drove back to work, which is what people often do in these situations, and stayed at the office for another two years.

There is no such thing as a "train of thought." Nope! Thought is an off-road vehicle. If thought were a train, it would crash and burn the moment it derailed. But thought behaves differently. Thought can veer many miles off the road. It can stop, but it probably won't. It will keep going until it runs out of gas or until something else changes. It is terrifying.

The side effect of being home that day when my grenade-brain self-destructed—which I add because I sometimes feel obligated to paint a silver lining on the mental illness narrative—is that, in the long run, I ended up with different ideas about how to write this book.

This description of mental illness is short and yet also roundabout, which must be a headscratcher given that much of this book is devoted to mental illness. I am leaving this gap in the story because I cannot talk about it now. We can pay our respects at the lip of the blast crater with a half-hour of archival silence. If someone figures out this part of my story someday, many years in the future, it will be because they are curious enough to do the work to resurrect it, and then — I am giving permission — the biomythographer will be entitled to the narrative they create from it.

Does it really matter, anyway, what was the energy inside the Big Bang? It matters to the physical universe (and perhaps this energy became matter itself), but after the Big Bang has happened, does its explanation still matter to us as we navigate our days?

For now, at least, it is necessary to have a gap. The gap is the *tzimtzum,* a Hebrew word for a constriction. This self-control is the act of Pre-Creation, yielding the cosmic darkness and emptiness (according to the Lurianic Kabbalah) wherein the Creator puts light and objects. If there weren't an opening on the chessboard, the pieces would have nowhere to move. In this theology, the gap is the place where someone still has free will.

#########

Of course he loved travel. Wouldn't you, if you didn't want a job and there weren't any to be had anyway, and you lived as a lodger in someone else's house, and your mother were in the next room, and your handwritten book didn't fit on your shelf? If the trains were your spiritual inheritance from your father?

I don't know for how long he planned to kill himself, or if suicide was something that just happened to him suddenly. I don't know if he wrote a suicide note.

His entire manuscript was his suicide note, in a couple non-literal senses.

First, reading between the lines, I can derive prosaic answers. "Characteristics of the individual who compensates," began one of Ned's lists. For one such characteristic: "He will not admit that he has failed though he feels that he has. This inconsistency is behind every compensation."[3]

And then, to be yet more diffusely symbolic about it: the warning lay in the fact that he wrote so many pages—at all, about anything—despite his inability to transform it into a finished product. He persisted in something that was unworkable. He did not get the help he needed. Stubbornness, as much as failure, is what I see in the artifact of his manuscript. Stubborn activity is what created the thing that failed.

////////////

In the 1990s, nearly 5 percent of suicides in New York City were related to the subway.[4] In 2017, the city reported 43 attempted or completed suicides involving subways,[5] apart from the hundreds of other people who end up too close to the trains for other reasons. The Cathedral Parkway station at 110th and Broadway, the place where Ned died, has about one such incident every year.[6]

I don't have any statistics on the number of writers who don't finish their books and whether they survive that.

////////////

Ned Cumming chose a train because he wanted his body to be unrecognizable in death. I don't know exactly how he felt about his body, but he wouldn't be the first eunuch to have asked for this fate.

He chose a train because he knew he was headed for his family plot, and he wanted a closed casket or cremation.

He chose a train because it was modern.

He chose a train because he was mad at the

engineers and the military for their inability to recognize and promote whatever makes a fulfilling human life. Never mind the example of the third Cornelius Vanderbilt who had studied both philosophy and mechanical engineering. He isn't a good example because he disinherited his son—the one whose wedding Felix probably attended because he had an invitation and Ned probably did not attend because he was likely out of the country[7]—for preferring the newspaper business.

He chose a train because the Nazis put their victims on trains direct to the death camps.

He chose a train because the world is an ethical dilemma of Nazism and he wanted to stop this philosophical trolley problem before anyone else was hurt.

He chose a train so it would take him to the ends of the earth. "He loved travel most," said his Harvard obituary.

He did not throw his manuscript in front of the train. His manuscript was too big to carry and might have derailed the train. He left his manuscript where others could find it.

He had attained the age of 39 years and 100 days.

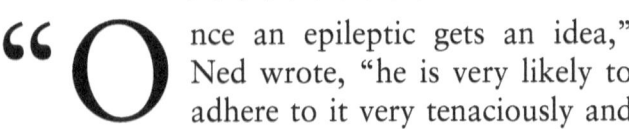

"Once an epileptic gets an idea," Ned wrote, "he is very likely to adhere to it very tenaciously and attempt to carry it out at all odds. He treats opposition in much the same manner that one would expect a spoiled child to treat it. He is as likely to persist in some trivial, senseless pursuit as in some activity that has worth. It is a blind persistence." By "epileptic," here, he was naming some personality type. Similarly, he said, "the Neurotic Personality" is compulsive and irrational, governed by personal inclinations.[8]

Many thrill-seekers "are engaged in a mild argument with the world" (as Rob Zaretsky put it)[9] and are not merely idly amusing themselves. Still, if Ned had wanted amusement, he could have gone to Coney Island, the site of the first roller coaster in the United States.[10] A roller coaster is a small train you ride for no particular purpose except to feel that you are about to die.

#########

Valeria Luiselli describes her work as a volunteer translator for children who enter the United States without documents.

> Sometimes, only sometimes, while we ride the subway back, we tell each other pieces of the stories we heard during the day. Telling stories doesn't solve anything, doesn't reassemble broken lives. But perhaps it is a way of understanding the unthinkable. If a story haunts us, we keep telling it to ourselves, replaying it in silence while we shower,

while we walk alone down streets, or in our moments of insomnia.[11]

K. Tait Jarboe wrote in short fiction:

> The important thing was that it made me notice the train station. There were lights in the building, and then there were more of them. It was a rare thing, but I had seen it before. The town wasn't dead, after all—it was haunted. There's a difference. Sometimes haunted things wake up: they repeat themselves, like an amnesiac with obsessive compulsive disorder. But sometimes, they know they've been gone, and they have these impossible insights. They'll offer them, buried in their twisted, obfuscating sense of humor.[12]

✄✄✄✄✄✄✄✄✄

Uncertainty: What form does mine take? Am I asking, after the physicist Erwin Schrödinger's famous "cat" question in 1935 about quantum indeterminacy, if it is possible that a dead man simultaneously *has and does not have* his scrotum until I get a chance to read everything on his cart and determine the reality once and for all? No—I don't think that's a valid form of the mystery.[13]

I know he identified with eunuchs. I know he jumped. I just know, though the proof is not recorded in any one sentence to which I can point. I don't need to have been there to know that. It's not a physical state or action that I see with my eyes. A jury wouldn't take it as proof "beyond a reasonable doubt." Nor is it something I know with power granted to me by colonialist authority. I know it only insofar as I have "attain[ed] a right understanding of the eunuch character," to quote his mission statement. Or, to be more specific and to avoid essentializing gender categories: a right understanding of *this* eunuch character, of Ned Cumming.

The mystery is not whether he viewed himself as part of eunuch-kind or whether he jumped, but how those two facts are connected.

"There is a mystery at the core of every suicide," the Columbia professor Mark Lilla wrote recently.[14] Lilla was diagnosing what he sees as the political self-harm of "identity politics." Why, he asked, do people insist on talking about sensitive, controversial, personal subjects, if we may assume that doing so collapses others' support for their broader political causes and shared needs? In disagreement with Lilla's position, and as a matter of individual psychology, I counter that people *literally* kill themselves when they *don't* talk about their identities. Talking about who we are is an opportunity to ask others to stop hurting us, for one thing, and it is an opening for us to participate in society in a way that renders us visible to ourselves. Talking about who we are *is* a shared political need. It is hard to talk about other shared political needs without first having

TEN PAST NOON

this one in place.

In describing Ned's early life before describing his suicide, I meant to show how his family connection to railroads determined the manner of his death. Who we are now determines what happens next. In a complex universe, the way this plays out is rarely obvious, and there are always open questions about the trajectories of our real lives. This piece of Ned's story, however, is apparent. His personal fate is narratively clear, which is part of the reason I chose to tell his story and why I chose to tell it this way.

If he wasn't going to die by self-castration (perhaps because he was already castrated), then he was going to die by train.

He heard and saw the trains crossing the country, over and over, for years. He knew this phenomenon before he knew what it meant. He may not have "heard" nor "saw" the meaning. Yet, at the end of the story, when he lands in front of a train, the one who reads the story may feel they have always known it would be so. Finally, in this architecture, the data is transformed into information: He jumped.

++++++++++

Nathaniel Hawthorne's story *The Great Stone Face*—the tale L. L. Nunn recommended over and over to the Deep Springs students—involves a fictional prophecy that there will come a great and noble man. It is predicted that the great man's face, in maturity, will resemble a certain rock formation in the mountain. A boy, Ernest, is fascinated by this prophecy. Eventually, as an old man, he finds his favorite poet to see if the poet meets the description. "All through life I have awaited the fulfilment of a prophecy," Ernest says wistfully, "and, when I read these poems, I hoped that it might be fulfilled in you." But alas, his revered poet looks nothing like the face in the mountain. The poet is amused, and finally gives old Ernest the answer, shouting, "Behold! Behold! Ernest is himself the likeness of the Great Stone Face!" Ernest cannot accept it, "still hoping that some wiser and better man than himself would by and by appear."[15]

If we try hard, we may grow into the nobility we are waiting for.

When someone tells us they can see an important part of who we really are, they are often right.

We know who Ned was because he left those fingerprints on his book.

It helps us feel connected to a manuscript when we have a backstory. Matthew Hutson said that "when people learned that an artist was eccentric—he mangled his ear, or carried stones on his head—they liked his work more." This is particularly true if they believed the artist was authentically eccentric (and not faking it for attention).[16] Ned's backstory feels authentically eccentric to me.

TEN PAST NOON

#########

Two days after Ned's death, the *New York Times* reported that several dozen prominent Catholics had signed a plea for the United States to help Great Britain against the Nazis.[17]

In December, Arthur Koestler's novel was published in English as *Darkness at Noon*. During his wartime exodus from France, his original German version had been lost, even though he had typed it with a carbon copy.[18] No one could find either of the copies.

In 1942, Ned's former employer, Stone & Webster, employed hundreds of engineers to determine how to obtain uranium for the atom bomb.[19]

As World War II intensified, his mother and sister—and, who knows, perhaps his cousin—would have had an opportunity to read and censor his handwritten papers before donating the manuscript to the New York Academy of Medicine. If Ned ever explained who he was, what happened to him, or why he cared about it, those pages were expurgated then. The heart and meaning was taken out. Volume 1 is bookmarked with a small page from a desktop calendar from Tuesday, June 30 and Wednesday, July 1, 1942, an interstitial date between Ned's suicide and the library's acquisition of his manuscript. Someone who wasn't Ned put their hands here. I don't know whose calendar it was.

His sister, who had studied secretarial skills in the months before his death, did not type up any of his manuscript for him.

Terms like "violence of the archive" or "archival silence," says Carmen Maria Machado, are used to describe the fact that "sometimes stories are destroyed, and sometimes they are never uttered in the first place."[20] It happens even to generally privileged people whose writing is nevertheless marginalized in some way.

The New York Academy of Medicine does not have a record of how the papers arrived. The binders are stickered with the information that the material is from the author's "estate." The family may have placed those stickers there, and "estate" is probably an informal designation, Ned having died likely without assets and, as they say, intestate. For all we know, someone hauled over two suitcases of papers in the rain in 1943, dropped them off, and zoomed away.

Having made the "intestate" joke, I feel I may as well go for broke and make the *"tzimtzum"* joke about withdrawing oneself to make space for a new creation. If I could ask Ned, he'd probably agree to it, because I am the editor and Ned would like to see this book published.[21]

#########

"If you go to a fortune-teller, you have to condense most of what you want to know into one or two fundamental issues or you'll be there all day. Anyway, there should always be a few large questions in your head," Wendy Plump wrote in her memoir *Vow*, "so you have something to think about while you're getting your car simonized."

Her large question, "if we would be all right," a question having to do with her marriage, was held at bay by throwing herself into her work, and it "became less an urgent question than a philosophical one. Which made it easier to see the answer, to see that 'Yes' answered back from a huge distance. It was an almost celestial, light-years, Oort cloud kind of distance. But it did answer back."[22]

The rocket scientist Robert Goddard, with cancer hushing his voice to a whisper, died in 1945. He was buried only an hour's stroll from the site of his first rocket launch.

The microbiologist Paul de Kruif's book *The Male Hormone* received publicity in national magazines.[23] He opened the book by admitting that, at age thirty-nine, he appreciated his own physical strength but felt "haunted by a scientific promise that it was not likely to be mine for many years longer...I remember lying awake nights dreading the approach of my fortieth birthday." But, he wondered, if testosterone injections had already caused hens to "strut" and "crow" like roosters and to stop laying eggs, then how might it enhance men's vitality? "What would the pure male hormone do for certain almost-men and certain broken men, eunuchoids," he mused, "who'd been deprived of their own natural hormone from birth or by disease or accident?"[24]

Ned's one-time traveling companion Walter Mairs submitted a copyright request for his song "Carol of Roses."[25]

Felix Kittredge became a Navy commander stationed in London as an attaché to exiled leaders during the final years of the war, and for several years after that he worked for the U.S. State Department.[26] In 1947, he and his family moved to his father's Cypress Gardens plantation in South Carolina and spent years restoring it before donating it to the city of Charleston.

Also in 1947, the members of the *Bulletin of the Atomic Scientists* created a "Doomsday Clock" to illustrate our likely proximity to global catastrophe. They set it to seven minutes before midnight.

Dr. Errol T. Engle's advice was sought by the U.S. government regarding the reproductive effects of the atom bomb on people in Japan and on the fertility of injured American veterans.[27]

A returning American soldier began taking estrogen and traveled to Copenhagen for a series of sex-reassignment surgeries that began in 1952. Newspapers that year reported on the debut of the New Yorker now known as Christine Jorgensen. The public was fascinated to learn not only that such surgeries were available but that hormones, too, could be be leveraged to physically feminize a male body.

TEN PAST NOON

The next year, Xie Jianshun made news in Taiwan. Xie was a soldier who lived as a heterosexual man (an identity with which he was happy) and whose body had intersex characteristics. Although he made it clear that he did not wish to be a woman, doctors were determined to assign his physical sex one way or the other, and they performed an exploratory surgery to determine which way they wished to go. While Xie was on the table, they determined that he should be turned into a female, a decision that was reported in the newspapers before it was disclosed to the recovering patient himself. "She is at present oblivious of her fate—that she is destined to become a lady," the newspaper printed.[28] This story has many interesting features, one of which is that Chinese society had always had a niche for men to become eunuchs, but at this moment—after the dissolution of the empire and the discovery of estrogen—popular interest leaned toward the possibility of medically changing men into women. This conceptual shift lies behind the title of Howard Chiang's book *After Eunuchs*.

Despite some historical adjacencies like this, transgender women are not eunuchs. They have different self-understandings and aspirations, and they explain themselves brilliantly.

Dr. Pershing, who had signed Ned's birth certificate and who survived smallpox contracted aboard an ocean liner, died at 90.[29]

"The night before my last session in therapy," Audre Lorde recollected of the year 1956 in *Zami,* "I dreamt that Muriel and I stood waiting for a train in a midnight-blue subway station. There are clusters of people about, but their backs are turned and I cannot see their faces. As the train pulls into the station, Muriel falls off the platform beneath its wheels. I stand on the platform as the train rolls over her, powerless to do anything, my heart breaking beneath the wheels. I awake to tears and a sense of mourning too deep for words, that would not go away."[30]

The late William Strunk's former student, E. B. White, revised the *Elements of Style* forty years after its initial publication. This partly posthumous collaboration resulted in the "Strunk & White" manual that writers celebrate today.

Katherine Johnson calculated a parabolic flight trajectory. She did it all the time. It was her job. She began her mathematical career for the U.S. government in a segregated unit for African-American women; her workplace desegregated when it was absorbed into NASA. "We wrote our own textbook, because there was no other text about space," she recalled. She remembered telling the NASA engineers: "You tell me when you want it and where you want it to land, and I'll do it backwards and tell you when to take off." Using her calculations, in 1961 Alan Shephard spent fifteen minutes in suborbital flight, becoming the first American in space. He reached an altitude of 187.5 kilometers and landed unscathed. Geometry had said he would. "It was easy to predict," Johnson said.[31]

≠≠≠≠≠≠≠≠≠≠

In a block in the southeastern part of Hillside Cemetery, near the forest line, there is a family plot with gravestones for Ned's maternal grandparents, and one sister of each of them; his mother's first cousin; his uncle and two aunts. There are flat crosses with his parents' initials and the stone for his infant brother Richard who died before Ned was born.[32]

Ned's sister Emily died in the surrounding Peekskill area in 1977. Neither of the siblings married nor had children. Hillside Cemetery reserved lots for them near their family members[33] but has no further records of whether their burials ever occurred. The cemetery may not have accepted remains if it did not receive payment. Grass grows over empty space here. I have never found a photograph of Emily, nor of their mother.

"My father once talked about having to identify someone who had killed themself," Felix's daughter, Carola Kittredge Lott, told me in 2013 in response to my inquiry. "He said the person had jumped and I assumed it was out a window."[34]

Ned could be anywhere, really. We leave behind a heap of carbon, a bit of phosphorus, maybe a couple milligrams of testosterone. I hear there's an island for New York City's unclaimed bodies.[35] I hear there's an afterlife. I hear it's made of the words we put out into the world and the way the world absorbs them.

"There are so many ghosts in our machines—their locations so hidden, their methods so ingenious, their motives so inscrutable," Walter Kirn wrote in 2015, "that not to feel haunted is not to be awake."[36]

NOTES TO "SUICIDE NOTE"

[1] Ace Boggess. *Displaced Hours.* Stirling, Scotland: Gatto, 2004. p. 12.

[2] Henry Adams. *The Education of Henry Adams.* The Massachusetts Historical Society, 1918. Chapter XXXIV: "A Law of Acceleration (1904)."

[3] MS Cumming, *Eunuchry.* "Text," black folder, unnumbered (probably meant to be Vol. 16, on psychology, not specific to castration).

[4] The data studied were from 1990 to 2003. "Epidemiology of suicide in the New York City subway system." Sandro Galea, MD, DrPH, Melissa Tracy, MPH, Tinka Markham Piper, MPH, CSW, Angela M. Bucciarelli, MPH, Ken Tardiff, MD MPH, Robyn Gershon, PhD, and David Vlahov, PhD. A recorded presentation at Public Health and Human Rights: APHA 134th Annual Meeting and Exposition. November 4-8, 2006, Boston, MA. https://apha.confex.com/apha/134am/techprogram/paper_133195.htm Accessed May 16, 2014.

[5] "Yet Another Worrisome Subway Statistic: More People Are Going on the Tracks." Emma G. Fitzsimmons. *New*

TEN PAST NOON

York Times. Sept. 17, 2018. https://www.nytimes.com/2018/09/17/nyregion/nyc-subway-tracks-delays.html

[6] I am extrapolating from the fact that, between 2010 and 2012, there were three incidents at the Cathedral Parkway station.

"Interactive Map Shows Where Subway Suicides And Other Injuries Happen Most." Aaron Marks. Oct. 24, 2013. http://gothamist.com/2013/10/24/map_subway_suicides_injuries.php#. Accessed May 16, 2014.

[7] The wedding invitation is saved in Felix's papers at the South Carolina Historical Society, but I have no evidence that Ned received an invitation or was meaningfully connected to the Vanderbilts.

[8] He said this under a heading: "Personality of Epileptics." MS Cumming, *Eunuchry*. "Text," black folder, unnumbered (probably meant to be Vol. 16, on psychology, not specific to castration).

[9] "Plunging to Earth." Rob Zaretsky. *The American Scholar.* Summer 2011. p. 59.

[10] "The History of the Roller Coaster." [No author named.] Davison. August 20, 2013. https://www.davison.com/blog/the-history-of-the-roller-coaster/ Accessed August 5, 2019.

[11] Valeria Luiselli. *Tell Me How It Ends: An Essay in Forty Questions.* Minneapolis: Coffee House Press, 2017. pp. 69–70.

[12] "Greenhorn." K. Tait Jarboe. Printed in *The Collection*, ed. Tom Léger and Riley MacLeod. New York: Topside Press, 2012. p. 124.

[13] Schrödinger attempted to strike down the idea of quantum indeterminacy with his famous hypothetical cat. If the life of a cat in a box depends on whether a particular atom has decayed, he asked, would the cat be simultaneously both alive and dead until you opened the box and took a look at the situation? He meant this as a *reductio ad absurdum*, but some people think it's correct.

[14] Mark Lilla. *The Once and Future Liberal: After Identity Politics.* HarperCollins: August 15, 2017. p. 60.
[15] "The Great Stone Face." Nathaniel Hawthorne. *The National Era,* January 24, 1850.
http://www.online-literature.com/hawthorne/139/ Accessed February 22, 2020.
[16] "What is art? Why we like what we like." Matthew Hutson. *The Atlantic.* July/August 2014. p. 28. Citing Jakesch and Leder, "Finding Meaning in Art." *The Quarterly Journal of Experimental Psychology,* Nov. 2009.
[17] "Catholics Appeal for Aid to Britain; 60 Prominent Members of the Clergy and Laity Issue Call to Send All Possible Help—Hitlerism is Attacked—Described as 'Denial of God' and 'Ruthless Without Honor'—Two Bishops Sign Plea." *New York Times.* Shipping and Mails, Weather Reports. October 28, 1940.
http://select.nytimes.com/gst/abstract.html?res=FB0C16FC3A5A11728DDDA10A94D8415B8088F1D3
[18] "After 80 years, *Darkness at Noon's* original text is finally translated." Alison Flood. *The Guardian.* September 24, 2019.
https://www.theguardian.com/books/2019/sep/24/darkness-at-noon-original-text-gets-first-english-translation-arthur-koestler Accessed January 28, 2020.
"A Different 'Darkness at Noon'." Michael Scammell. *New York Review of Books.* April 7, 2016.
https://www.nybooks.com/articles/2016/04/07/a-different-darkness-at-noon/ Accessed January 28, 2020.
[19] "Stone & Webster." Wikipedia. Accessed June 1, 2014.
[20] "Dream House as Prologue." Carmen Maria Machado. *In the Dream House: A Memoir.* Minneapolis: Graywolf, 2019. The term "violence of the archive" is credited to Saidiya Hartman. See Hartman's essay, "Venus in Two Acts." Small Axe (2008) 12 (2): 1–14.
https://doi.org/10.1215/-12-2-1
[21] Refer back to "Tracks 37-39: No Book": "Unanswered Questions."
[22] Wendy Plump. *Vow: A Memoir of Marriage (and Other*

Affairs). New York: Bloomsbury, 2013. pp. 211, 212-213.
[23] "Sympathy for the Devil." Steven Kotler. *LA Weekly.* July 28, 2005. https://www.laweekly.com/sympathy-for-the-devil/ Accessed February 22, 2020.
[24] Paul de Kruif. *The Male Hormone.* New York: Harcourt, Brace, and Co., 1945.
    "...the approach of my fortieth birthday." pp. 3-4.
    "...eunuchoids..." pp. 86-87.
[25] Library of Congress Copyright Office. ID number 401968, listed in the Catalog of Copyright Entries, 1945 Music, New Series, Vol. 40, Part 3, No. 1.
[26] "Benjamin Kittredge, 81, Dies; Restored Southern Plantation." *New York Times.* Nov. 1, 1981. https://www.nytimes.com/1981/11/01/obituaries/benjamin-kittredge-81-dies-restored-southern-plantation.html
[27] From his eulogy by Dr. John K. Lattimer at the meeting of the New York Society of the American Urological Association.
Errol [Earl] T. Engle papers, 1896-1970 (bulk 1922-1930), Health Sciences Library Archives and Special Collections, Columbia University.
[28] "Xie Jianshun kaidaohou zuori qingkuang zhengchang," [Xie Jianshun's operation proceeded normally yesterday], *Lianhebao [United Daily News],* August 22, 1953. Quoted by Howard Chiang. *After Eunuchs: Science, Medicine, and the Transformation of Sex in Modern China.* New York: Columbia University Press, 2018. p. 246.
[29] "Dr. Pershing Leaves Hospital." Wireless. New York Times. Oct. 20, 1938.
https://www.nytimes.com/1938/10/20/archives/dr-pershing-leaves-hospital.html
He died in 1955.
https://www.findagrave.com/memorial/13029039/edward-hamilton-pershing
Accessed January 29, 2020.
[30] Audre Lorde. *Zami: A New Spelling of My Name.* Berkeley: Crossing Press, 1982. Chapter 30.
[31] "Katherine Johnson." *Encyclopedia Britannica.*

https://www.britannica.com/biography/Katherine-Johnson-mathematician Accessed February 24, 2020.

"She Was a Computer When Computers Wore Skirts." Jim Hodges. *NASA.* August 26, 2008.

https://www.nasa.gov/centers/langley/news/researchernews/rn_kjohnson.html Accessed February 24, 2020.

[32] Benjamin L. Kittredge and Lucy (Dana) Kittredge; Benjamin's sister Elizabeth (Kittredge) Eaton and her daughter Elizabeth K. Eaton; Lucy's sister Mary Willard Dana; Sarah Kittredge; and Samuel Dana Kittredge and his wife Anna Mattison. There are flat crosses with the initials for Lucy (Kittredge) Cumming and George Miller Cumming, and the stone for their infant son Richard.

[33] Hillside Cemetery, "Beech block." Lots 8 and 38.

[34] Personal email correspondence with Carola Kittredge Lott. September 29, 2013.

[35] "New York City's Island of the Dead." Margaret McCormick. *Failed Architecture.* 12 May 2015. http://www.failedarchitecture.com/new-york-citys-island-of-death/

[36] "If You're Not Paranoid, You're Crazy." Walter Kirn. *The Atlantic.* November 2015.

https://www.theatlantic.com/magazine/archive/2015/11/if-youre-not-paranoid-youre-crazy/407833/ Accessed August 6, 2019.

NOW ARRIVING ON TRACK 40

NOW ARRIVING
ON TRACK 40

I have ideas for what Ned Cumming might have done differently.

He could have cultivated, curated, and focused on his correspondence.

With his talent for languages—his native English, plus French, German, and Latin—he could have examined intercultural transmission of ideas and pinpointed possible mistranslations.

Or—I am making suggestions—why not interview the guardians of living history? When he was writing, there were still elderly people who remembered the Emancipation Proclamation as a formative event in their lives, as well as younger people who had experienced the slow transition of Southern Reconstruction. In 1927, Zora Neale Hurston interviewed Kossola (known as Cudjo Lewis), the last known survivor of the last slaveship that arrived in America before the Civil War.[1] The Works Progress Administration hired interviewers between 1936 and 1938 to speak to thousands of formerly enslaved people.[2] If Ned really wanted to understand slavery's effect on personality, actual interviewees would have given him insight into trauma and resilience. This could potentially have been of service to others, which incidentally would have been of service to himself.

Although his obituary claimed that he enjoyed travel, there's no evidence that he aspired to travel for research. He knew from the reports of the contemporary English author of *The Holy Cities of Arabia* that the mosques were still staffed by young eunuchs,[3] but he didn't add a note that he wished to go and speak to them himself. He was probably aware that such a trip in itself would have justified a book, but I don't know if he realized it would likely have made a *better* book than his failed encyclopedia. He seemed to prefer secondhand Orientalism to firsthand. He doesn't have what Katherine Boo calls "the earned fact" (the information acquired through wholehearted "immersion journalism" in difficult circumstances),[4] nor even a travel story.

Here's another option, closer to home, and skirting the problem: Why not attend one of the deliriously fabulous crossdressing parties that caused the word "gay" to refer exclusively to homosexuality? He was living in that place, in that moment: 1930s New York.[5] Why not put his manuscript aside, gay or no gay, and just get happy-drunk?

He could have gone to Coney Island. He could have stayed away from the roller coaster and gotten an ice cream.

But I rather doubt he did.

"Too many people die with their music still in them," said Oliver Wendell Holmes.[6]

My advice is worth a nickel. The *Peanuts* character Lucy first opened her "Psychiatric Help, 5¢" booth in a comic strip published in 1959. Charlie Brown confided that he was depressed, and her advice was that he should "snap out of it!"[7] There is a reason this advice was in a comic strip and was priced less than a contemporary cup of coffee.

You can save your nickels and go somewhere. When Lucy opened her booth, three nickels could be exchanged for a token to get through the turnstile of the New York City subway.[8] The value of your nickel depends on what you use it for. Don't trade it for bad advice.

Irrespective of whether my advice is good, I also lack what is commonly referred to as the "moral authority" to give it, meaning that my own life is not exemplary for its work, wisdom, trauma survival, or any other form of saintliness.

Right now, every year, hundreds of thousands of Central Americans, many of them children, grab the roof or side of a freight train that runs north through Mexico.[9] When they cross the border into the United States, they are often detained. Andrea Pitzer defines a "concentration camp" as a place of "mass civilian detention without trial" where a government generally aims to deprive its prisoners of dignity and power.[10] These Latino migrants are in concentration camps in the United States.

I am a U.S. citizen; Colombians have begun to inform me that I actually do speak Spanish; and I have free time. I have spent precious years writing about a dead white man's list of eunuchs. So I don't have the moral authority to tell other people what they should do (or should have done) with their lives.

Making the best of the work I *have* done, however, I can publish it. I can write it with the self-awareness of its limits. I do not have solutions to large problems that threaten millions of people, but I have insight into certain matters with which a few people intensely concern themselves, and I may as well share that insight for their benefit. Someone out there right now is asking, "What are the *Eunuchry* papers at the New York Academy of Medicine?" and I'm letting them down if I hide my answer on my own cart. If I believe I'm letting them down, I can't sleep. Then neither of us are happy. I finish a book so that others can learn from it and so that I can move on. These are not the only steps one should take in a lifetime, but they are important first steps.

#########

TUCKER LIEBERMAN

"That's one small step for a man, one giant leap for mankind," an astronaut said when he put his boots on the moon.[11] It is believed now that it is done. Machines calculated the path. Ned would have been sixty-eight, watching it on television.

Some months after Felix and his daughter attended Emily's funeral in 1977, the Northeast was buried in snow. People still remember that blizzard. I wasn't born yet.

Kathleen Chang published a children's picture book, *The Iron Moonhunter*, about 19th-century Chinese workers in the Sierra Nevada who built a special train to carry the spirits of their fellow workers who died on the job.

I was born 100 days before what would have been Ned's 79th birthday. Felix died the following year, in 1981.

My birthplace is two-and-a-half degrees of longitude east of Ned's birthplace. Our views of the sun are ten minutes apart.

1983 brought the suicide of Arthur Koestler, who was terminally ill, and simultaneously the suicide of his wife, who was not.

Halley's Comet came back. I was five. I might see it again someday. It will come again when I am eighty-one. It runs on a predetermined track. The wedding invitations are sent out, the guests show up for the cake, and there it is, at exactly the appointed hour, the enormous, one-of-a-kind cake on a revolving table, more delicious for its evanescence, here it comes, there it goes.

I was a teenager when the last surviving Chinese palace eunuch, Sun Yaoting, died in his old age in Beijing, just as Ned had been a teenager when that same Sun Yaoting (who was the same age as Ned) was serving the abdicated emperor in the Forbidden City.[12]

There was a real Great Stone Face, probably the one on which Nathaniel Hawthorne based his story. It was a natural rock formation in New Hampshire. I saw it at least once as a child because I grew up in the region. It stayed intact while I was studying philosophy at college, and it collapsed in 2003.

"When a man dies," Anne Michaels wrote in her novel *Fugitive Pieces,* "his secrets bond like crystals, like frost on a window. His last breath obscures the glass."[13]

"There's no use getting morbid," as Felix's father's friend Herman Duryea had written to him not long before Duryea's death. "They will never come back again and I will try to write of the present."

‡‡‡‡‡‡‡‡‡

In 2015, a graduate student discovered the original German version of Arthur Koestler's novel, previously believed to have been lost when his girlfriend translated it rapidly into English as they prepared to flee the Nazis. The German version was published for the first time several years later as *Sonnenfinsternis [Solar*

Eclipse]. A new English translation of *Darkness at Noon* was then created by a translator who had more time.[14]

########

One of the first things my husband ever told me, shortly after we met in 2016, was that he aspired to travel to see a particular eclipse. Astronomers predict the exact time and place at which such phenomena will be visible. The planet from which we orbit and view the sun is on a predetermined track. The moon that orbits our planet and that may obstruct our view of the sun is on a predetermined track. Thus I knew three years in advance that, if he and I married, we would be together in Asia viewing this eclipse on December 26, 2019.

########

When I was thirty-six, he and I married on the eightieth wedding anniversary of Felix Kittredge and Carola Kip.

Figure 26 – I gave him this ring. It is supposed to look like an annular eclipse "ring of fire."

That year, the date fell on the third Monday in January, which I have always known during my lifetime as Martin Luther King, Jr. Day, the national holiday celebrating Dr. King's birthday. Dr. King would have been eighty-eight. It is a holiday in the United States where I grew up, but not in Colombia where I married.

A promise is a bond you accept around your life, and it changes everything that happens next.

✂✂✂✂✂✂✂✂✂

When I was thirty-eight, I self-published my own book on eunuchs in literature, *Painting Dragons*. It wasn't "complete" in the sense that it did not include all possible information on the subject; no book is ever complete that way. The set of all sets would have to contain itself, and such a library will expand infinitely, analyzing itself forever. My book was "complete" in the sense that I finished a thought and let go of it. Two months later, I self-published a memoir of suicidality, *Bad Fire*. I typed those books myself. Alan Turing whispers through the machine.

Through these projects, I came to understand something that Ned never did: my "eunuch" book and my "mental illness" book were not the same. (And neither of them is the same as this biomythographic hypno-saga.) Had I tried to weave them together, inventing some complex way in which a discussion of mental illness is "supplemental" to a discussion of castration, I would never have finished, and my handwritten papers would still be sitting on my cart. I realized they could be published separately. Let them be separate stars. Anyone can plug them into any constellation.

Also, a book needs to be written only if it does not already exist. I am writing this book now because no one else has written it. I am not trying to rewrite anything. There is nothing to be photocopied, and I am not a photocopy machine. Once I see the specific need to be filled, my words flow into those corners. I consulted the dead trees of some dead men, probably enough carbon for a whole sequoia when I add them up, but that's not what a book is. The soul is gathered from spiderweb and spins itself.

I have come to understand the importance of knowing how to write about myself before tackling a topic I care about. When the person who cares about the topic hides themselves in a dishonest or ignorant way, it is hard to develop a good thesis statement. My language ends up sounding like a man's idea of how a university wants him to write, or how a university would write if universities had hands and typewriters. Universities are not people and they do not care about their topics because they have no feelings. They would write boring books. People write books. We study at universities not to become universities but to learn to think for ourselves. I have to be willing and able to acknowledge myself in my role as an author; that is a distinct skill from writing about some external topic.

TEN PAST NOON

For years, I had an itch to rewrite Ned's book for him because of my mistaken assumption that he and I aspired to write the very same book. It took time for me to have a chance to read enough of his manuscript to understand what he was doing and why I needed to do something different. When I finally wrote my own *Painting Dragons*—which was about eunuch characters in fiction, but otherwise bore no relation to Ned's work—I understood that my book was specific to who I am, and that Ned's book would have had to be specific to who he was. Since he didn't do all his work, no one can ever finish his book for him. It doesn't need to be finished now. It was about him, and his time has passed, as have the 1930s, that narrow window in which his inquiry had roots.

Even his individual words would be hard to pick up again. The conditions under which we live give our words their meanings. Once the word is spoken, its original context slips away, and it can never form again exactly as it was. This was what Bakhtin meant, in his essay on the chronotope, by his use of the word "heteroglossia": every repetition of a sentence conveys a slightly different meaning.[15] Words aren't static. They're "ours" in the sense that they are particular to our lives, but we don't control the passage of time nor what eventually becomes of us and our words.

I had to experience completing a couple books of my own before I could have better insight into what Ned failed to do with *his* project. I thought I would learn how to rehabilitate his project; instead, I learned why it doesn't need to be saved.

I finally wrote the books in my own future. I can pick them up and read them. When I read my own book, I am

> creating a copy of it, in a very real sense I'm generating a new version...I am making the book my own, in retyping a book that already exists in the future, producing the very book I will eventually write. I am transcribing a book that I have, in a sense, not yet written, and in another sense, have always written, and in another sense, am currently writing, and in another sense, am always writing, and in another sense, will never write.
>
> —Charles Yu, *How To Live Safely in a Science Fictional Universe*[16]

I also had to destroy a handwritten manuscript from my own past, one of my teenage journals, to understand how letting go of some irredeemable sentences makes space for the theses I want to cultivate. As I wrote in *Bad Fire:*

> I made a final decision. The journal was not historically valuable. Even if I become historically significant someday, no librarian should ever have to curate that notebook in any manuscript collection and no well-meaning grad student should ever have to stumble across it. The journal had to die. I uncurated it. I

murdered all one hundred and twenty pages with scissors and a recycle bin.[17]

Through repetition in our minds and in our journals, words gain an illusory power, and when we examine the exact words we are repeating, we realize that many of them need to be cut. The manuscript shrinks. It has fewer words, and they are better words.

I could collect all the starlight in one place, but then I would have infinite starlight and it would not be very useful. It would be like standing in a tunnel and looking directly at an oncoming train.

Editing is repetitive. *Is that right? Is that right?* I ask over and over. *How do I know? What's a better way to explain it?* I feel as if I know the answers to my own questions, yet they are hard to pinpoint or explain. This is a contradiction; surely I do not really know what I cannot yet articulate. The process of writing, editing, and rewriting is, in this way, a kind of learning process. It is not like learning from someone else's book. I pull my own book out of myself. It is more like coming to know something for the first time that I always knew all along. An epiphanic architecture.

The manuscript is finished and is let go like the rope that tethers a balloon. Whoever is standing in the balloon at that moment will ride off in it. Whoever isn't will be left behind.

I learned that the proper use of molasses is as a slow-moving, sugary liquid in a small glass jar that can be licked off a spoon to fuel my body for a couple hours. Molasses should not be hoarded in a tank of great size. Nothing good will come of that. (Profit, possibly, if I assume that I will be the one who trades the final product rather than the one who harvests the raw sugar with my hands. But that capitalist hierarchy raises a whole category of ethical concern.) Regarding the tank as a work of engineering, I worry about its structural integrity. And, as I was saying, it remains the case that the purpose of molasses, its alpha and omega, its *telos*, has always been simply for someone to eat it. When we taste molasses, we immediately know that this is true. Being eaten is what molasses is for. The taste is an onto-epistemic revelation, incontrovertible, Grade A, pure.

This insight is not what I originally expected to get from meeting Ned, but friends often reveal our true selves to us in unexpected ways.

> ...it is important not to restrict the idea of friendship to people who are alive at the same time, despite this being the main category. For one can have friendships with writers long dead...One good way to know what sort of person someone is, is to examine the kinds of friendship he or she has maintained through time, including these non-standard ones.
>
> —A. C. Grayling, *Friendship* (2013)[18]

#########

TEN PAST NOON

It does not matter if you have been kissed by Harvard. It does not matter how far you develop your character and industriousness. If you are not an expert in the subject, you cannot authenticate the Nampa Image. You are in the middle of the desert looking at bits of clay from when the dinosaurs roamed the Earth and you are telling us how old you think humanity is based on a graven image the size of your finger that you happen to hold in your hand. You do not know what you are talking about. Your whiteness carries a tiny bit less social currency once someone calls it out for what it isn't, and your whiteness won't give you the answer. It takes so long just to see the whiteness, to name it with the same words with which it named you.

Being accepted to Harvard at age fifteen conveys illusions about how much effort will be required to write your book. The book is on a complex and personal topic. There is infinite light in the sky, but you have to wait for it to reach you. When it arrives, you will still have to interpret the constellations because their apparent position depends on where you stand.

You can take one of your binders off your cart and publish it. You should acknowledge that it is limited, that it is not the only binder on the cart, that it would be different if you'd published it earlier or later because all the binders always change, and that someone else would have written it differently and probably will someday. You don't have to finish reading or writing the encyclopedia. The acknowledgment of the limitation of your work *is what makes it good* and is what sets you free of it. Your acceptance of your limitation also eases you into your fate so you don't end up as a tragedy. Do pick up the binder, see how it is limited, and finish it. Fear to die with all your binders on your cart.

The Sphinx asks: *What walks on four legs in the morning, two legs at noon, and three legs in the evening?* You already know. You are allocated one orbit of Halley's Comet, no more. One *sæculum.* If you lived an extra half-rotation, you'd make medical history.

"*Ickira,*" says my hip, loudly, when I get off the couch.

Time will be measured by the Earth's movements in relation to the sun. Years will pass, as surely as there will be morning, noon, and evening. Ecclesiastes wrote more than two millennia ago that there is a time to be born and a time to die; a time to wreck stuff and a time to create; a time to sit on your archives and a time to send them to the landfill; a time to shut your mouth and a time to speak up because you discovered something useful to say.

We often arrive at these junctures according to patterns, some of which are consequences of our private feelings and others that are shared behavioral patterns of the nations to which we belong. We have chronotopes. Bits and pieces of the stories can surprise us. But no one gets broad

TEN PAST NOON

exemptions from the rules. You start by crawling and then you grow up, and if you survive until the comet comes back, you'll be tired and leaning on a crutch. Some people have more or less physical mobility, but that is not the point. The point is that no one has a *radically* different experience. Some people are born with an extra limb or lose a limb in the war, and some infants are left for dead in a Greek tragedy and are named after their mutilated feet, but no one has multiple-horsepower angel wings and a dorsal fin and shoots themselves into space beyond the orbit of Halley's Comet. None of us is transgender enough to pull that off. We may try, but we do not achieve it. There is no hour whatsoever when that will happen. It's a chronotope that exists only in fiction. If you don't want to become a real-life tragedy, don't lie to yourself that you're going there. You will fail the riddle. The Sphinx will eat you. When you know your general limits, your train will glide more gracefully down the track.

"How many more years I shall be able to work on the problem," the rocket scientist Robert Goddard once wrote to the science fiction novelist H. G. Wells, "I do not know; I hope, as long as I live. There can be no thought of finishing, for 'aiming at the stars,' both literally and figuratively, is a problem to occupy generations..."[19]

In Dr. Martin Luther King, Jr.'s final sermon, he says: "If I were standing at the beginning of time, with the possibility of taking a kind of general and panoramic view of the whole of human history up to now, and the Almighty said to me, 'Martin Luther King, which age would you like to live in?,' I would take my mental flight..." King imagines various important eras he'd like to appreciate and the long life he'd hope to have. What's most important to him, he says, is his belief that collective liberation will come someday. Comparing himself to Moses who wandered forty years in the desert and could only look down from the mountain, he assures the crowd, "I've seen the promised land. I may not get there with you. But...we, as a people, will get to the promised land!"[20] No one has the opportunity to witness everything as an individual. But if we feel linked to others in the past and future, we experience the meaning of life beyond our own limits.

≠≠≠≠≠≠≠≠≠

The first time I went to see Ned's papers, I was eager to read everything and was alarmed that the hands of the clock were moving. The library was only open for a few hours. At ten past noon, the librarian needs a lunchbreak, in which case I must also exit the reading room. And then I had to return to Boston.

Seven years later, I knew when I was done. I recognized my own finish line because my attention had shifted. I no longer wanted or needed to ensure that I'd read every last piece of paper on the cart. It wasn't that my project was done; *I* was done, and therefore my project needed to wrap up. On my last day at the New York Academy of Medicine library, I did not want to be there anymore. I went mostly just to feel what it was like to sit there and *not* feel that hunger for those particular papers. To flip through them and acknowledge that I finally understood them at least as well as, and in some respects better than, their author did. To confirm that I had graduated. The feeling of being done is the feeling of walking to the library on my last day, arriving deliberately an hour after the doors open, no laptop under my arm, no existing notes with my own manuscript-in-progress, no agenda, nothing but a cell phone without a charger and a pocket notebook and pencil for whatever thoughts might pop up. "Being done" is the feeling of knowing that the answers are in *me*. It feels like wanting to scribble my own ideas in my pocket notebook rather than read Ned's manuscript. It feels like not feeling sad about this.

"My lesson is in reaching and honoring limits, not in ignoring them," DeWitt Henry wrote of running marathons. "If it is given for the run to be ten miles, fifteen, twenty, then it is. If it is not given, then it is not. It is not for me to force or will the outcome. Strength is not the issue. The run itself is the issue."[21]

Not having feelings about a stack of papers I don't need is a good kind of doneness. We all prefer that to the kind of doneness that makes a person jump in front of a train. That's a hard one. But we don't always have a choice in how our endings shake out.

I can't transcribe Ned's entire manuscript because I don't have it. It is in New York; I am not. Also—although this is still hard for my whiteness to grasp—it isn't mine. White men are always trying to steal each other's stuff as well as everyone else's. The papers belonged to Ned, and now they belong to the New York Academy of Medicine. There's no way I can have them even if I believe they would benefit me.

These days, even the books I have I don't really have. They're not physical. They're on an e-reader. They can display as black text on a white background for reading during the daytime or as white text on a black background for reading after dark. The battery-powered electric light comes through the machine. The books are made of light.

##########

Earlier, I presented a new riddle: *When train engineers go home and relax with a novel, what do they always see in the book?*

Here is the promised answer: People who drive trains are generally sighted and have hands that can grasp objects. When they physically pick up a book—whether it's made of printed pages or is a display on a small electronic device—there is

TEN PAST NOON

something in their field of vision that is always the same, no matter what they're reading: It's their own hands. Their fingers are wrapped around the book they're holding. And whether they realize it or not, their individual personhood affects how they perceive the book's content. Every book they have ever read has been interpreted a certain way because of who they are. They have hands that can hold a book; their wrists and knuckles are hairy, or their nails are painted, or both, or neither; their skin is a given color. They'd see something different in the book were they different people with different hands.

Anything that facilitates or interferes with the way you absorb the book is part of your experience of the book and also your experience of yourself. Maybe you use an assistive device to hold the book or turn the pages, or maybe a human or robot reads the book aloud to you. Maybe you read in a fancy living room, in a sleeping bag under a bridge, or on a passenger train. Everything that goes into your reading experience affects what you learn from the book, and what you learn when confronted with this book, in whatever conditions you engage it, tells you more about who you are. You train your attention on the book and you learn more about what your attention is.

#########

TUCKER LIEBERMAN

In December 2019, as I reclined on a sleeper train departing Indore, two tall women in saris made their presence known. They walked down the aisle with performance energy, clapped their hands, and yelled something brief in a language I did not know. "Ten rupees," one of the women specified in English for my benefit. This was the same price as the tiny paper cups of tea and milk that the *chai-wallahs* carried through the stations. The men near me on the train quickly grabbed their wallets and handed over their small bills to the women.

I recognized this situation from books, though I had never experienced it, as it involves a social category that is not part of American culture. These people may be intersex or transgender; they may call themselves *kinnar* or *hijra*; at some point, they may have been called "eunuch" in English. They may identify as women or as something else. They live and work together, demand money in exchange for blessings, and are seen as simultaneously holy and sexually threatening. That is the stereotype I'd learned, and it helped me navigate the situation I was in.

Very likely they are not the only people I encountered in India who had marginalized genders or interesting gender stories. They are simply the only two people whom I was able to recognize as such, because they happened to fit a broad category of which I was already aware.

One of the women touched my head gently

and muttered something. When I did not immediately respond, she grabbed my inner thigh sharply and yelled in her language. All the other passengers could see and hear that I was being groped. I produced ten rupees. She softened, touched my head gently again, repeated the blessing, and she and her friend left the train car.

Of course, there is more to any individual than a stereotype or social category, and my foreigner's understanding of the category must be shallow. Because they were dressed as women, I assume they prefer feminine pronouns in English, if they have an opinion about English. Apart from that, I don't know how to refer to their gender.

To know the correct way to refer to their gender, I would have had to ask those individuals how they want others to describe them. It was not my place to ask. I don't even know their names, so it is not my prerogative to have details about their gender. That knowledge was not part of our transaction. The exchange was ten rupees for a blessing. It was not an invitation to discuss other people's outmoded words for us. They didn't ask what kind of "transsexual" I am, so I didn't ask what kind of "eunuch" they are.

If we priced that information, it would cost a lot more than ten rupees. Maybe they would not make theirs available at any price. Maybe it is more valuable for me not to have it. Generalizations can be useful, but there is wisdom in not tightening the screw to pin down people with whom I'm not in dialogue. There is value in stepping back and letting go of things that are not mine to have.

This story is partly about someone else, and partly about me. I think of a line by Vijay Seshadri, an American poet who was born in India and grew up in Ohio.[22] In his poem "Enlightenment," an unnamed man trades hedonism for personal kindness, and violence for political compromise. "The world," the poet's voice chimes in, pivoting in a stunning way, "is only its own membrane."[23] He gives no further explanation. A membrane is what contains and defines each cell in our bodies while remaining porous to allow the functions of life. Membranes surround an entire human embryo. Our skin is a membrane. A membrane allows a living being to be distinct from others, but it also allows interchange and the growth that will result. It creates the opportunity for a label while simultaneously serving as the grounds on which to challenge the label. We are part of the Earth on which we depend. Of course, "your compassion for our kind" also serves a role in enlightenment, somehow, according to the poet; "our kind," insofar as we have similar membranes by which to identify "our kind."

There's no taxonomy here. It's just a travel story. People are not merely data in the encyclopedia. We are passengers on the same train.

TEN PAST NOON

#########

My husband and I had traveled to India, as I mentioned before, to see the annular solar eclipse on December 26, 2019, exactly as we were determined to do.

In this kind of eclipse, the sun appears as a bright ring around the dark center of the moon passing in front of it. We changed our position and, for a minute, we saw the opposite of what we'd always seen in the sun: a circle of darkness.

Figure 27 – "Ring of Fire," December 26, 2019. U.S. National Weather Service.[24]

#########

The e-reader casts light over dark water.

Over the ocean, a reflection is a line that seems to travel directly from the beacon to the eyes of the person who is looking at it. The person's vision follows the line back to the beacon again.

What they see when they study a book in their e-reader tells them who they are.

A different person standing somewhere else would see the reflection cast a different path. They'd see the path that leads to them. The same book tells them who they are, too.

#########

Deep Springs remains a two-year school for a small number of students who like abstract thought, geographic isolation, and occasional jokes in German. A young man who graduated in 2006 explained that L. L. Nunn was still invoked as a kind of guiding spirit, if not exactly as an authority. At Student Body meetings, he said, one might hear: "Nunn says X, I take that to mean Y, so let's do Z. There is a sense that Nunn is at every S.B. meeting. There's a Nunn in all of us." Another student, discussing agricultural techniques, explained that he was using the word "today" to mean "in the outside world"—"inadvertently revealing," the journalist editorialized, "something about the Deep Springs conception of time."[25]

Deep Springs welcomed its first women students in 2018.[26]

I try to spend part of my time in "today." It is often a good place to be.

Bogotá, the Colombian city where I live now, is currently managing a population the size of New York City's with no trains. The contract for its first train system was awarded to a Chinese consortium consisting of China Harbour Engineering and Xi'An Rail Transportation Group.[27] After much debate, it was decided that the trains will be elevated. It is perhaps not appropriate to call it a "subway," then; here, it is more generically called a "metro." More important than how we compare it with trains elsewhere is that the city will finally build it after a whole comet orbit of talking about it. "Yo como que todavía no me lo creo," said the mayor.[28] *I don't quite believe it yet myself.*

Meanwhile, we wait for the bus. The metro *will be believed,* as some have said, *when it is done.*

"Time exists in order that everything doesn't happen all at once," said Susan Sontag, "and space exists so that it doesn't all happen to you."[29]

A scene change in my own life story was my move from Boston to Bogotá, and a chronotope change is the project to build a metro. In the first home, trains already existed before I was born; in the second home, trains will be built again.

"And now you're probably thinking: That's an amazing amount of coincidence," said Gemma Files in *Experimental Film.*

> Which is true, I guess, but history thrives on coincidence, as does archaeology. Sometimes all it takes is being in the right place for the wrong reasons, then moving

just a little only to find you're standing on top of something you weren't even looking for, something you never would have found otherwise.[30]

I have never seen the Nampa figurine, the piece of clay pressed into a human shape that was pulled out of the dig site for a water well in 1889. The Idaho State Historical Society has it, maybe in storage, maybe on display; sources differ. I don't plan to travel to see it. Ned Cumming's father once touched it, but I don't need to touch it to tell its story.

Memoirists, says Carmen Maria Machado, "braid the clays of memory and essay and fact and perception together, smash them into a ball, roll them flat. They manipulate time; resuscitate the dead. They put themselves, and others, into necessary context."[31] For that purpose, the Nampa figurine is not the clay I want. I hear it's a hoax. If it was indeed sculpted with a thumbprint in the chest to indicate breasts, it could have depicted a woman or maybe a eunuch. There's a potential story right there. But I can't hold on to every story someone's fathers' colleagues made up while they were managing the trains in the middle of a desert I've never seen.

We often fixate on points behind us, and we see them, out the train window, receding into the distance. It's like watching a movie. Our brains collate distinct images into the impression of continuous movement.

TEN PAST NOON

People have watched movies for enjoyment since the kinetoscope in the 1890s. At first, only one person at a time could look into the box, and that was a solitary experience. Inventors found ways to project the image on a screen so the experience could be shared. We watch the movie and feel as though we are moving together—maybe forward, maybe backward—though really we are armchair travelers.

Then maybe we have an idea that we could experience a kind of motion that is more than an illusion. More, even, than a chronotope, which is a set of individual illusions. We could experience a motion that hacks the chronotope. We could go truly forward.

#########

"Se propone una escala ética superior: la del fin de la memoria humana," the educator Félix González Montejo writes.

> Y mientras llega el momento donde no se pueda decir que existimos alguna vez, hay que empoderar al individuo y a las comunidades para construir y destruir sus memorias en un ciclo en el que en cada giro de todo desaprendizaje sea escrutado con más vigor que el precedente.[32]

> *[One might propose a superior ethical scale: that of the end of human memory. And, as the moment approaches in which we can't say whether we ever existed, it's*

necessary to empower individuals and communities to build and destroy their memories in a cycle in which each rotation of every unlearning is scrutinized more vigorously than the one before.]

╪╪╪╪╪╪╪╪╪╪

The 1920s became the 1930s, and still Ned couldn't leave the 19th century behind. Though I don't know if he was physically able to grow a handlebar Monopoly mustache like his father's, he could nonetheless have been president of a dozen railroads. He had access to his father's business network and didn't want it. He thought of himself as a classicist but didn't want to go to school. He was living in some fantasy inside a binder. He wouldn't own the trains, and he let the train own him.

╪╪╪╪╪╪╪╪╪╪

When we compare two people to evaluate who is older and who is younger, sometimes we look only at their dates of birth, and other times we also consider what happens afterward.

To illustrate the former method: Ned had an older brother he never met, a baby who only lived five days, who is eternally five days old, but who will always be older than Ned by virtue of his date of birth. Ned has always been and will always be older than I in that way.

Ned used to be older than I in the latter sense,

TEN PAST NOON

too, but he no longer is. We say that people "outgrow their friends" when their interests and capacities diverge, but they also outgrow their friends when they've hacked the calendar. Ned is eternally 39 years and 100 days old. I am still growing.

##########

Today, my husband, Arturo Serrano, is writing his alternate history novel, *To Climates Unknown*, in which the United States never existed.

#########

We fixate our vision on a series of points. We pay attention to what has always mattered. What we choose to care about is the story of who we are. Who we are might also matter to someone else.

Modern movements like Black Lives Matter, Trans Lives Matter, and Black Trans Lives Matter, says C. Riley Snorton, activate a hope that someday people who have been marginalized for these identities "*will have mattered* to everyone." That renegotiation might "end the world" as we know it, "but worlds end all the time."[33]

And so it will be, until the Second Coming: *in sæcula sæculorum*, world without Ned.

I am finishing the book I was always going to write in this science nonfictional universe. There's a one-way mirror on the wall. They're used in observation chambers. Depending on what side I'm on and the lighting conditions, I might see through the glass or I might only see my own face. This mirror is stamped "Hammermill Bond" after the American paper company. For years, I wrote what I saw, and, finally, what I see is what I wrote. I suppose the book looks a lot like me. I hope someone can see through it.

Thomas Mann said of his protagonist in *The Magic Mountain*:

> If he does not find the Grail, yet he divines it, in his deathly dream, before he is snatched downwards from his heights into the European catastrophe. It is the idea of the human being, the conception of a future humanity that has passed through and survived the profoundest knowledge of disease and death. The Grail is a mystery, but humanity is a mystery too.[34]

We are entering the 2020s, and it is time for me to leave the 20th century behind. The Doomsday Clock reads two minutes to midnight, and I am needed for other projects.

The train rolls slowly into the station according to a precise schedule and the wheels click until it reaches its resting place. The people at the station have been waiting for me.

The train can go back where it came from. If you read this book backwards, you will see all

TEN PAST NOON

the same things and they will look familiar, but this time they will mean something different to you. You can try it.

The train doesn't have to return exactly where it came from. At the railway switch, if someone pulls the lever, a little piece of track moves and connects the train to another major piece of track. Someone already has the lever in their hand.

The entrance to the New York Academy of Medicine bears the motto *"Post mille secula præscindetur occasia aliquid adjiciendi."* That is, even "after a thousand ages" pass, there will always be time—a top-shelf opportunity, specially reserved, *præscindetur,* "scissored off" like a slice of wedding cake—for another person to toss their part into the mountain of knowledge. Thousands of *sæcula,* snowballing into a world without end, effectively—the unending larger world beyond the smaller worlds whose time must come to a close.

By 2140, Manhattan has been drowned by a dramatic sea level rise, and wealthy New Yorkers have adapted to life in the tops of skyscrapers. This is the premise of *New York 2140,* a novel by Kim Stanley Robinson.[35]

TUCKER LIEBERMAN

Zen and the Art of Motorcycle Maintenance suggests, as mentioned once before, that we stop examining the sand and shift attention to the place "from which the sand is taken."[36] I also note that, if the sand is part of the world, so is the person walking over the horizon; thus, another approach is to notice the person who enters, takes something, and leaves, the person who has expectations about how long sand can be held in the fist.

As usual, the journey teaches more than whatever broken clay figurine is at the beginning or the end of it, especially if someone made the figurine to mislead us. The initial questions—*What is it? Who made it?*—are impossible to answer, and any answers I might invent won't address my underlying questions. If I'm on a train and I want to know where I'm going, I can look out the window—there goes another milemarker! Whether my ways of knowing are colonizing, colonized, or something else depends in part on what I choose to give and take. If I want to know where I am now, I have to look beyond the object I'm grasping and instead begin to notice, with openness and curiosity, the thing that does the grasping: my fingers, my palm lined with thousands of bulls that I can engage or let be, the solidity and the function of my own hand.

—Tucker Lieberman
Information Architect and Product Manager
Age 39 Years, 100 Days

TEN PAST NOON

NOTES TO
"NOW ARRIVING ON TRACK 40"

[1] Zora Neale Hurston. *Barracoon: The Story of the Last 'Black Cargo.'* HarperCollins, 2018.
[2] "WPA Slave Narratives." Neil R. McMillen. *Mississippi History Now.* February 2005. http://mshistorynow.mdah.state.ms.us/articles/64/wpa-slave-narratives Accessed July 18, 2019.
[3] The author was Eldon Rutter. He traveled in 1925–6. Mentioned in MS Cumming, *Eunuchry.* "Text" (black folder), Vol. 10.
[4] "The Earned Fact: PW Talks with Katherine Boo." Robert Avila. *Publishers Weekly.* Dec. 9, 2011. https://www.publishersweekly.com/pw/by-topic/authors/interviews/article/49803-the-earned-fact-pw-talks-with-katherine-boo.html Accessed January 17, 2020.
[5] See: George Chauncey. *Gay New York: Gender, Urban Culture, and the Making of the Gay Male World, 1890-1940.* Basic Books, 1994.
[6] Oliver Wendell Holmes, first quoted in Huffingtonpost.com, then quoted in *The Week,* July 26, 2013, p. 17.
[7] Charles M. Schulz. *Peanuts.* March 27, 1959. https://peanuts.fandom.com/wiki/March_1959_comic_strips Accessed February 19, 2020.
[8] "All the MTA Fare Hikes of the Last 100 Years." Diane Pham. *6sqft.* March 23, 2015. https://www.6sqft.com/all-the-mta-fare-hikes-over-the-last-100-years-plus-a-video-of-when-it-cost-just-15-cents/ Accessed February 19, 2020.
[9] Valeria Luiselli. *Tell Me How It Ends: An Essay in Forty Questions.* Minneapolis: Coffee House Press, 2017. pp. 18-19.

[10] Andrea Pitzer. *One Long Night: A Global History of Concentration Camps.* Introduction: "Sailing to Guantánamo." New York: Hachette, 2017. p. 6, p. 5.
[11] "Armstrong's famous 'one small step' quote—explained." Associated Press. *Navy Times.* July 13, 2019. https://www.navytimes.com/news/your-navy/2019/07/13/armstrongs-famous-one-small-step-quote-explained/ Accessed Oct. 21, 2019.
[12] "The Death of the Last Emperor's Last Eunuch." Seth Faison. *New York Times.* December 20, 1996. https://www.nytimes.com/1996/12/20/world/the-death-of-the-last-emperor-s-last-eunuch.html Accessed February 19, 2020.
[13] Anne Michaels. *Fugitive Pieces: A Novel.* New York: Alfred A. Knopf, 1997. p. 114.
[14] Matthias Wessel was the graduate student who found the German manuscript, after which Philip Boehm translated it into English.
[15] The glossary entry for "heteroglossia" *[raznorecie, raznorecivost]* at the end of M. M. Bakhtin, *The Dialogic Imagination,* ed. Michael Holquist. Trans. from the Russian by Caryl Emerson and Michael Holquist. (1981) Austin, Texas: University of Texas Press, 2008.
[16] Charles Yu. *How to Live Safely in a Science Fictional Universe.* Pantheon, 2010. p. 104.
[17] Tucker Lieberman. *Bad Fire: A Memoir of Disruption.* Bogotá, Colombia: Glyph Torrent, 2019. p. 10.
[18] A. C. Grayling. *Friendship (2013).* New Haven: Yale, 2013. p. 171.
[19] "The Stuff of Goddard's Dreams: Goddard's Legacy & NASA's Journey to Mars." Remarks by NASA Administrator Charles Bolden. Goddard Memorial Symposium, Greenbelt, Maryland. February 9, 2016. https://www.nasa.gov/sites/default/files/atoms/files/bolden_goddard_2016.pdf Accessed January 16, 2020.
[20] "The story of how Michael King Jr. became Martin Luther King Jr." DeNeen L. Brown. *Washington Post.* Jan. 15, 2019.

https://www.washingtonpost.com/history/2019/01/15/story-how-michael-king-jr-became-martin-luther-king-jr/ Accessed February 2, 2020.

[21] DeWitt Henry, "On Aging," in *Safe Suicide: Narratives, Essays, and Meditations.* Los Angeles, California: Red Hen Press, 2008.

[22] "Vijay Seshadri (1954–)." Poets.org. https://poets.org/poet/vijay-seshadri Accessed February 17, 2020.

[23] Vijay Seshadri. "Enlightenment." Originally published in Poem-a-Day on January 1, 2018, by the Academy of American Poets. https://poets.org/poem/enlightenment Accessed February 17, 2020.

[24] National Weather Service photo (public domain) posted to Twitter, December 26, 2019. This photograph was taken from Guam, where the same eclipse was visible. https://twitter.com/NWSKeyWest/status/1210223364943405057

[25] "The Searchers: The fate of progressive education at Deep Springs College." Dana Goodyear. *The New Yorker.* August 28, 2006. https://www.newyorker.com/magazine/2006/09/04/the-searchers-dana-goodyear Accessed Oct. 1, 2019.

[26] "Coeducation." Deep Springs. https://www.deepsprings.edu/coeducation/ Accessed Oct. 1, 2019.

[27] "Pesos pesados de la ingeniería, los socios del consorcio chino Apca Transmimetro." *El Tiempo.* 18 de octubre de 2019. p. 1.2.

[28] "Bogotá ya tiene quien construya y opere la primera línea del metro." *El Tiempo.* 18 de octubre de 2019. p. 1.2.

[29] Susan Sontag, *At the Same Time: Essays and Speeches.*

[30] Gemma Files. *Experimental Film.* Toronto, Canada: ChiZine, 2015. p. 73.

[31] "Dream House as Prologue." Carmen Maria Machado. *In the Dream House: A Memoir.* Minneapolis: Graywolf, 2019.

[32] "La formación de la competencia comunicativa intercultural en la clase de lenguas extranjeras: un ciclo de transformación integral del ser." Félix A. González Montejo. *Interculturalidad y formación de profesores: Perspectivas pedagógicas y multilingües.* ed. Beatriz Peña Dix, Isabel Tejada-Sánchez y Anne-Marie Truscott de Mejía. Bogotá, Colombia: Universidad de los Andes, 2019. p. 169.
The English translation is mine. (The original article has "hemos existimos"; the author confirms that this was a publishing error.)

[33] C. Riley Snorton. *Black on Both Sides: A Racial History of Trans Identity.* Minneapolis: University of Minnesota Press, 2017.

[34] "The Making of *The Magic Mountain.*" Thomas Mann. *The Atlantic,* January 1953. Reprinted in *The Magic Mountain* (originally S. Fischer Verlagberlin, 1924). Translated from the German by H. T. Lowe-Porter. England: A. Wehaten and Co., Exeter, 1971. p. 729.

[35] Kim Stanley Robinson. *New York 2140.* New York: Orbit, 2017.

[36] Robert M. Pirsig. *Zen and the Art of Motorcycle Maintenance.* (1974) New York: Bantam, 1975. p. 76.

CABOOSE

ACKNOWLEDGMENTS

Thank you to my early onboarders. I received help from **Cit Callahan; Claire Schwartz; Sydney Fowler; Emma Grae; Jesus MacLean; Félix González Montejo; Rebecca Sullivan; Denise Rayman; Tom Johnson; Richard Wassersug; Craig Hanscom;** my parents, **Marc and Linda Lieberman;** and my husband, **Arturo Serrano.** I value **Robbie Samuels'** tips on self-publishing.

All errors, shortcomings, and sins are mine.

I am grateful to **Arlene Shaner,** the Historical Collections Librarian at the New York Academy of Medicine, for granting me access to the E. D. Cumming *Eunuchry* papers, and to my sister and brother-in-law, **Brooke and Reed Collins,** for hosting me during those visits to Manhattan.

I thank **Valerie Simpson** at St. George's School Archives and **Carola Lott** for their assistance by email.

I appreciate my readers, too, for the gift of your limited time. You are driving the train now.

ABOUT THE AUTHOR

Haunted by his acquaintance with the late author of *Eunuchry*, **Tucker Lieberman** wrote the ghost story "Exit Interview" for DefCon One's "imaginary friends" fiction anthology, *I Didn't Break the Lamp*. His recent books include *Painting Dragons: What Storytellers Need to Know About Writing Eunuch Villains* and *Bad Fire: A Memoir of Disruption*.

At Brown University, he received the Casey Shearer Memorial Award for Creative Nonfiction and a bachelor's degree in philosophy. He earned a postgraduate degree in journalism from Boston University.

Originally from Boston, Massachusetts, he lives with the science fiction writer Arturo Serrano in Bogotá, Colombia.

This book has one page for every month of his life up to this point. He is turning forty.

WWW.TUCKERLIEBERMAN.COM

PRIMARY TEXTS

MS Cumming, Edward Dilworth. *Eunuchry; the history of human castration with notes on the personalities of eunuchs.* 59 boxes.
Housed at:
New York Academy of Medicine
New York, New York
http://nyam.org

Kittredge, Benjamin Sr. (1859–1951) and Benjamin Jr. (1900–1981). Kittredge family papers, ca. 1888–1958. SCHS 1228.00, Containers 25/12-22.
Housed at:
South Carolina Historical Society
Charleston, South Carolina
https://schistory.org

Deep Springs College records, 1913-1999. Collection Number: 6428.

Lucien L. Nunn papers, 1863-1971. Collection Number: 37-4-1770.

Housed at:
Division of Rare and Manuscript Collections
Cornell University Library
Ithaca, New York
https://rare.library.cornell.edu

Norman Mosley Penzer papers, 1919-1928.

Housed at:
Rare Book & Manuscript Library Collections
Butler Library, Columbia University
New York, New York
http://www.columbia.edu

Errol [Earl] T. Engle papers, 1896-1970 (bulk 1922-1930).

Housed at:
Health Sciences Library Archives and Special Collections
Columbia University Medical Center
New York, New York
http://www.columbia.edu

SELECTED BOOKS

Adams, Henry. *The Education of Henry Adams.* The Massachusetts Historical Society, 1918.

Akers, Floyd [L. Frank Baum]. *The Boy Fortune Hunters of China.* Reilly and Britton, 1909.

Aklekar, Rajendra B. *A Short History of Indian Railways.* New Delhi: Rupa, 2019.

Alighieri, Dante. *La divina commedia [The Divine Comedy].* Foligno, Italy: Johann Numeister and Evangelista Angelini da Trevi, 1472.

Bakhtin, M. M. *The Dialogic Imagination.* (1975) Translated from the Russian by Caryl Emerson and Michael Holquist (1981). Austin, Texas: University of Texas Press, 2008.

Barker, Dan. *Free Will Explained: How Science and Philosophy Converge to Create a Beautiful Illusion.* New York: Sterling, 2018.

Bly, Robert and Marion Woodman. *The Maiden King: The Reunion of Masculine and Feminine.* New York: Henry Holt and Company, 1998.

Brody, Jules. *'Fate' in Oedipus Tyrannus: A Textual Approach*. (Arethusa Monographs, XI.) Buffalo, New York: SUNY Buffalo, 1985.

Burton, Robert. *On Being Certain: Believing You Are Right Even When You're Not*. New York: St. Martin's Griffin, 2008.

Chang, Gordon H., and Shelley Fisher Fishkin, eds. with Hilton Obenzinger and Roland Hsu. *The Chinese and the Iron Road: Building the Transcontinental Railroad*. Stanford, Calif.: Stanford University Press, 2019.

Covert, Abby. *How to Make Sense of Any Mess*. Amazon, 2014.

Drager, Lindsey. *The Archive of Alternate Endings*. Ann Arbor, Mich.: Dzanc, 2019.

Dzmura, Noach, ed. *Balancing on the Mechitza: Transgender in Jewish Community*. North Atlantic Books: 2010.

Egri, Lajos. *The Art of Dramatic Writing: Its Basis in the Creative Interpretation of Human Motives*. (1942) New York: Touchstone, 1972.

Files, Gemma. *Experimental Film*. Toronto, Canada: ChiZine, 2015.

Fleming, Crystal M. *How To Be Less Stupid About Race*. Boston: Beacon Press, 2018.

Freud, Sigmund. *Die Traumdeutung [The Interpretation of Dreams]*. Leipzig and Vienna: Franz Deuticke, 1900.

Grayling, A. C. *Friendship*. New Haven: Yale, 2013.

Haverington, Christine with the Middletown Historical Society and the Newport Historical Society. *Middletown*. Arcadia, 2012.

Hurston, Zora Neale. *Barracoon: The Story of the Last 'Black Cargo.'* HarperCollins, 2018.

Jen, Gish. *Tiger Writing: Art, Culture, and the Interdependent Self.* Cambridge, Mass.: Harvard University Press, 2013.

Jones, Ann. *They Were Soldiers: How the Wounded Return from America's Wars—The Untold Story*. Haymarket/Dispatch, 2013.

Kaldera, Raven. *Hermaphrodeities: The Transgender Spirituality Workbook*. USA: XLibris, 2001.

Koestler, Arthur. Three versions of the same book:

Darkness at Noon. Translated by Daphne Hardy. London: Jonathan Cape, 1940.

Sonnenfinsternis. Coesfeld, Germany: Elsinor Verlag, 2018.

Darkness at Noon. Translated by Philip Boehm. New York: Scribner, 2019.

de Kruif, Paul. *The Male Hormone*. New York: Harcourt, Brace, and Co., 1945.

Leuchtenburg, William E. *The Perils of Prosperity: 1914-32*. Chicago and London:

University of Chicago Press, 1958.

Lieberman, Tucker. *Painting Dragons: What Storytellers Need to Know About Writing Eunuch Villains.* Bogotá: Glyph Torrent, 2018.

Lorde, Audre. *Zami: A New Spelling of My Name.* Berkeley: Crossing Press, 1982.

Luiselli, Valeria. *Tell Me How It Ends: An Essay in Forty Questions.* Minneapolis: Coffee House Press, 2017.

Mann, Thomas. *Der Zauberberg [The Magic Mountain].* S. Fischer Verlagberlin, 1924.

Millant, Richard. *Les Eunuques à travers les ages.* Paris: Vigot Frères, 1908.

Most, Doug. *The Race Underground: Boston, New York, and the Incredible Rivalry That Built America's First Subway.* New York: St. Martin's Press, 2014.

Newell, L. Jackson. *The Electric Edge of Academe: The Saga of Lucien L. Nunn and Deep Springs College.* Salt Lake City: The University of Utah Press, 2015.

Painter, Nell Irvin. *The History of White People.* New York: W. W. Norton, 2010.

Penzer, N. M. *The Harem.* (1936) New York: Dorset Press, 1993.

Pirsig, Robert M. *Zen and the Art of Motorcycle Maintenance.* (1974) New York: Bantam, 1975.

Pitzer, Andrea. *One Long Night: A Global*

History of Concentration Camps. New York: Hachette, 2017.

Poe, Edgar Allan. "Eureka: A Prose Poem." New York: Putnam, 1848.

Schechter, Harold. *The Mad Sculptor: The Maniac, The Model, and the Murder that Shook the Nation.* Seattle: Amazon Publishing, 2014.

Schwartz, Rosalie. *Pleasure Island: Tourism and Temptation in Cuba.* Lincoln and London: University of Nebraska Press, 1997.

Serrano, Arturo. *To Climates Unknown.* It will be believed when it is done.

Steinberg, Ted. *Gotham Unbound: The Ecological History of Greater New York.* New York: Simon and Schuster, 2014.

Snorton, C. Riley. *Black on Both Sides: A Racial History of Trans Identity.* Minneapolis: University of Minnesota Press, 2017.

Tharoor, Shashi. *An Era of Darkness: The British Empire in India.* New Delhi: Aleph, 2016.

Vivian, Daniel J. *A New Plantation World: Sporting Estates in the South Carolina Lowcountry, 1900-1940.* Cambridge, U.K.: Cambridge University Press, 2018.

Wolmar, Christian. *The Subterranean Railway: How the London Underground Was Built and How It Changed the City Forever.* London: Atlantic, 2004.

Wright, G. Frederick. *The Nampa Image.* Boston Society of Natural History, 1890.

Yu, Charles. *How to Live Safely in a Science Fictional Universe.* Pantheon, 2010.

Zoellner, Tom. *Train: Riding the Rails That Created the Modern World—From the Trans-Siberian to the Southwest Chief.* New York: Viking, 2014.

www.ingramcontent.com/pod-product-compliance
Lightning Source LLC
Chambersburg PA
CBHW031053080526
44587CB00011B/666